A COMMENTARY

ON

HEGEL'S LOGIC

A COMMENTARY
ON
HEGEL'S LOGIC

BY

JOHN McTAGGART ELLIS McTAGGART

NEW YORK

RUSSELL & RUSSELL · INC

1964

FIRST PUBLISHED IN 1910
REISSUED, 1964, BY RUSSELL & RUSSELL, INC.
BY ARRANGEMENT WITH CAMBRIDGE UNIVERSITY PRESS
L. C. CATALOG CARD NO: 64—10391

PRINTED IN THE UNITED STATES OF AMERICA

PREFACE

CHAPTERS II, III, VIII, IX, and X of this book are based on articles which appeared in *Mind* (Oct. 1902; April, 1904; April and July, 1897; Jan. 1899; and April, 1900). In many cases, however, both the interpretation and the criticism as now published are materially different from the earlier versions.

I am much indebted to my wife for her aid in reading this book in proof, and for many valuable suggestions, as also to Mr Bertrand Russell for his kindness in reading Chapter III, and for giving me much assistance in the treatment of the categories of Quantity. I owe much, too, to the criticisms and suggestions of the pupils to whom I have lectured on Hegel's philosophy.

TRINITY COLLEGE, CAMBRIDGE.
January, 1910.

TABLE OF CONTENTS

CHAPTER I

INTRODUCTION

CHAPTER II

QUALITY

CHAPTER III

QUANTITY

CHAPTER IV

MEASURE

CHAPTER V

ESSENCE AS REFLECTION INTO ITSELF

CHAPTER VI

APPEARANCE

CHAPTER VII

ACTUALITY

CHAPTER VIII

SUBJECTIVITY

CHAPTER IX

OBJECTIVITY

CHAPTER X

THE IDEA

CHAPTER I

INTRODUCTION

1. In this book I propose to give a critical account of the various transitions by which Hegel passes from the category of Being to the category of the Absolute Idea. I shall not describe or criticise the method which he employs, nor his applications of the results of the dialectic to the facts of experience. With these subjects I have dealt, to the best of my ability, in my *Studies in the Hegelian Dialectic* and *Studies in Hegelian Cosmology*. I hope that my present work may serve two purposes—that those students of Hegel who have read the *Greater Logic* may find it useful as a commentary, and that it may serve as an account of the *Greater Logic* for those who are prevented by want of time or ignorance of German from reading the original.

2. The dialectic process of the Logic is the one absolutely essential element in Hegel's system. If we accepted this and rejected everything else that Hegel has written, we should have a system of philosophy, not indeed absolutely complete, but stable so far as it reached, and reaching to conclusions of the highest importance. On the other hand, if we reject the dialectic process which leads to the Absolute Idea, all the rest of the system is destroyed, since Hegel depends entirely, in all the rest of the system, on the results obtained in the Logic.

Yet the detail of the Logic occupies a very small part of the numerous commentaries and criticisms on Hegel's philosophy. They are almost entirely devoted to general discussions of the dialectic method, or to questions as to the application of the results of the Logic to the facts of experience. The most elaborate of the expositions of Hegel's system—that which Kuno Fischer gives in his *History of Philosophy*—allows to the detail of the Logic less than one-ninth of its space.

There are, however, two admirable accounts of the Logic, category by category—*Hegel's Logic*, by Professor Hibben of Princeton, and *La Logique de Hegel*, by the late M. Georges Noël, which is less known than its merits deserve. I owe much to these commentators, but my object is rather different from theirs. I propose, in my exposition, to give frequent references to the passages in Hegel's text on which I base my account, and to quote freely when necessary. When the meaning of the text is doubtful, I shall not only give the view which I think preferable, but shall discuss the claims of other interpretations. I shall also add a certain amount of criticism to my exposition.

Professor Hibben follows the *Encyclopaedia* in his exposition, while M. Noël follows the *Greater Logic*[1]. I shall adopt the *Greater Logic* as my text, but shall note and discuss any point in which the *Encyclopaedia* differs from it.

3. The *Greater Logic* and the *Encyclopaedia* agree much more than they differ, but they do differ on various important points. When this happens, the advantage is not always on the same side, but is, I think, more often on the side of the *Encyclopaedia*. But, whichever is the more correct, there is no doubt that the *Greater Logic* is much clearer. The Logic of the *Encyclopaedia* is excessively condensed. The treatment of the categories, as distinct from preliminary questions, is, in the *Encyclopaedia*, only one-fourth as long as it is in the *Greater Logic*. Some room is gained in the *Encyclopaedia* by the elimination of certain sub-divisions, and also by the omission

---

[1] By the *Greater Logic* I mean the work published in 1812—1816. Hegel himself calls this simply the *Logic*, but I use the adjective to distinguish it from the *Logic* which forms part of the *Encyclopaedia*. My references to the *Greater Logic* are to the *pages* of the complete edition of Hegel's works, in which the *Greater Logic* occupies Vols. 3, 4 and 5 (quoted as *G. L.* i., *G. L.* ii., *G. L.* iii.) published in 1833—1834. My references to the *Encyclopaedia* are to *Sections*, and in quoting from it I have generally, though not always, availed myself of Professor Wallace's valuable translation. When, in expounding the *Greater Logic*, I give references both to the *Greater Logic* and to the *Encyclopaedia*, the latter merely indicates that it is in this Section of the *Encyclopaedia* that the corresponding point is treated, and not that the treatment is the same as in the *Greater Logic*.

of the notes on mathematics which fill a disproportionate space in the *Greater Logic*, but in spite of this the categories in the *Encyclopaedia* are in some parts of the process crowded so closely together, that the arguments for the transition from the one to the other almost disappear.

With regard to the relative authority of the two *Logics*, as expressing Hegel's final views, nothing very decisive can be said. The last edition of the *Logic* of the *Encyclopaedia* published by Hegel appeared in 1830. In 1831 he published a second edition of the Doctrine of Being in the *Greater Logic*. His death prevented him from carrying this edition further. It would seem, therefore, as if the *Greater Logic* was the best authority for the Doctrine of Being, and the *Encyclopaedia* for the Doctrines of Essence and the Notion.

But many of the points in the Doctrine of Being in which the first edition of the *Greater Logic* differs from the *Encyclopaedia* are repeated in the second edition. We can scarcely suppose that in each of these cases Hegel had abandoned by 1831 the view he held in 1830, and returned to the view he held in 1812. And thus it seems impossible to attach any superior authority to the second edition of the *Greater Logic*. But if, to the end, he regarded the changes in the *Encyclopaedia* as improvements, at any rate he cannot have regarded them as very important, since he did not alter the second edition of the *Greater Logic* to correspond with then.

The actual language, however, of the *Greater Logic* has a much greater authority than much of the language of the *Encyclopaedia*. For every word of the *Greater Logic* was written and published by Hegel himself. But in the *Encyclopaedia* a part of the supplementary matter added, with the title of Zusatz, to many of the Sections, is compiled from students' notes or recollections of what Hegel had said in his lectures[1].

4. A few points about terminology must be mentioned. The whole course of the dialectic forms one example of the dialectic rhythm, with Being as Thesis, Essence as Antithesis, and Notion as Synthesis. Each of these has again the same

---

[1] Cp. the editor's Preface to the *Logic* of the *Encyclopaedia* in Vol. 6 of the *Collected Works*.

moments of Thesis, Antithesis, and Synthesis within it, and so on till the final sub-divisions are reached, the process of division being carried much further in some parts of the dialectic than in others.

Hegel has no special name for the system formed of a Thesis, Antithesis, and Synthesis. A name, however, is convenient, and I propose to speak of such a system as a triad. Being, Essence, and Notion I shall call primary categories; their immediate divisions (*e.g.* Quality, Quantity, and Measure) I shall call secondary, and so on with smaller sub-divisions.

One difficulty of terminology arises in writing about Hegel from the fact that he uses so many terms as names of particular categories that none are left to be used more generally. For example, to what does the whole dialectic process apply? According to one view, the subject-matter of the process is what is commonly called Being or Reality. According to another view it is what is commonly called Existence. But Hegel has already appropriated these names. Being and Existence are the names of particular categories in the process, while Reality, according to Hegel, is a term only applicable after a certain stage in the process has been reached. (*G. L.* i. 120; *Enc.* 91.)

Again, after a few categories we reach the result, which persists through the rest of the process, that the subject-matter under consideration is a differentiated unity. It would be very convenient to have a name by which to designate these differentiations, irrespective of the category under which we were viewing them. But here, again, every name is already appropriated. One, Thing, Part, Substance, Individual, Object—each of these is used by Hegel to indicate such a differentiation as seen under some one particular category. To find a name for more general use is not easy.

To meet this difficulty so far as possible, I have always used a capital initial when a term indicates one of Hegel's categories, and a small initial when the term is applied more generally. I have distinguished in the same way between those of Hegel's categories which are named after concrete facts, and the concrete facts after which they are named—*e.g.* I have written Life when I meant Hegel's category, and life when I meant the biological state.

5. With regard to the Logic as a whole, I believe, for reasons which I have explained elsewhere[1], that the dialectic method used by Hegel is valid—that, if the categories do stand to one another in the relations in which he asserts them to stand, he is entitled to pass from one to another in the way in which he does pass. And I believe that in many cases this condition is fulfilled, and that therefore, in these cases, the actual transitions which he makes are justified.

The points on which I should differ from Hegel are as follows. In the first place I think that he falls into serious errors in his attempts to apply the results gained by the Logic in the interpretation of particular concrete facts. In the second place I think that he did not in all respects completely understand the nature of that dialectic relation between ideas which he had discovered. And in the third place there seem to be certain errors which vitiate particular stages in the process.

I have considered the first of these points elsewhere[2]. With regard to the second there are two fundamental questions as to which I believe that Hegel to some extent misunderstood the nature of the dialectic process. I think that he exaggerated both its objectivity and its comprehensiveness.

By his exaggeration of its objectivity, I mean that he did not merely hold that the dialectic process conducted us to a valid result, and that the lower categories of the process were contained, so far as they were true, in the Absolute Idea which synthesised them. So much he was justified in holding, but he went further. There is no doubt, I think, that he held that if that chain of categories, which was given by him in the Logic, was correct at all, it was not only *a* valid way of reaching the Absolute Idea, but the only valid way. He would have held it to be *à priori* impossible that two valid chains of dialectic argument, each starting from the category of Being, should each lead up to the Absolute Idea, so that the goal could be attained equally well by following either of them. And he would also have rejected the possibility of alternative routes over smaller

---

[1] *Studies in the Hegelian Dialectic*, Chapters I. to IV., but cp. below, Sections 10—13.

[2] *op. cit.* Chapter VII.

intervals—the possibility, *e.g.*, of passing from the beginning of Quantity to the beginning of Essence by two alternative dialectic arguments.

Now I do not assert that such alternative routes are to be found, but I cannot see that their possibility can be disproved. And, if there were such alternatives, I do not think that the dialectic process would lose its value or significance. In rejecting the possibility of equally valid alternatives, it seems to me that Hegel exaggerated the objectivity of the process as expounded by himself.

6. His exaggeration of the comprehensiveness of the dialectic lies in the fact that, having secured, as he rightly believed, an absolute starting point for the dialectic process in the category of Being, he assumed that this was not only the absolute starting point of the dialectic, but of all philosophy. No preliminary discussion was required, except negative criticism designed to remove the errors of previous thinkers, and to prevent misunderstandings. Nothing in philosophy was *logically* prior to the dialectic process.

Here again there seems to be an error. For example, what is the subject-matter to which the whole dialectic applies? It is, I think, clear that Hegel regards it as applying to all reality, in the widest sense of the term. But, when we examine various stages of the process it becomes clear that he is only speaking of what is existent, and that his results do not apply, and were not meant to apply, to what is held by some philosophers to be real but not existent—for example, propositions, the terms of propositions, and possibilities[1]. The apparent inconsistency is removed if we hold, as I believe we should, that Hegel, like some later philosophers, held nothing to be real but the existent. I do not mean that he ever asserted this explicitly. Probably, indeed, the question was never definitely considered by him, if we may judge from the fact that his terminology affords no means of stating it. (Reality and Existence, as used by Hegel, refer, as was mentioned above, to particular stages of the dialectic.) But it seems to me that the view that nothing

---

[1] I had not realised this distinction with sufficient clearness when I wrote my *Studies in the Hegelian Dialectic*, but what is said there is not inconsistent with my present view. Cp. Sections 17, 18, and 79 of that work.

is real but the existent is one which harmonises with his general position, and that he would have asserted it if confronted with the problem.

But the view that nothing but the existent is real, whether right or wrong, is one which cannot be assumed without discussion.   It is a difficult and disputed point, and Hegel had no right to take a dialectic of existence as equivalent to a dialectic of reality until the question had been carefully considered. Moreover, the absence of such consideration leaves Hegel's position, not only unjustified but also rather vague.   Generally, as I have said, the categories seem clearly intended to apply to the existent only, but there are some steps in which he seems to change his position unconsciously, and to take the categories as applicable to some other reality in addition to the existent.

There is another point on which preliminary discussion was needed and is not given. Hegel's arguments assume that, when a thing stands in any relation to another thing, the fact that it stands in that relation is one of its qualities.   From this it follows that when the relation of one thing to another changes, there is a change in the qualities of each of them, and therefore in the nature of each of them.   Again, it follows that two things which stand in different relations to a third thing cannot have exactly similar natures, and on this a defence might be based for the doctrine of the Identity of Indiscernibles.

This is a doctrine of the greatest importance, and by no means universally accepted. It is possible to conceive a dialectic process which should contain a proof of it, but, so far as I can see, Hegel's dialectic does not contain any such proof, direct or implied.   In that case he had no right to use the doctrine in the dialectic unless it had been proved in some preliminary discussion, and he does not give such a discussion.

7.   Passing to the errors in certain particular transitions, there are some, I think, which cannot be traced to any general cause, but are simply isolated failures.   But other errors appear to be due to certain general causes.   In the first place some errors have, I believe, been caused by Hegel's failure to realise explicitly that his dialectic is a dialectic of the existent only, and by his treatment of some categories as applying also to

some non-existent reality. This is unjustifiable, for he would
have no right to pass in this way from the smaller field to the
more extensive, even if the more extensive field were in being.
And, as I have said, it seems implied in his general treatment
that there is no such wider field, but that existence is co-extensive with reality, in which case any attempt to apply the
dialectic beyond existence is obviously mistaken.

8.   Another general cause of error may be found in a desire
to introduce into the dialectic process as many as possible of the
conceptions which are fundamentally important in the various
sciences. It is, doubtless, a fortunate circumstance when a conception which is important in this way does occupy a place
among the categories of the dialectic. For then the dialectic
will assure us that such a conception is neither completely valid
of reality, nor completely devoid of validity—an important
result. Moreover, its place in the dialectic process shows us
how much, and in what respects, its validity falls short of the
validity of the Absolute Idea, and whether it is more or less
valid than those other conceptions which are also categories of
the dialectic. And this also may be of much importance.

But there is no reason to believe that this fortunate state of
things will always occur. We have no right to anticipate that
every category of the dialectic will be a conception of fundamental importance in one or more of the particular sciences.
Nor have we any right to anticipate that every conception of
fundamental importance in a science will be a category of the
dialectic. In several cases I think that Hegel has distorted the
course of his argument, and made an invalid transition, moved
by an unconscious desire to bring into the process some conception of great scientific importance[1].

9.   This is connected with another source of error, which
arises from Hegel's practice of designating many of his categories by the names of concrete states which are known to us
by empirical experience. Thus we find a category of Attraction

[1] It has lately been objected to Hegel's treatment of Quantity that it does
not include the conception of Series, which is of such great importance in
mathematics. If the dialectic process can go from Being to the Absolute Idea
without passing through the conception of Series, then the omission of that
conception is no defect in the dialectic. But this truth is obscured by Hegel's
anxiety to bring all important scientific conceptions into the dialectic process.

and Repulsion, and categories of Force, Mechanism, Chemism, Life, and Cognition[1].

This practice does not necessarily involve any error in the dialectic process. For when Hegel names a category in this way, he does not suppose that he has deduced, by the pure thought of the dialectic, all the empirical details which can be determined with reference to the corresponding concrete state. He merely expresses his belief that the category is manifested in a special manner by the concrete state whose name it bears. For example, in giving a category the name of Mechanism he does not assert that it is possible to determine by the dialectic process any of the laws of the finite science of Mechanics. All that the use of the name implies is that, when we perceive the existent in such a way that it appears[2] to include bodies obeying the laws of Mechanics, then the category in question will be manifested with special clearness in the facts as they appear to us.

There is thus nothing unjustifiable in the use of such a nomenclature, and it has the advantage of making the meaning of the category clearer, by informing us where we may look for clear examples of it. But in practice it turns out to be extremely difficult to use such names without being led by them into error.

There is, in the first place, the possibility of choosing a wrong name—of taking a concrete state which manifests the particular category less clearly than another state would, or which itself manifests more clearly some other category. But this is a mistake which, so far as I can see, Hegel never makes.

But there is a second possibility. The concrete states which give their names to the categories contain, as has been said, much other content beside the categories in question. Hegel does not suppose that the dialectic process could help him to

---

[1] The use of logical terms as names for the categories of Subjectivity is an example of the same practice, though in this case the conceptions are not borrowed from empirical knowledge. But, relatively to the dialectic process, they are concrete, for the logical processes, which give the names, have characteristics not to be found in the categories which they exemplify.   Cp. Chapter VIII.

[2] Such a perception would, of course, be held by Hegel to be more or less erroneous. Nothing really exists, according to his system, but Spirits. Bodies only appear to exist.

deduce this other content.   But in practice he sometimes confuses the two sides—the pure conception which he had deduced,
and the remaining content which he had not.   And thus he
introduces into the dialectic process, in connection with certain
categories, some characteristics illegitimately transferred from
the concrete states after which they are named.   In Judgment,
in Syllogism, in Life, in Cognition, we find sub-divisions introduced and transitions made, which rest on characteristics which
are found in the judgments and syllogisms of ordinary logic, in
the life of biology, or in the cognition of psychology, but which
have no justification as applied to the categories of the
dialectic.

These cases, of course, lend support to the theory, which I
have discussed elsewhere[1], that the dialectic process, while professing to be a process of pure thought, does, in fact, always
rest on empirical elements illegitimately introduced.   But the
categories of the process which are named after concrete states
are comparatively few, and it is not in all of them that an
illegitimate element has been transferred to the category.

In several of those cases where the illegitimate transference
has taken place, it seems to me that the process, so far from
being dependent on the transference, would have gone better
without it.   The transition Hegel does make, with the aid of
the element illegitimately introduced, is in these cases one
which would be invalid even if the element it was based on had
itself been legitimately deduced.   And sometimes, I think, a
perfectly valid transition was available, which was only obscured
by the intrusion of the illegitimate element.

Whenever a particular transition seems to be invalid, I have
given the reasons which prevent me from accepting it.   In
some cases I venture to think that I could suggest a valid
substitute.   When this does not involve a reconstruction of
more than a single category I have generally made the suggestion, but any more extensive alteration would, I think, be
beyond the scope of a commentary.

10.   I wish to take this opportunity of correcting some
errors as to Hegel's method in my *Studies in the Hegelian*

---

[1] *Studies in the Hegelian Dialectic*, Sections 41—43.

Dialectic. (The correction of errors on other points would be irrelevant here.) In Section 19 of that book, after giving an account of the method which I still think correct, I added "It will be seen that this argument is strictly of a transcendental nature. A proposition denied by the adversary...is shown to be involved in the truth of some other proposition which he is not prepared to attack." But this is not a description confined to a transcendental argument, but applies to all attempts to convince an adversary. I failed to see that the proposition with which a transcendental argument, in Kant's sense of the term, starts, is always a proposition which asserts that some other proposition is *known* to be true. (For example, Kant's transcendental argument on Space does not start from the truths of geometry, but from the truth that we know the truths of geometry *à priori.*) Hegel's argument does not start from a proposition of this kind, and I was wrong in supposing it to be of the class which Kant calls transcendental.

11. In Section 109, I pointed out two characteristics in which the method in the later part of the dialectic process differed from the method at the beginning. Firstly, at the beginning the Antithesis is the direct contrary of the Thesis. It is not more advanced than the Thesis, nor does it in any way transcend it. But, as the process continues, the Antithesis, while still presenting an element of contrariety to the Thesis, is found to be also an advance on it. It does, to a certain extent, transcend the inadequacy of the Thesis, and thus shares with the Synthesis that character which, in the earlier type, belonged to the Synthesis only.

The second change follows as a consequence of the first. In the first triad of the dialectic the movement to the Synthesis comes from the Thesis and Antithesis together, and could not have been made from the Antithesis alone. But later on, when the Antithesis has transcended the Thesis, and has the truth of it within itself, it is possible to make the transition to the Synthesis from the Antithesis alone, without any distinct reference to the Thesis.

12. In Sections 112—114 I enquired whether these changes were sudden or continuous, and came to the conclusion that they were both continuous. And here I think I was partly

wrong. The first change *is* continuous. As we proceed through
the dialectic there is on the whole (there are a few exceptions)
a steady diminution in the element of contrariety to be found in
the Antitheses, and an increase in their synthetic functions.
But the second change cannot be continuous. For the direct
transition must either be from both the Thesis and Antithesis,
or from the Antithesis only. There is no intermediate
possibility.

The truth seems to be that the direct transition is from the
Antithesis alone whenever the Antithesis is at all higher than
the Thesis—that is, in every triad after the first. (The
Particular Notion, and the Negative Judgment of Inherence,
seem, however, to be exceptions to this rule, since, contrary
to the general character of the dialectic, they are not higher
than their respective Theses.)

13. In Section 80 I said of the transition from the
Synthesis of one triad to the Thesis of the next. " It is, in fact,
scarcely a transition at all. It is...rather a contemplation of
the same truth from a fresh point of view—immediacy in the
place of reconciling mediation—than an advance to a fresh
truth." This needs some qualification. In the first place, it is
only true when the Synthesis and new Thesis are categories of
the same order of subdivision. Thus, in Essence as Reflection
into Self, we have Determining Reflection as a Synthesis, to
which Identity, which is a Thesis, immediately succeeds. But
Determining Reflection is a category of the fifth order, while
Identity is only of the fourth order—produced by four successive processes of analysis instead of five. And the content in
these two categories is not an identical content looked at from
two different points of view.

In the second place, the identity of content is only to be
found when the two categories are not further divided. Thus
Actuality is the Synthesis of Essence, and Subjectivity the
Thesis of the Notion. They are contiguous categories of the
same order—the third. But each is subdivided, and the content
of the two is not identical.

Finally, although with these two qualifications the statement
is generally true of the dialectic, there are several cases, which
I have noted when they occur, in which it does not apply.

CHAPTER II

14. The Logic is divided into Being (Sein), Essence (Wesen), and Notion (Begriff). Being is divided into Quality (Qualität), Quantity (Quantität), and Measure (Maass). The divisions of Quality are as follows:

I. Being. (Sein.)

    A. Being. (Sein.)

    B. Nothing. (Nichts.)

    C. Becoming. (Werden.)

II. Being Determinate. (Dasein.)

    A. Being Determinate as Such. (Dasein als solches.)

        (*a*) Being Determinate in General. (Dasein überhaupt.)
        (*b*) Quality. (Qualität.)
        (*c*) Something. (Etwas.)

    B. Finitude. (Die Endlichkeit.)

        (*a*) Something and an Other. (Etwas und ein Anderes.)
        (*b*) Determination, Modification and Limit. (Bestimmung, Beschaffenheit und Grenze.)
        (*c*) Finitude. (Die Endlichkeit.)

C.   Infinity.   (Die Unendlichkeit.)

 (*a*) Infinity in General.   (Die Unendlichkeit überhaupt.)

 (*b*) Reciprocal Determination of the Finite and Infinite.   (Wechselbestimmung des Endlichen
   und Unendlichen.)

 (*c*) Affirmative Infinity.   (Die affirmative Unendlichkeit.)

III. Being for Self.   (Das Fürsichsein.)

 A. Being for Self as Such.   (Das Fürsichsein als solches.)

  (*a*) Being Determinate and Being for Self.   (Dasein
    und Fürsichsein.)

  (*b*) Being for One.   (Sein für Eines.)

  (*c*) One.   (Eins.)

 B. The One and the Many.   (Eines und Vieles.)

  (*a*) The One in Itself.   (Das Eins an ihm selbst.)

  (*b*) The One and the Void.   (Das Eins und das Leere.)

  (*c*) Many Ones. Repulsion.   (Viele Eins. Repulsion.)

 C. Repulsion and Attraction.   (Repulsion und Attrak-
   tion.)

  (*a*) Exclusion of the One.   (Ausschliessen des Eins.)

  (*b*) The one One of Attraction.   (Das Eine Eins der
    Attraktion.)

  (*c*) The Relation of Repulsion and Attraction.   (Die
    Beziehung der Repulsion und Attraktion.)

We must notice the ambiguity with which Hegel uses the word Being. It is used (i) for one of the three primary divisions into which the whole Logic is divided; (ii) for one of the three tertiary divisions into which Quality is divided; and (iii) for one of the three divisions of the fourth order into which Being, as a tertiary division, is divided. In the same way Quality, besides being the general name for the secondary division which forms the subject of this Chapter, is also the name for a division of the fifth order, which falls within Being Determinate as Such. And Finitude, again, is the name of a division of the fourth order, and also of a division of the fifth order.

I. Being.

A. Being.

15. (*G. L.* i. 77. *Enc.* 86.) I do not propose to discuss here
the validity of the category of Being. Since the dialectic
process starts with this category, its validity is rather a question
affecting the whole nature of the process than a detail of the
earliest stage, and I have treated it elsewhere[1]. If, then, we
begin with the category of Being, what follows?

It must be remembered that the position is not merely that
we are affirming Being, but that, so far, we are affirming nothing
else. It is to indicate this absence of anything else that Hegel
speaks of Being in this division as Pure Being (reines Sein),
though the adjective does not appear in the headings.

Pure Being, says Hegel (*G. L.* i. 78. *Enc.* 87) has no
determination of any sort. Any determination would give
it some particular nature, as against some other particular
nature—would make it X rather than not-X. It has therefore
no determination whatever. But to be completely free of any
determination is just what we mean by Nothing. Accordingly,
when we predicate Being as an adequate expression of existence,
we find that in doing so we are also predicating Nothing as
an adequate expression of existence. And thus we pass over to
the second category.

B. Nothing.

16. (*G. L.* i. 78. *Enc.* 87.) This transition, which has
been the object of so much wit, and of so many indignant
denials, is really a very plain and simple matter. Wit and
indignation both depend, as Hegel remarks (*G. L.* i. 82. *Enc.*
88), on the mistaken view that the Logic asserts the identity
of a concrete object which has a certain definite quality with
another concrete object which has not that quality—of a white
table with a black table, or of a table with courage. This is
a mere parody of Hegel's meaning. Whiteness is not Pure
Being. When we speak of a thing as white, we apply to it

Cp. Section 6. Also *Studies in the Hegelian Dialectic*, Sections 17, 18, 79.

many categories besides Pure Being—Being Determinate, for
example. Thus the fact that the presence of whiteness is not
equivalent to its absence is quite consistent with the identity
of Pure Being and Nothing.

When the dialectic process moves from an idea to its
Antithesis, that Antithesis is never the mere logical contradictory of the first, but is some new idea which stands to the
first in the relation of a contrary. No reconciling Synthesis
could possibly spring from two contradictory ideas—that is,
from the simple affirmation and denial of the same idea. In
most parts of the dialectic, the relation is too clear to be
doubted. But at first sight it might be supposed that Nothing
was the contradictory of Being. This, however, is not the case.
If we affirmed not-Being, in the sense in which it is the mere
contradictory of Being, we should only affirm that, whatever
reality might be, it had not the attribute of Being. And this
is clearly not the same as to say that it has the attribute of
Nothing. It may be the case that wherever the predicate
Being can be denied, the predicate Nothing can be asserted,
but still the denial of the one is not the affirmation of the
other.

Hegel says, indeed (*G. L.* i. 79) that we could as well say
Not-being (Nichtsein) as Nothing (Nichts). But it is clear
that he means by Not-Being, as he meant by Nothing, not the
mere denial of Being, but the assertion of the absence of all
determination.

If the identity of Being and Nothing were all that could be
said about them, the dialectic process would stop with its
second term. There would be no contradiction, and therefore
no ground for a further advance. But this is not the whole
truth (*G. L.* i. 89. *Enc.* 88). For the two terms originally
meant different things. By Being was intended a pure
positive—reality without unreality. By Nothing was intended
a pure negative—unreality without reality. If each of these
is now found to be equivalent to the other, a contradiction has
arisen. Two terms, defined so as to be incompatible, have
turned out to be equivalent. Nor have we got rid of the
original meaning. For it is that same characteristic which
made the completeness of their opposition which determines

their equivalence. A reconciliation must be found for this contradiction, and Hegel finds it in

C. Becoming.

17. The reconciliation which this category affords appears to consist in the recognition of the intrinsic connexion of Being and Nothing (*G. L.* i. 78. *Enc.* 88). When we had these two as separate categories, each of these asserted itself to be an independent and stable expression of the nature of reality. By the affirmation of either its identity with the other was denied, and when it was found, nevertheless, to be the same as the other, there was a contradiction. But Becoming, according to Hegel, while it recognises Being and Nothing, recognises them only as united, and not as claiming to be independent of one another. It recognises them, for Becoming is always the passage of Being into Nothing, or of Nothing into Being. But, since they only exist in Becoming in so far as they pass away into their contraries, they are only affirmed as connected, not as separate, and therefore there is no longer any opposition between their connexion and their separation.

But, Hegel continues, this is not the end of the matter. Being and Nothing only exist in Becoming as disappearing moments. But Becoming only exists in so far as they are separate, for, if they are not separate, how can they pass into one another? As they vanish, therefore, Becoming ceases to be Becoming, and collapses into a state of rest, which Hegel calls Being Determinate (*G. L.* i. 109. *Enc.* 89).

18. I confess that I regret the choice of Becoming as a name for this category. What Hegel meant seems to me to be quite valid. But the name of the category suggests something else which seems to me not to be valid at all.

All that Hegel means is, as I have maintained above, that Being is dependent on Nothing in order that it should be Being, and that Nothing is dependent on Being in order that it should be Nothing. In other words, a category of Being without Nothing, or of Nothing without Being, is inadequate and leads to contradictions which prove its falsity. The only truth of the two is a category which expresses the relation of the two. And this removes the contradiction. For there is no contradiction in the union of Being and Nothing. The previous contradiction was between their identity and their difference.

Hegel seems to have thought it desirable to name the new category after a concrete fact. But, as I have said above (Section 9), the use of the names of concrete facts to designate abstract categories is always dangerous. In the present case, the concrete state of becoming contains, no doubt, the union of Being and Nothing, as everything must, except abstract Being and Nothing. But the concrete state of becoming contains a great deal more—a great deal which Hegel had not deduced, and would have had no right to include in this category. I do not believe that he meant to include it, but his language almost inevitably gives a false impression.

When we speak of Becoming we naturally think of a process of change. For the most striking characteristic of the concrete state of becoming is that it is a change from something to something else. Now Hegel's category of Becoming cannot be intended to include the idea of change.

Change involves the existence of some permanent element in what changes—an element which itself does not change. For, if there were nothing common to the two states, there would be no reason to say that the one had changed into the other. Thus, in order that anything should be capable of change, it must be analysable into two elements, one of which does not change. This is impossible under the categories of Quality. Under them each thing—if the word thing could properly be used of what is so elementary—is just one simple undifferentiated quality. Either it is itself—and then it is completely the same—or its complete sameness vanishes, and then the thing also vanishes, since its undifferentiated nature admits no partial identity of content. Its absolute shallowness leaves no room for distinction between a changing and an unchanging layer of reality.

This was recognised by Hegel, who says that it is the characteristic of Quantity that in it, for the first time, a thing can change, and yet remain the same (*G. L.* i. 211. *Enc.* 99). He cannot therefore have considered his category of Becoming, which comes before Quantity, as including change.

But, it may be objected, although Hegel's category of
Becoming is incompatible with fully developed change, may
it not be compatible with change in a more rudimentary form?
Is it not possible that, even among the categories of Quality,
a place may be found for a category which involves, not the
change of A into B, but the disappearance of A and the
appearance of B instead of it?   To this I should reply, in the
first place, that if such replacement of A by B was carefully
analysed, it would be found to involve the presence of some
element which persisted unchanged in connexion first with
A and then with B.   The case would then resolve itself into
an example of change proper.   To defend this view would,
however, be an unnecessary digression here.   For it is clear
that, if such a replacement could exist without being a change
of A into B, then A would be quite disconnected with B.   But
in Hegel's category of Becoming the whole point lies in the
intrinsic and essential connexion of Being and Nothing.   The
category could not, therefore, be an example of such replacement.

19.   Thus Becoming, as a category of the Logic, cannot
consistently involve change.   And when we look at the transition by which Hegel reaches it, we see, as I said above, that
the essence of the new category lies in the necessary implication
of Being and Nothing, and not in any change taking place
between them.

But the name of Becoming is deceptive in itself, and so is
Hegel's remark that the category can be analysed into the
moments of Beginning (Entstehen) and Ceasing (Vergehen)
(*G. L.* i. 109).   If the implication of the two terms is to be
called Becoming, there is, indeed, no reason why these names
should not be given to the implication of Being in Nothing,
and of Nothing in Being.   It all tends, however, to strengthen
the belief that we have here a category of change.   The same
result is produced by the mention of the philosophy of
Heraclitus in connexion with the category of Becoming.   Of
course a philosophy which reduced everything to a perpetual
flow of changes would involve the principle of the implication
of Being and Nothing.   But it would also involve a great deal
more, and once again, therefore, we meet the misleading

suggestion that this great deal more is to be found in the category of Becoming.

20. For these reasons I believe that the course of the dialectic would become clearer if the name of Becoming were given up, and the Synthesis of Being and Nothing were called Transition to Being Determinate (Uebergang in das Dasein). This follows the precedent set by Hegel in the case of the last category of Measure, which he calls Transition to Essence (Uebergang in das Wesen) (*G. L.* i. 466).

When we have taken this view of the category, the transition to the next triad becomes easy. So long as the third category was regarded as involving change, it might well be doubted whether Hegel had succeeded in eliminating, in Being Determinate, the change he had introduced in Becoming. And to do this was necessary, since Being Determinate is certainly not a category of change. But on the new interpretation change has never been introduced, and does not require to be eliminated.

The assertion that Being Determinate contains Being as an element is simple enough. But to say that it contains Nothing as an element seems strange. The difficulty is, however, merely verbal. The Antithesis to Being should rather have been called Negation than Nothing. The word Being involves a positive element, but does not exclude a negative element—unless we expressly say Pure Being. But Nothing is commonly used to designate a negative element combined with the absence of any positive element. It corresponds to Pure Being, while Being corresponds to Negation.

Now Being Determinate contains Being as a moment, but not Pure Being, since Pure Being means "Being and nothing else." In the same way, then, we must say that Being Determinate contains as an element, not Nothing, but Negation. Hegel recognises this, for he says (*G. L.* i. 81) that in Being Determinate we have as moments Positive and Negative, rather than Being and Nothing. But he fails to see that Being and Nothing are not in ordinary usage correlative terms, and that, while, when he came to the Synthesis, he had to substitute Negative for Nothing, he could just as well have kept Being instead of Positive. It seems to me that it would have been better if he had spoken of the Thesis and Antithesis as Being and Negation. He could then have said in this triad, as he does in other cases, that it was the Thesis and Antithesis themselves which are the moments of the Synthesis.

21. It is easy to see that in Being Determinate Being and Negation are synthesised. If anything has a definite quality, this involves that it has not other definite qualities, inconsistent with the first. A thing cannot be green unless it is not red, and thus its greenness has a negative aspect, as well as a positive one.

II. Being Determinate.

A. *Being Determinate as Such.*

(a) *Being Determinate in General.*

(*G. L.* i. 112. *Enc.* 89.) This, as the first subdivision of the first division of Being Determinate, has, as its name implies, no other meaning except the general meaning of Being Determinate, namely, that in all existence Being and Nothing are united.

And now, for the first time, we get the possibility of differentiation and plurality. Being and Nothing did not admit of this. Whatever simply Is is exactly the same. And this is also true of whatever simply Is Not. But under the category of Being Determinate, it is possible to have an *a* which is not *b*, and is thus distinguished from *b*, which is not *a*. And not only the possibility of such differentiation, but also its necessity is now established. For whatever is anything must also not be something, and cannot be what it is not. It must therefore not be something else than what it is. And thus the reality of anything implies the reality of something else. (The validity of this will be discussed in Section 25.) Hegel calls the various differentiations by the name of Qualities, and so we reach the second subdivision of Being Determinate as Such, namely

(b) Quality.

22. (*G. L.* i. 114.) We must not be misled by the ordinary
use of the phrase "a Quality." As a rule, when we speak of
a Quality or of Qualities, we mean characteristics which inhere
in a Thing, and of which one Thing may possess many. Hegel
calls these, when he comes to treat of Essence, by the name of
Eigenschaften. We have not yet got any idea so advanced as
this. It is not until Essence has been reached that we shall
be able to make a distinction between a Thing and its characteristics. And, although we have now attained a plurality, we
have not yet acquired the idea of plurality in unity, which
would be necessary before we could conceive one Thing as
having many characteristics.

The Qualities of which Hegel speaks here are simply the
immediate differentiations of Being Determinate. They do not
inhere in anything more substantial than themselves; they, in
their immediacy, are the reality. Consequently they are not
anything separate from the Being Determinate. Each Quality
has Determinate Being, and the universe is nothing but the
aggregate of the Qualities. There is not one Being Determinate with many Qualities, but there are many Determinate
Beings. These may be called, not inappropriately, Somethings. And this is the transition to the third division of
Being Determinate as Such, namely,

(c) Something.

23. (*G. L.* i. 119.) At this point, says Hegel, we first get
the Real (*G. L.* i. 120. *Enc.* 91). The reason for this is not
very obvious. Reality seems to be taken as a matter of degree
—a thing is more or less Real in proportion as it is regarded
under a more or less true category. Something is, no doubt,
a truer category than those which preceded it, but it is less
true than those that follow it, and I cannot see why Reality
comes in here, if it did not come in before. Something is not
even the first Synthesis.

24. Looking back on the two last transitions—from Being
Determinate in General to Quality, and from Quality to Some-

thing—they must, I think, be pronounced to be valid. A doubt might perhaps arise as to the necessity of passing through them. Is it not clear, it might be asked, that the differentiations cannot lie on the surface of Being Determinate (since that would involve a distinction between Essence and Appearance) but must be in it? And in that case could we not have simplified the process by taking Something as the immediate form of Being Determinate, and so forming the undivided first moment of it[1]?

But between simple Being Determinate and Something there is a difference—namely the explicit introduction of plurality. The fact that the name Something is in the singular number (inevitable with the German word Etwas) may obscure. this if we confine ourselves to the titles, but in reading the demonstrations it soon becomes evident that, between Being Determinate in General and Something, plurality has been introduced. In the idea of Something, therefore, we have more than is in the simple idea of Being Determinate, and a transition between them is required.

We can also see why there should be two steps between Being Determinate in General and Something, and why the road from the one to the other should lie through the category of Quality. The transition to plurality takes place in the transition to Quality, since Hegel speaks of one Being Determinate in General, but of many Qualities. Now we can see, I think, that it is natural that, in passing from what is singular to a plurality, we should first think that what is plural is something different from that which had previously been before us (and in Quality the suggestion is that they are different) and that we should require a fresh step of the process to show us that

---

[1] This objection may be made clearer by a table.

I. Hegel's division of Being Determinate.	II. Division proposed by Objection.
A. Being Determinate as Such.	A. Something
(a) Being Determinate in General.	(without any sub-divisions).
(b) Quality.	
(c) Something.	
B. Finitude.	B. Finitude.
(et cetera.)	(et cetera.)

the plurality is the true form of what we had previously taken
not to be plural (and this is what is gained by the transition to
Something).

We have, then, a plurality, and a plurality which does not
inhere in anything else. It must therefore be regarded as
a rudimentary form of plurality of substance, rather than of
plurality of attributes. Now the categories are assertions about
the nature of existence. So, when we have got a plurality of
Somethings, we have got a plurality of existence. Is this
justified ?

25. It may be objected that we are not entitled to argue in
this way from the existence of one Something to the existence
of others. No doubt, it may be said, if this Something is x,
there must, by the results we have already reached, be some y,
which x is not, but it does not follow that y exists. If (to take
an example from a more complex sphere than that of Something) an existent object is red, it must be not-green, but it
does not follow that any green object exists. Thus, it is urged,
there might, for anything we have proved to the contrary, be
only one existent Something, whose definite nature consisted in
the fact that it was x, and was not y, z, etc.

I do not, however, think that this is valid. For if we get
the definiteness of the Something out of the fact that it is x and
not y, not z, etc., then it will have a plurality of qualities, x, not-
y, not-z, etc. This requires the conception of a thing as a unity
which holds together a plurality of attributes, and is not
identical with any one of them. And this is a conception which
we have not yet reached, and have no right to use. Thus the
negative element in each Something cannot fall within it, and
must fall outside it, and so we are compelled to follow Hegel in
asserting the plurality of existent Somethings.

It may be replied that what belongs to the nature of anything cannot be wholly outside it, and that if two existent
Somethings are distinguished from each other by being respectively x and y, then after all it must be true of x that it is not-
y, and of y that it is not-x, and so that there will be the plurality
of attributes in each Something, in which case the possibility
that there is only one Something has not been effectively
refuted.

It is quite true, no doubt, that the existence of a plurality
of substantial beings does involve a plurality of attributes in
each of them. But the recognition of this forms a further stage
of the dialectic, in which we shall have passed beyond the
category of Something. We have not yet reached this stage,
and at present, since there is no plurality of attributes in a
Something, each Something can only find its determinateness in
another existent Something.

When we do reach to the conception of a thing with a
plurality of attributes, we shall no longer have our present
reason to believe in a substantial plurality. For that reason,
as we have seen, is that plurality is necessary, and that no other
plurality is possible, and this becomes invalid when a plurality
of attributes in one thing has been established. If the conception of a substantial plurality is finally retained, it must rest on
considerations not yet before us[1].

Thus we have a plurality of Somethings. Each of these is
dependent for its nature on not being the others. It may thus
be said, in a general sense, to be limited by them. (Limit, as a
technical term in the dialectic, denotes a particular species of
limitation in the more general sense.) With this we pass to the
second division of Being Determinate, which is

B. Finitude.

(a) Something and an Other.

26. (*G. L.* i. 122.) This category should be a restatement,
in a more immediate form, of the category of Something. This
is exactly what it is. For the category of Something, as I have
said, included the idea of a plurality of such Somethings. And,
from the point of view of any one of these, the other Somethings
will be primarily not itself. So we get the idea of Something
and an Other.

Since each Something is dependent for its own nature on an
Other, its nature may be called a Being-for-Other. (Sein für
Anderes.) But this is not the only aspect of its nature. The
relation to an Other is what makes it what it is. And thus

---

[1] Cp. Sections 101—102.

this relation is also what it is By Itself or implicitly (An Sich[1]). And thus this relation is also a quality of the Something itself. (*G. L.* i. 129. Cp. also *Enc.* 91, though the explanation is here so condensed as scarcely to be recognisable.) This takes us to the next subdivision, Determination, Modification and Limit. (I admit that Modification is not a very happy translation of Beschaffenheit, but it is impossible to get really good names for so many meanings which differ so slightly.)

(b) Determination, Modification and Limit.

27. (*G. L.* i. 129.) Not content with the analysis of his subject-matter by five successive trichotomies, Hegel further analyses this category into a triad of the sixth order, the terms of which are Determination, Modification, and Limit. The subtlety of the distinctions at this point is so great that I must confess to having only a very vague idea of what is meant. So far as I can see, Determination is the character of the Something viewed as its inner nature, and Modification is that character viewed as something received by it from outside—is, in fact, the Being for Other come back again. It follows then, naturally enough, that Determination and Modification are identical. And from this again it follows that, as the Something was conceived as having a nature which was both a characteristic of itself and of its Other, that nature should be conceived as a Limit. In such a sense a meadow is limited by the fact that it is not a wood, nor a pond. (*Enc.* 92.) Now it is clear that we only get such a Limit when the nature of the Something is seen to be both in itself and in its relation to an Other. The conception of a Limit implies that it makes the Something what it is—no more and no less. That it should be no less than itself requires that its nature should be in itself, so that it should maintain itself against the Other. That it should be no more than itself requires, at the present stage of the dialectic, that its nature should also be outside itself, that the Other should maintain itself against it.

---

[1] It is, so far as I know, impossible to find any one English phrase which will adequately render An Sich. I have followed Prof. Wallace's example in using either By Itself or Implicitly, according to the context.

The correctness of this interpretation is, no doubt, very problematic. But whatever Hegel's meaning may have been in this obscure passage, we can see for ourselves that the category of Limit would necessarily have come in at this point. For, in the category of Something and an Other, the nature of each Something lay in the Other. But it is also true, as Hegel points out without any obscurity, that the nature of Something must also lie in itself. And, since the nature of Something lies both in itself and in its Other, we have the idea of a Limit—of a characteristic which, while it belongs both to Something and to its Other, keeps them apart.

Here, as Hegel remarks (*G. L.* i. 133), we get for the first time the conception of Not-being for Other. In the category of Something and an Other we had the conception of Being for Other, but now in Limit the Something has its nature in itself as well as in the Other, and so it has a certain stability and exclusiveness.

At this point, therefore, we may be said to get the first glimpse of the conception of Being for Self. But it is not yet seen to be the truth of Being for Other. On the contrary it appears to be in opposition to it, and this opposition produces fresh contradictions, which cannot be solved until the true nature of Being for Self is discovered in the category which bears that name.

We now come to Finitude in the narrower sense. That this conception should only be reached at this point will not seem strange if we realise the meaning which Hegel always gives to this term. For him the Finite is not simply that which has something outside it, and the Infinite is not simply that which has nothing outside it. The Infinite for him is that whose nature and, consequently, whose limits, are self-determined. The Finite, on the other hand, is that whose nature is limited by something outside itself. The essential feature of the Infinite is free self-determination. The essential feature of the Finite is subjection to an Other.

This explains why Finitude only becomes explicit at this point. Two things are necessary for subjection to an Other— the Other, and a definite nature in the Something to be subjected to it. The conception of plurality was only reached at the end of Being Determinate as Such, and till then there could be no question of Finitude. When this point was reached, Finitude began to appear, and accordingly the second division of Being Determinate, which we are now considering, is, as we have seen, called Finitude. But Finitude does not become fully explicit till the Something's nature is seen to be also in itself, and not only in the Other. For till then there can scarcely be said to be anything to be subjected to the Other. Only with the conception of Limit does Finitude become fully explicit. And therefore the next category—the last subdivision of Finitude in the wider sense—is called in a special sense

(c)   Finitude.

28. (G. L. i. 137.) This category is merely a restatement of the last moment of the previous subdivision—that is to say, of Limit. The idea of a Limit is, as has already been said, the idea of Finitude, since they both mean that the limited thing has a nature of its own, and that its nature is in subjection to an Other. This conception takes the form of Limit when we view it as overcoming the difficulties which arise from the opposition between the nature as in an Other and the nature as in the object itself. When the conception is taken as a more immediate statement of the truth, it takes the form of Finitude.

Finitude is the Synthesis of a triad of which Something and an Other is Thesis, and Determination Modification and Limit is the Antithesis. The Thesis asserted that the nature of the Something lay in its Other, the Antithesis asserted that the nature of the Something lay in itself. These assertions are reconciled in Finitude.

29. On looking back we can see, I think, that the subdivisions found within the category of Determination Modification and Limit are useless. Modification is only a repetition of Something and an Other[1], while Limit is identical with Finitude. The only idea remaining is Determination. It would have been better, therefore, if Determination by itself had been the Antithesis of Something and an Other. The

---

[1] Hegel denies this, but I cannot see that he has shown any difference between them.

name of Limit, not being wanted for a subdivision of the Antithesis, would be set free, and could be used, instead of Finitude, as the name of the Synthesis, and this would avoid the inconvenience of using Finitude here, for a division of the fifth order, when it is also used for a division of the fourth order.

30. In Finitude, as was said above, there are two sides— the internal nature of the finite Something and the relation in which it stands to the Other. These Hegel calls respectively the Ought and the Barrier. (Das Sollen und die Schranke.) (*G. L.* i. 140.) The Barrier seems an appropriate name. But why the internal nature of the Something should be called the Ought is not so clear. It may be said that a conscious being, when he feels himself limited by something, says that the limit ought to be removed, and that he ought to have room to develop freely. But the resemblance between such a conscious being and a limited Something is very slight, and far less important than the difference. When a man says that he ought to be able to do what, in point of fact, external circumstances do not allow him to do, he has an ideal of some course of action different from the one which he is forced to take, and he judges that his ideal course would fulfil his true nature more completely than the other. The position here is entirely different. The content of the two opposed sides is here the same, for the Something has only one nature, which may be looked at either as in itself or in the Other, and the opposition is only between the two ways of looking at it.

Why then did Hegel use the word Ought? I believe he did so because it gave him a chance of introducing an attack on the ethics of Kant and Fichte (*G. L.* i. 142; *Enc.* 94). This was a temptation which he was never able to resist.

31. But the inner nature of the Something now bursts its Barrier. The Other which limits it has no nature which is not expressed in the limitation itself. And the limitation belongs to the nature of the Something. So that it now finds its own nature beyond the Barrier, which it has, therefore, passed. (*G. L.* i. 147. The line of the argument in the *Encyclopaedia* is different, and will be considered later on.) To go back to Hegel's own example, a meadow is limited by the fact that it is not a wood. Not to be a wood is a part, and an essential part,

of the nature of the meadow. Thus the nature of the meadow is to be found in the nature of the wood, and is thus no longer something bounded and confined by the wood's nature—for what is left to be bound ?

We thus pass to

C. *Infinity*

the third division of Being Determinate (*G. L.* i. 147). For, the Barrier being abolished, the Something is no longer determined by anything outside itself. Thus we have got rid of Finitude, and so attained Infinity, though only, so far, in a very rudimentary form.

The transition here, it will be noticed, is a distinct advance. Infinity is a fresh conception from Finitude. This is not what might have been expected, for Finitude (in the narrower sense of the word) is a division of the fifth order, and stands to the next division of the fifth order (Infinity in general) as the Synthesis of one triad to the Thesis of the next. According to the general scheme of the dialectic, therefore, their content should have been the same.

And the transition seems to me to be invalid. I cannot see that anything which Hegel has said entitles him to conclude, as apparently he does, that in this category we have got rid of Limit and Barrier. The nature of the meadow is determined by that of the wood—but it is determined negatively. It is its nature not to be the wood. And this determination, while it relates the two, does not in any way destroy the difference between them, so that there is no justification for concluding that the second of them has ceased to limit the first, or to act as its Barrier. For the proper transition at this point, we must, I believe, adopt the view of the *Encyclopaedia*, rather than that of the *Greater Logic*.

Continuing the treatment of the subject in the *Greater Logic*, we find that when, in the first place, the Something passes over its Barrier, it finds itself outside the Barrier, and so unlimited. Thus the first stage is

(a) Infinity in General.

32. (*G. L.* i. 148.) And now Hegel proceeds to restore the limitations which, if I am right, he ought never to have discarded. What, he asks (*G. L.* i. 153), is this Infinity ? It has been gained by negating Finitude, and passing beyond it. Now nothing can negate anything definite, except by being definite itself. But we have seen that a thing can only be definite if it has a limit and is finite. And thus the Infinite which we seemed to have reached turns out to be another Finite. A meadow, for example, cannot be negated by pure Being, or by Nothing. It must be by some other Being Determinate. And this must be finite.

The Infinity, which had been reached, thus turns out to be finite. But, being finite, it will have its nature outside itself, and so again passes the Barrier, and becomes infinite—only once more to become finite. This process goes on without end, and thus we have the second subdivision (*G. L.* i. 149)

33. (*b*) *Reciprocal Determination of the Finite and Infinite*

which may be called more briefly Negative Infinity (cp. *Enc.* 94).

It must be noted that this is not a category of change. A category of change would assert that the reality, when viewed under that category, is viewed as changing its nature. This is not the case here. The reality—the nature of the Something— is not conceived as changing. All that changes is the way in which we judge it. We conceive its nature, first as being generally outside itself, then as being in another Something, then as generally outside that other Something again. We oscillate endlessly between these two views. But this does not involve any judgment that the reality changes. It is only a change of judgment about the reality.

This involves a contradiction. The nature of the Something is first seen not to be Finite, but Infinite. But it is then seen to be, not Infinite, but Finite again. And the second step does not transcend the first, for the second leads back again to the

first.   Therefore a part of the nature of the Something—that
part which lies outside the Something—cannot be pronounced
either Finite or Infinite.   Thus it can be found nowhere—for
the category recognises no third alternative.   And since this part
of the nature of the Something has been shown to be essential
to the Something, there can be no Something, and so (so far as
can be seen under this category) no Determinate Being at all.
And so there is a contradiction.

It is sometimes said that Hegel holds that an Infinite Series
is *as such* contradictory.   But this is a mistake.   He denies that
there is anything sublime in endless repetition, and asserts that
its only important feature is its tediousness (*Enc.* 94), but he
does not assert it to be intrinsically impossible.   It is only
Infinite Series of particular kinds which are contradictory, and
then only for some reason other than their infinity.   In the case
of the present series, as we have seen, there is such a reason.

34.   How do we get rid of this contradiction ?   Hegel points
out (*G. L.* i. 155) that the same fact which produced the contradiction has only to be looked at in a rather different light to
give the solution.   That fact is the unity of the Finite and
Infinite—or, in other words, of what is within any finite Something and of what is outside it.   It was this which produced the
contradictory infinite series, for it was this which made the
content of the Something first overstep its Barrier.   But if we
put it in another way—that the content of the Something is in
part its relation to what is outside it, then the Something has an
internal nature which is stable through its relation to what is
outside it, and the contradictory infinite series never begins.
Instead of saying that the nature of the Something must be
found in what is outside it, we must now say that it has its
nature through what is outside it.   The conception of relatively
self-centred reality thus reached is called by Hegel (*G. L.* i. 155)

(c)   Affirmative Infinity.

35.   The treatment of the subject in the *Encyclopaedia* is
different.   After establishing the category of Limit, Hegel
continues (*Enc.* 93) "Something becomes an Other: this Other
is itself Something : therefore it likewise becomes an Other,

and so on *ad infinitum."* The transition here is not alternately from Finite to Finite. The only Infinite is the infinite number of such Finites.

This seems to me to be better than the argument in the *Greater Logic.* In the first place, the categories are so arranged in the *Encyclopaedia* as to avoid the difference of content between a Synthesis and the succeeding Thesis—which, as we saw above, occurs in the *Greater Logic.*

In the second place, the *Encyclopaedia* avoids the transition from the limited to the unlimited, which I have maintained above to be invalid. And the transition which it substitutes is, I think, valid. Part of the nature of A is found in its Other, B, since it is part of its nature not to be B. But this can only be a definite characteristic of A, if B is definite. Now part of B's nature, on the same principle, must be found in *its* Other C. Thus the nature of A will be partly found in C, since it is part of its nature to be not-B, while B's nature includes being not-C. A similar argument will prove that the nature of A is partly in C's Other, D, and so on without end.

Here, again, we get an infinite series which is a contradiction. A, as a Something, must have a definite nature. But part of this nature is not to be found in itself. It must, according to the category, be found in one of the series of Others. But it cannot be found in any one of them, for whichever we take proves to have part of its own nature, and therefore of A's nature, in yet another. Thus this indispensable part of A's nature is to be found in none of the series of Others, and therefore, according to this category, can be found nowhere. Thus A has no definite nature, though it is a Something. And this is a contradiction.

Nor can we escape from this contradiction by saying that the part of A's nature which is external to itself is found in the whole series, though it is not found in any one term of it. For nothing which we have yet reached entitles us to regard the series as a unity with which A can enter into relations. Its relations can only be to some particular Something which forms part of the series.

It will be seen that the contradiction does not rest on the impossibility that a mind working in time should ever reach the

end of an infinite series. This impossibility might prove that
the full nature of any Something could never be known to any
mind working in this way, but in this there would be no
contradiction.

36. From this contradiction we are freed by passing to the
category of True Infinity. Hegel says that the Something
stands in the same position to its Other, as the Other stands
to the Something. The Something is the Other of its own
Other, and, therefore, "Something in its passage into Other only
joins with itself" (*Enc.* 95). This means that, while the nature
of *A* is partly to be found in *B*, and the nature of *B* is partly to
be found in something other than *B*, this need not be a third
Something, *C*, but can be *A*, which is after all other than *B*. So
the infinite series, with its contradiction, is avoided. *A* and *B*
are each determinate through the fact of not being the other.
Thus we reach Being for Self. *A*'s nature is now wholly in
itself. It no longer has part of its nature in its Other, but its
nature within itself is what it is because of its relation to its
Other. (The *Encyclopaedia* is very condensed here, but it
seems to be certain that this is the meaning.)

This position, Hegel says, is that of True Infinity, and it is
identical with what was called, in the *Greater Logic*, Affirmative
Infinity. The name of Infinity may appear inappropriate. For
here all assertion of Infinity, in the ordinary sense of the word,
has disappeared, since the necessity for an Infinite Series of
Somethings has disappeared. According to the category we
have just reached there must be at least two Somethings, and
there may be any number, but, so far as I can see, there may be
only two.

It is very characteristic of Hegel's thought that he should
call this concept True or Affirmative Infinity. According to
him the essence of Infinity lies in the fact that it is what is
unconstrained, unthwarted, free. And freedom, according to him,
can only be found, not in being unbounded, but in being self-
bounded. That is truly infinite whose boundaries are determined
by the fact that it is itself, and not by mere limitation from
outside. It is through applications of this principle that Hegel
holds that a conscious spirit has more true infinity than endless
space or endless time. Now in this category we have reached

self-determination, though only as yet in a very rudimentary form. And therefore, in comparison with what has gone before, Hegel calls it True Infinity.

37. From this point the *Greater Logic* and the *Encyclopaedia* again coincide in their treatment. It is here, says Hegel, that we first get Ideality (*G. L.* i. 164. *Enc.* 95) and that Idealism becomes possible (*G. L.* i. 171). Idealism, he says, consists in maintaining that the Finite is Ideal (das Ideelle, not das Ideal), and this, again, means that the Finite is recognised "not truly to be." For this it is necessary that the Finite should have been reached, and should have been transcended, and that we should recognise that what is merely Finite is impossible. (Finite is, of course, used in Hegel's own sense, and means, not that which is bounded, but that which is not self-bounded.) This is the first category in which such a recognition is involved.

Affirmative Infinity gives us, as we saw when dealing with the *Encyclopaedia*, Being for Self. In the *Greater Logic* they form two separate categories, but the content of Affirmative Infinity—the final Synthesis of Being Determinate—is identical with the content with which the new division of Being for Self begins. The Something has now its whole nature inside itself.

III. BEING FOR SELF

(*G. L.* i. 173. *Enc.* 96) is the last of the three tertiary divisions to be found in Quality. Its first subdivision is called by Hegel

A. *Being for Self as Such*

(*G. L.* i. 174), while the first subdivision of this again is named

(a) *Being Determinate and Being for Self.*

(*G. L.* i. 175.) The position here is that a thing has *both* Being Determinate and Being for Self. (This seems to me to be invalid, but the discussion of its validity had better be postponed until we reach the end of Being for Self as Such.) Since it has both, it is qualitatively differentiated from its Other, while the Being for Self gives it stability and saves it from the infinite series of Others, in which Being Determinate, taken by itself, is compelled to seek the nature of each differentiation.

But the position, Hegel continues (*G. L.* i. 176), cannot be maintained. For Being Determinate has, by the previous transition, been transcended in Being for Self, and is a moment of Being for Self. In so far as it is valid at all, its validity is summed up in Being for Self. In so far as it claims to be anything distinct from, and supplementary to, Being for Self, it is not valid. Therefore all Being for Other has now disappeared, and Being for Self is not for an Other. Being for Self has not negation "an ihm" as a determinateness or limit, and therefore not as a relation to a Being Determinate other than itself.

We have no longer a Something, since Hegel confines that term to the sphere of Being Determinate. At the same time we are not yet entitled to speak of a One. Let us for the present call the reality, which was previously called the Something, by the neutral name of X. The point of the present argument is that the relation of the X to the not-X has become more negative than before.

We must not exaggerate the change. The relation of the Something to the Other was already, in a sense, negative, for the Something was limited by its Other, and was what the Other was not. And, again, X is still related to the not-X. For it is only by distinguishing itself from the not-X that it got Being for Self at all, and this distinction is itself a relation, as will appear more explicitly when we come to the categories of the Many and of Attraction. (When Hegel says that Being for Self does not contain negation "as a relation to a Being Determinate other than itself" (*G. L.* i. 176), the emphasis is, I believe, on the last five words. There *is* a relation, but it is not a relation to a Being Determinate, nor to anything which is, in the technical sense, the "Other" of the Being for Self.)

But the change is there, and is important. When the Something was determined by its Other, the positive nature of the Other was essential to the determination. The Something was this quality, and not any other, and it was determined in this way because the Other was what it was, and nothing else. Now it is different. In Being for Self all that is essential is that there should be something else which is not X. Whatever this other thing may be, X can determine itself by means of a relation to it. It has no longer its own peculiar Other. This increased independence of X is the natural consequence of X being more individual and self-centred than before.

The new category to which we now pass is called by Hegel

(b) Being for One.

38. (*G. L.* i. 176.) We ought, I think, to consider the significance of this category as mainly negative, in spite of its positive name. Its essence is that Being for Self is *not* also Being Determinate, and it might not unfairly have received the name of Not-Being for Other.

Hegel has then no difficulty in proving that the One, for which the X is, can only be itself. If it were anything else the Being for One would be Being for Other. And this is impossible, since Being for Other has already been transcended. The Being for One of X, then, is Being for Self.

This takes us to a new category which consists in the re-statement of Being for Self, but this time by itself without Being Determinate. To this Hegel (*G. L.* i. 181) gives the name of

39.   (c) One,

which emphasises the negative and exclusive character of Being for Self.

It seems to me that Hegel was wrong in subdividing Being for Self as Such. The category of Being Determinate and Being for Self is unjustified, for he only reached Being for Self by transcending Being Determinate. Being Determinate, therefore, in so far as it is true at all, is contained in Being for Self and cannot properly be put side by side with it. The Thesis of the triad must thus be rejected, and the Antithesis must go with it, since the only thing done in Being for One is to remove the Being Determinate which had been improperly introduced in the Thesis. There only remains the Synthesis of the triad—namely, One. Now Hegel's conception of One is just the same as his conception of Being for Self. So the Thesis and Antithesis are removed, and the Synthesis is the same as the undivided category. Thus all the sub-divisions are removed. It would be convenient to call this undivided category One, rather than Being for Self as Such, as this distinguishes it more clearly from the wider tertiary category of Being for Self of which it is a subdivision. This is the course actually taken by Hegel in the *Encyclopaedia* (*Enc.* 96), where an undivided category of One is the Thesis in the triad of Being for Self.

We now pass to the second division of Being for Self,

40. B. *The One and the Many*

(*G. L.* i. 182. *Enc.* 97) of which the first subdivision is

(*a*) *The One in Itself.*

(*G. L.* i. 183.) The first subdivision here is, as is to be expected, a restatement of the last subdivision of the previous division. The two bear, in this instance, almost the same name. Now the One, since it is Being for Self, has its nature by relating itself to, and distinguishing itself from, something other than itself. But this other is at first only determined negatively in regard to the One. The relation of the other term to the One is simply that the other term is not the One. This other term has therefore, to begin with, a merely negative nature. The One is limited by the not-One, by which is meant, so far, not the Many, but only something which is not the One. Thus we get

(*b*) *The One and the Void.*

41. (*G. L.* i. 184.) The name of this category is appropriate enough as a metaphor, but we must remember that it is nothing but a metaphor. If it were a Void, in the literal sense of the term, which was thus related to the One, the One could only be an atom in space, which is not the case.

But the One can only be negated by something like itself (*G. L.* i. 187). The One is definite, and its definiteness depends on a definite relation with the other term. And the relation between them cannot be a definite relation to a definite One, unless the other term is itself definite. Now it has been shown that nothing can be definite, unless it is for itself, and so is a One. Thus the One can only be negated by another One, which bring us to the category of

42.   (c) *Many Ones*

(*G. L.* i. 186), to which Hegel gives the additional name of
Repulsion, since the relation of the Ones to each other is mainly
negative.

Since the conception of the Many has been reached, the
natural question to ask is How Many? Hegel does not regard
this, I think, as a question which can be answered by pure
thought. Pure thought has proved the necessity for a plurality—
has proved, that is, there must be at least two Ones, but not
that there must be more than two. The proof of that would
rest on the empirical fact that we are presented with more than
two differentiations of our experience. So far as the dialectic
can tell us, the number of Ones may be any number not less
than two. There is no reason, that I can see, why the number
should not be infinite, since the contradiction in the infinite
series in Being Determinate did not depend on the infinity of
the series but on the way in which its members were connected.
This, of course, leaves the question undetermined whether, as we
advance in the dialectic, we shall discover objections to an
infinite number of differentiations[1].

Hegel says that the deduction of the Many Ones from the
One must not be considered a Becoming "for Becoming is a
transition from Being to Nothing; One, on the other hand,
only becomes One" (*G. L.* i. 187). And he also warns us
(*G. L.* i. 188) that the plurality is not to be regarded as Otherbeing, for each One is only externally related to all the other
Ones—while in Other-being the whole nature of the Something
was found in its Other.

The divisions of the One and the Many may perhaps be
condemned as superfluous. If we start with the conception of a
One determined by its relation to something else, it might be
possible to conclude directly that this must be another One, and
so reach the Many without the intervening stage of the One
and the Void. At the worst, however, the subdivisions here
only are superfluous, and not, as in Being for Self as Such,
positively erroneous.

[1] It might be said that any question of the number of Ones is improper, since
Hegel does not introduce Number till he comes to Quantum. But it seems to
me that what he introduces in Quantum is only the conception of a number of
units less than the whole, and that therefore even before Quantum it is legitimate
to enquire about the total number of Ones. (See below, Section 54.)

We now pass to the last division of Being for Self which is

43.   *C.   Repulsion and Attraction,*

(G. L. i. 190.   *Enc.* 98) of which the first subdivision is

(a)   *Exclusion of the One.*

(G. L. i. 190.) This is a restatement of the category of Many Ones, which, as was said above, involves the Repulsion by each One of the rest of the Many. But what is the nature of this Many which the One repels? They are other Ones, and thus the One in Repulsion only relates itself to itself *(G. L.* i. 191). The Repulsion thereupon becomes Attraction, and the Many Ones come together in a single One.

The new category thus obtained is called by Hegel *(G. L.* i. 194)

(b)   *The one One of Attraction.*

44. It shows itself to be as untenable as its opposite. If there were only one One there could be no Attraction. For what would there be to attract it, or to be attracted by it? And, again, that there should be only one One is impossible, because as has been shown already, One implies many Ones.

The truth is, as we now see, that Attraction is only possible on condition of Repulsion, and Repulsion is only possible on condition of Attraction. They must be united, and so we reach

45. (c)   *The Relation of Repulsion and Attraction*

(G. L. i. 195) which concludes the categories of Quality.

It seems to me that the subdivisions of Repulsion and Attraction, like those of Being for Self as Such, are positively erroneous. No doubt that which each One repels is other Ones, but this does not make them identical with it. Each One has Being for Self, each has its own nature, and the fact that they are all Ones does not destroy their plurality. If this is correct, we must reject the transition to the Antithesis, and therefore Hegel's deduction of the Synthesis must be invalid.

The Relation of Repulsion and Attraction, which Hegel makes the Synthesis of the triad of Repulsion and Attraction, ought really, I think, to be the whole content of the undivided category of Repulsion and Attraction. And, if so, it may be very easily deduced. The previous category—the last in One

and Many—was Repulsion. But Repulsion is impossible by
itself. Two things cannot have *merely* negative relations to one
another. If *A* is itself only on condition of not being *B*, then
the existence of *B* is essential to *A*, and the relation is positive
as well as negative. To take an example from a more concrete
field, the relation of a combatant to his antagonist is negative.
But it is also positive, for, if he had no one to fight, he could not
be a combatant. Thus the relation of each One to the other
One which it repels is positive as well as negative, and we have
arrived at Hegel's conclusion, though in a simpler and more
valid manner.

We must, of course, here, as elsewhere, be on our guard
against confusing Hegel's categories of Repulsion and Attraction
with the far more concrete ideas of Physics after which he has
named them. The Repulsion and Attraction of Physics may
exemplify these categories, but they also contain empirical
elements which Hegel has not deduced, and which he does not
think that he has deduced.

46. The dialectic has now reached Quantity. Quantity
involves that the units should be so far indifferent to one another,
as to be capable of combination or separation without any change
in their nature. This is rendered possible by the equipoise
between Repulsion and Attraction which has now been established. The Ones are sufficiently under the influence of
Attraction to be brought together in aggregates. They are
sufficiently under the influence of Repulsion to retain their
separate existence in their aggregates, so that the quantity of
the aggregate varies according to the number of its units.

The dialectic thus regards it as an advance to pass from
Quality to Quantity. This may seem to conflict with the
ordinary view that quantitative determinations are more
abstract and less profound than qualitative. But it must be
remembered that this is said with reference to those qualitative
relations which have transcended and absorbed Quantity, while
Hegel, as we have seen, means by Quality only the simplest and
most rudimentary form of what usually goes by the name. The
most abstract Quantity may be an advance on this, although
such Quantity may be very inadequate as compared with more
complex qualitative determinations.

CHAPTER III

QUANTITY

47. Quantity is divided as follows:

I. Quantity. (Die Quantität.)

   A. Pure Quantity. (Die reine Quantität.)

   B. Continuous and Discrete Magnitude. (Kontinuirliche und diskrete Grösse.)

   C. Limitation of Quantity. (Begrenzung der Quantität.)

II. Quantum. (Quantum.)

   A. Number. (Die Zahl.)

   B. Extensive and Intensive Quantum. (Extensives und intensives Quantum.)

     (*a*) Their difference. (Unterschied derselben.)

     (*b*) Identity of Extensive and Intensive Magnitude. (Identität der extensiven und intensiven Grösse.)

     (*c*) The Alteration of Quantum. (Die Veränderung des Quantums.)

   C. The Quantitative Infinity. (Die quantitative Unendlichkeit.)

     (*a*) Its Notion. (Begriff derselben.)

     (*b*) The Quantitative Infinite Progress. (Der quantitative unendliche Progress.)

     (*c*) The Infinity of Quantum. (Die Unendlichkeit des Quantums.)

III.   The Quantitative Ratio. (Das quantitative Verhältniss.)

   A.   The Direct Ratio.   (Das direkte Verhältniss.)

   B.   The Inverse Ratio.   (Das umgekehrte Verhältniss.)

   C.   The Ratio of Powers.   (Potenzenverhältniss.)

It will be noticed that Quantity is used in an ambiguous manner, since it is the name both of the whole secondary division, and of the first of the tertiary divisions contained in it. The tertiary division might be distinguished if we gave it the name of Undivided Quantity, which, as we shall see, would be appropriate to it.

The treatment of Quantity is not one of the most successful parts of the *Greater Logic*. It occupies a greater space than any of the other eight secondary divisions. Yet the transitions are frequently obscure, and often appear to owe their obscurity to excessive compression. By far the greater part of the 186 pages which are employed on Quantity are occupied with Notes on collateral points. Some of these, indeed, throw additional light on the main argument, but the rest only contain criticisms of Kant's views on Quantity, and of certain mathematical doctrines. Hegel is never at his best when criticising Kant, and the mathematical discussions are too purely technical to give us much assistance in comprehending the course of the dialectic.

48.   Again, were Hegel's mathematics correct? Was he right about the mathematics of his own time, and, if so, would he be right about the mathematics of the present day? To answer these questions requires a knowledge of mathematics which I am very far from possessing. Mr Bertrand Russell—one of the few philosophers who are also mathematicians—says: " In Hegel's day, the procedure of mathematicians was full of errors, which Hegel did not condemn as errors but welcomed as antinomies; the mathematicians, more patient than the philosophers, have removed the errors by careful detailed work on every doubtful point. A criticism of mathematics based on Hegel can, therefore, no longer be regarded as applicable to the existing state of the subject[1]."

---

[1] *Mind*, 1908, p. 242.

But the value of Hegel's treatment of Quantity would only be slightly affected by the fact that his criticisms of mathematics were based on ignorance or by the fact that they had been invalidated by the progress of that science. The main object of the dialectic, after all, is to reach the Absolute Idea, and so to demonstrate what is the true nature of reality. Thus the principal function of the lower categories is to lead on to the Absolute Idea. And for this it is only requisite that each of them should logically follow from the one before it, and lead on to the one after it.

Now the question whether Hegel's various categories of Quantity do perform this function is not affected by any mathematical mistakes which he may have made, nor can it be settled in the negative by any mathematical criticisms. The only question is whether Hegel was justified in starting the dialectic with the category of Pure Being, and whether the validity of the Hegelian categories of Quantity can be shown to be involved in the validity of the category of Pure Being. And this is a question for metaphysics and not for mathematics.

It is true that Hegel's main aim in the dialectic was not his only aim. He wished, not merely to deduce an absolutely valid conception of reality, but to account for other less valid conceptions, and to range them in the order of their relative validity. He probably believed that the categories with which he deals in the sphere of Quantity were identical with the fundamental notions of mathematics. In so far as they were not so, he must be considered to have failed in his subordinate purpose, and, in so far as he has failed, to have introduced additional obscurity by the fact that he has called his categories by the names of the mathematical notions.

But the purpose in which he may have failed is, as I have said, only of subordinate importance for him. And his failure if there is one[1], would not be a sign of any metaphysical flaw in his system, but only of mathematical ignorance. If the dialectic process is correct, it will be true of all mathematical conceptions, as of all others, that the way in which we can judge of the

---

[1] Whether there is such a failure or not is left undetermined by Mr Russell's criticisms, since these do not deal with the main course of the argument but with one of the mathematical Notes.

degree of their validity will be by means of the dialectic process. If the ideas are themselves stages in that process, the place which they occupy in it will give us their relative validity. If they are not stages in the process, their relative validity can be found by ascertaining the point in the dialectic at which it becomes clear that they are not absolutely valid. For example, if the absolute validity of mathematical ideas implied the absolute validity of the general conception of Quantum, as given in the dialectic, then, as the dialectic transcended Quantum, it would become evident that the mathematical ideas could not be absolutely valid. Thus, even if Hegel's judgments about mathematics were all wrong, that would not prevent his dialectic from being the foundation of right judgments on the same subject to a person more skilled in mathematics.

I. (UNDIVIDED) QUANTITY.

A. Pure Quantity.

49. This stage (*G. L.* i. 212. *Enc.* 99) appears to be identical in content with the last stage of Quality, though expressed with greater immediacy. The two elements, Repulsion and Attraction, which were recognised as inseparable in the final category of Quality, here receive the names of Discreteness and Continuity.

Pure Quantity is a category of the fourth order, while the category immediately preceding it (Relation of Repulsion and Attraction) is of the fifth order. Thus, according to the general method of the dialectic they should not be identical in content. If, however, the subdivision which produced categories of the fifth order at this point is excessive, as I have maintained above (Section 45), this objection would disappear in an amended dialectic.

But, although Discreteness and Continuity are recognised as inseparable, it is still possible to lay a greater emphasis on one of them than on the other. And we begin, Hegel tells us (*G. L.* i. 213), by laying the greater emphasis on Continuity. The reason appears to be that this element is more characteristic of Quantity, though not more essential to it, than Discreteness. For as long as we had only Repulsion the process remained within Quality, but, as soon as Attraction was added, the transition to Quantity took place. And there is always a tendency to put most emphasis on the element last reached.

B. *Continuous and Discrete Magnitude.*

50. (*G. L.* i. 229.) By a somewhat abrupt transition we come to this category, in which Magnitude is to be taken first as Continuous. Here there is as yet no plurality of Quantities, and the one Quantity is indefinite. A plurality of Quantities would require that they should be Discrete from one another. And, again, no Quantity can be definite unless by its having fixed boundaries—that is to say by being Discrete from the Quantity beyond those boundaries. It is true that, as was said above, all Quantity has an element of Discreteness. But, so far, the only things which are Discrete from one another are the units—the Ones—which are alike Discrete from and Continuous with one another.

Now a One, taken by itself, is not a Quantity at all. For it has no plurality in it. And Ones have no possibility of varying in magnitude. All variations of magnitude are only variations in the number of the Ones. These characteristics are essential to Quantity, and they are not possessed by isolated Ones. And the isolated Ones being, so far, the only Discrete things, we have as yet no definite Quantity, and no plurality of Quantities.

(It may appear incorrect to say that a One admits of no plurality. Can we not, it may be asked, conceive an isolated One as consisting of two halves, four quarters, and so on? But a One which consists of parts is no longer a *mere* One, which is all that the dialectic has got at present. It is something which, while from one point of view a unit, is, from another point of view, an aggregate of two or four units. And this involves the higher conception of Discrete Magnitude, which has not yet been reached.

In the same way, we may conceive the units of which an aggregate is made up as having magnitude, and as being capable of having different magnitudes, and of varying in magnitude. But we can only do this in so far as we conceive each of them as made up in its turn of parts, and so as not being *mere* Ones.)

The position at present is that we have a plurality of Ones—of the number of which we know nothing—which form a single Quantity. But within this single all-embracing Quantity there are as yet no minor Quantities. Each One is qualitatively different from each of the others, but all these qualitative differences are as yet unique. There are no qualities common to more than one One—except, indeed, the quality, if it may be called a quality, of being a One. And this is common to all Ones.

Continuous Magnitude was formed by passing from One to One in virtue of their Continuity. (Continuity, it will be remembered, is what was previously called Attraction. It is the capability, possessed by Ones, of being united in an aggregate.) We now pass to Discrete Magnitude (*G. L.* i. 229). Each One is as really Discrete from all the others as it is continuous with them. Thus a Quantity, less than the whole, can be formed by taking certain Ones together, in virtue of their Continuity, and cutting them off from all others in virtue of their Discreteness. And this Quantity, being cut off by its Discreteness from the indefinite Quantity beyond it, will be a finite Quantity. In the indefinite Quantity, again, other finite Quantities can be formed, and thus we get a plurality of finite Quantities.

51. In the form of this stage, as presented by Hegel, there appear to be two defects. The first is that no reason is given why we should pass from Pure Quantity to the new stage. The second is that, although Continuous and Discrete Magnitude is not divided into a subordinate triad, yet there is a distinct dialectic advance within it—namely from Continuous to Discrete Magnitude.

These defects seem to me to be merely a matter of arrangement. Continuous Magnitude is not really a fresh stage, or part of a fresh stage, at all. It is nothing but Pure Quantity, since, as we have seen, it does not permit of definite Quantity, or of a plurality of Quantities.

On the other hand Discrete Magnitude is not merely correlative with Continuous Magnitude. It is distinctly a more advanced conception. It gives us the distinctness and plurality which were lacking before, and it gives them to us by differentiating the relation between Ones—by joining some of them to

others, and disjoining them from others again, instead of making
the relation uniform.

It is, then, in reality, to Discrete Magnitude that the
advance from Pure Quantity is made. This is evident in
Hegel's text, but is misrepresented by his headings. In order
that these should correspond with his argument, he should have
dealt with Continuous Magnitude under the head of Pure
Quantity, and should have made his second stage simply
Discrete Magnitude, instead of Continuous and Discrete.

It should be remarked that, although the transition to
Discrete Magnitude lies in the possibility of breaking off the
Quantity at any One, this does not mean that it is merely
a possible transition. Continuous Magnitude is that which
cannot be broken off at any point. Discrete Magnitude is that
which can be broken off at any point. When we are forced to
admit the possibility of breaking Magnitude off at any point,
this is a necessary transition to the category of Discrete
Magnitude.

We can break it off, then, at any point we like. But no
reason has been given why we should break it off at one point
rather than at another. Nor can any such reason be given
until we have passed out of the sphere of Quantity into
Meas're. To this point we shall recur later on.

C. Limitation of Quantity.

52. (*G. L.* i. 231.) Hegel says that Discrete Magnitude as
such is not limited. It is only limited as separated from the
Continuous. By this, I conceive, he means that, if the Discrete
Magnitude were taken in isolation, its final One would not be
a Limit, because it would not divide the Discrete Magnitude
from anything else. It is only in so far as it is regarded as in
connexion with the indefinite Continuous Magnitude from which
it has been carved out, that its final term is to be considered
a Limit. (On Hegel's use of Limit cp. above, Section 27.)

The Discrete Magnitude, then, shares its Limit with the
Continuous Magnitude outside it. It is thus in a definite relation
to that which bounds it, and has itself a definite amount. To
definite Quantities Hegel gives the name of Quanta, and so we
pass to the second main division of Quantity.

II. Quantum.

A. *Number.*

53. (*G. L.* i. 232. *Enc.* 101.) In reaching the conception of a limited and definite Quantity we have, according to Hegel, reached for the first time the possibility of Number. While Quantity is merely continuous it cannot be numbered. For then there is no intermediate term between the separate Ones and the whole indefinite Quantity. And the separate Ones in their separateness cannot have any Number, since each of them is only One. But now that we have a definite Quantum, it consists of those Ones which are included between certain Limits, and can therefore be numbered.

54. It may be admitted that, up to this point, there could be no Number of anything less than the whole Quantity. But why could not this have a Number? We do not know how many Ones there are. But this does not prevent them from having a Number, though the dialectic cannot tell us what it is.

Hegel would probably have said that what was infinite could have no Number, and he does not seem to have considered the possibility that there should be a finite number of Ones. But I cannot see that this possibility can be neglected. Each One has—or rather is—a separate Quality. I cannot see anything in the dialectic to exclude the possibility that there should be just twenty such Qualities, and so twenty such Ones, no more and no less.

We must remember that the Ones are not Somethings. The latter had to be infinite in number, since each of them required a fresh Something beyond it. But the Ones have Being for Self, and so avoided, as we saw, this infinite series. Again, if Ones were always divisible into other Ones, their number would necessarily be infinite, but each One is a simple Quality, which is not divisible. Nor does each One involve an endless chain of derivative Ones in the same way, *e.g.*, that every relation is related, so that the number of relations is infinite.

It is true that the Number of the whole Quantity of Ones could not have a Limit, in the Hegelian sense, since there would be nothing outside it. But a Limit, in this sense, does not seem necessary, since the Ones which are numbered have

Being for Self. They can reciprocally determine each other, and when their natures are given, the number of them is given also.

Thus it seems quite possible that all the Ones, taken together, should have a definite and finite Number. That this possibility should have escaped Hegel may very well, I think, be due to the fact that he did not keep sufficiently in his mind the precise significance of his categories of Quantity.

These categories, like all others in the dialectic, refer only to what is existent. (Cp. above, Section 6.) He is not dealing with the purely abstract conception of quantity, which can be applied to anything which can be thought of at all. His categories of Quantity are attempts to explain the nature of what is existent by the conception of quantities of existent Ones—the nature of each One being, as we saw in the last chapter, a simple and unique Quality.

So far as I can see, he never definitely asserts anything inconsistent with this view of the categories of Quantity—the only view which he is entitled to take—except when he deals with Quantitative Ratio. (Cp. below, Section 66.) But his expressions often suggest that he is thinking rather of abstract quantity than of a Quantity of existent Ones. This may account for his failing to see the possibility of the total number, under the categories of Undivided Quantity, being limited. For of course there is no limit to a purely abstract quantity.

What Hegel says, however, in reaching his category of Number, only requires a verbal correction. For it is true that Hegel's category of Number is the first point at which any Quantity, less than the whole Quantity of Ones, could have a number.

55. "Quantity is Quantum" says Hegel, "or has a Limit, both as Continuous and as Discrete Magnitude. The difference of these species has here no meaning" (*G. L.* i. 232). This must not be taken as an assertion that Continuity and Discreteness have no longer meaning as different *moments* in any Quantity. It is only the distinction between Continuous and Discrete *Magnitudes* which has no longer any meaning. And this result was brought about in Limitation of Quantity. For there we saw that a Discrete Magnitude could only be Discrete in so far as it was positively related to that which was outside it. And this positive relation is what Hegel calls Continuity.

Quantity is now indifferent to its Limit, but not indifferent to having a Limit, for to have a Limit is identical with being a Quantum (*G. L.* i. 232). The distinction seems to be that it is always essential to a Quantum to have a Limit, but never essential to it to have a particular Limit. Of course, if it had a different Limit, it would be a different Quantum. But then there is no reason why it should not be different. This will be explained when we reach the Quantitative Infinite Progress.

Hegel further says that the Ones which make up any Quantum are indifferent to the Limit, but that the Limit is not indifferent to the Ones (*G. L.* i. 234). As the Limit is that which determines the Quantum to be what it is, it follows that the Ones in a Quantum are indifferent to the Quantum, while the Quantum is not indifferent to them.

This superiority of the units to the aggregate is essential to Quantity, and is implied in all quantitative statements. When we say, for example, $7 = 5 + 2$, we assume that each of the units dealt with will remain unchanged, whether it is combined with more or fewer others. If not, the proposition would not be true. But the aggregates do not remain the same, regardless of the units. If, for example, we take one unit away from 7, what remains is no longer equal to $5 + 2$.

B. *Extensive and Intensive Quantum.*

(a) *Their Difference.*

56. (*G. L.* i. 252.) Extensive and Intensive Quanta differ from each other in a manner analogous to the difference between Continuous and Discrete Quantity. The distinction between the two pairs of terms is that Extensive and Intensive refer to Quantitative *Limits* only, and, as the Quantum is identical with its Limit, they apply to Quanta, while, since no Quantities except Quanta have Limits, they apply to no Quantities except Quanta. Continuous and Discrete, on the other hand, apply to all Quantities.

We have first Extensive Quantum. This conception is identical with that of Number, except that its determination is now explicitly posited as a plurality (Vielheit) (*G. L.* i. 253).

I do not see why plurality is more explicitly posited in the conception of Extensive Quantum than in that of Number, nor does Hegel give any reason why it should be so. The idea of Extensive Quantum has the same content with the idea of Number. The Extensive Quantum is looked on as primarily a plurality. It is not exclusively a plurality, for, since it is a Quantum, it must be definite, and, being definite, must be Discrete. It is therefore a unity as well as a plurality, but its distinctive mark is plurality. Now this is also the case with Number. A Number is a unity, or it could not be definite. But it is conceived as more essentially a plurality. In Number, as we saw above, the Ones are indifferent to the Quantum, but the Quantum is not indifferent to them. The plurality is thus more essential than the unity.

But since the Quantum is a unity it can also be taken with the greater emphasis on the unity, and when this is done we get the conception of Intensive Quantum (*G. L.* i. 253. *Enc.* 103).

The difference between Intensive and Extensive Quantum is thus one of comparative emphasis[1]. Extensive Quantum has a certain unity, but its unity is subordinate to its plurality. It is comparatively Continuous with what is outside it, and comparatively Discrete within itself. Intensive Quantum is more Discrete from the external, more Continuous within, and its unity is therefore greater than that of Extensive Quantum. The Limit of an Intensive Quantum is called its Degree (*G. L.* i. 254. *Enc.* 103). The Degree of such a Quantum is rather Mehrheit than Mehreres, and while it may be spoken of as a Number (Zahl), it must not, since it is simple, be regarded as a Sum (Anzahl) (*G. L.* i. 254).

(b)   *Identity of Extensive and Intensive Magnitude.*

57. (*G. L.* i. 255.) The treatment of this point is rather obscure. Hegel says " Extensive and Intensive Magnitudes are thus one and the same determination of Quantum; they are only separated by the fact that one has its Sum inside itself, the other has its Sum outside itself. Extensive Magnitude passes over into Intensive Magnitude, since its plurality falls

---

[1] Hegel's use of the term Intensive Quantum differs considerably from that of most other writers.

inherently into a unity, outside which plurality is found.   But on the other hand this unity only finds its determination in a Sum, and in a Sum which is regarded as its own; as something which is indifferent to Intensities otherwise determined, it has the externality of the Sum in itself; and thus Intensive Magnitude is as essentially Extensive Magnitude " (*G. L.* i. 256).

Does this mean that the two terms are strictly correlative— that they stand side by side in the dialectic process, and that the transition from Intensive to Extensive is of precisely similar nature to the transition from Extensive to Intensive ?   Or does it mean that Intensive Quantum stands higher on the scale than Extensive, and that the transition from Extensive to Intensive is the transition of the dialectic process, while the transition from Intensive to Extensive only means that what is seen under a higher category can, if we choose, also be regarded under a lower one ?

The words quoted above suggest the first of these alternatives.   And this is supported by the passage which immediately follows them (*G. L.* i. 257).   In this we are told that with this identity we gain a Qualitative Something, since the identity is a unity which is formed by the negation of its differences.   This on the whole suggests that the two terms are to be taken as on an absolute equality.

Nevertheless it seems to me that the weight of the evidence is on the whole in favour of the view which finds Intensive Magnitude a more advanced stage of the dialectic process than Extensive Magnitude.   To this conclusion I am led by three reasons.

In the first place we cannot safely lay much weight on Hegel's expressions about the Qualitative Something.   For the mention of a Qualitative element here seems very casual.   It is dropped as soon as it has been made.   We hear nothing more of it while we remain in the division of Quantum.   The next mention of a Qualitative element comes in the division which succeeds Quantum—namely Quantitative Relation.   And when it comes in there, it is introduced quite independently, with no reference to the passage on p. 257, and in quite a different way.   That passage cannot therefore be considered as of much importance.

In the second place, the transition to the next category (Alteration of Quantum) does not start from the identity of Extensive and Intensive Magnitudes, but from the consideration of Intensive Magnitude taken by itself. This will, I think, be evident when we come to consider the transition, and it would follow that Intensive Magnitude must be above Extensive in the scale of categories, since the possibility of advancing from the Intensive alone implies that the Intensive has absorbed the Extensive.

In the third place, this view is supported by several passages. Hegel says (*G. L.* i. 279, 280) that the notion of Quantum reaches its reality as Intensive Magnitude, and is now posited in its Determinate Being as it is in its Notion. This agrees with the *Encyclopaedia*, where he says (*Enc.* 104) that in Degree the notion of Quantum is explicitly posited. Also there is not the slightest doubt that, in the *Encyclopaedia*, Intensive Quantum is higher than Extensive Quantum, since it falls in the third subdivision of Quantity, while Extensive Quantum falls in the second.

58. On the whole, therefore, although the evidence is certainly conflicting, I think that the *Greater Logic* regards Intensive Quantum as higher than Extensive Quantum. We can see why this should be so. Intensive Quantum emphasises the unity of the Quantum rather than its plurality. In other words, it emphasises the Limit. This carries us further away from the indefinite Quantity with which the treatment of Quantity began. Intensive Quantum is thus the more developed idea of the two.

The necessity of the transition does not lie in any contradiction in Extensive Quantum which forces us to pass to Intensive. The contradiction would lie in denying that a Quantum which was Extensive was also Intensive. For any Quantum must be Continuous within itself, and Discrete from what is outside it. In virtue of this it is a unity, and so is Intensive. Thus the previous conclusion that the universe is such that the conception of Extensive Quantum is applicable to it, involves that the conception of Intensive Quantum is likewise applicable, and anything else which is involved in the conception of Intensive Quantum.

Hegel's titles, then, do injustice to the course of his argument. The real advance is not from the difference between Extensive Quantum and Intensive Quantum to the identity between them. It is rather from Extensive Quantum to Intensive Quantum. And thus the two first subdivisions of Extensive and Intensive Quantum should have been (a) Extensive Quantum, (b) Intensive Quantum.

Thus, for the second time in this chapter, we find that Hegel's titles are misleading. In each case the defect arose from the titles taking as correlative two conceptions, of which his argument shows one to be superior to the other. In the first case it was the Continuous and Discrete; in the second case it was the Extensive and Intensive. It may perhaps be the case that the confusion arose from following in the titles the usage of mathematics, for which each of these pairs is a pair of two correlatives which are strictly on an equality with one another. Should this be the true explanation, it would add another to the cases in which the consideration of the finite sciences, so far from rendering assistance to the dialectic, has distorted it, and injured its cogency.

59. We now come to the transition to the next category. Of this Hegel says: "The Quantum is the determination posited as transcended, the indifferent limit, the determination which is equally the negation of itself. This discrepancy is developed in Extensive Magnitude, but it is Intensive Magnitude which is the determinate being of this externality, which constitutes the intrinsic nature of the Quantum. It is posited as its own contradiction, as being the simple determination relating itself to itself, which is the negation of itself, as having its determination, not in itself, but in another Quantum.

"A Quantum is therefore posited as in absolute Continuity, in respect of its Quality, with what is external to it, with its Other. It is therefore not only *possible* that it should go beyond any determination of Magnitude, it is not only *possible* that it should be altered, but it is posited as *necessarily* alterable. The determination of Magnitude continues itself in its Other being in such a way that it has its being only in its Continuity with an Other; it is a limit which *is* not, but *becomes*" (*G. L.* i. 261. Cp. also *Enc.* 104).

That is to say, there is nothing to decide why, when there is a Quantum, it should be one Quantum, with one Magnitude, rather than another Quantum, with another Magnitude. Magnitudes can only be fixed by non-quantitative considerations. There is an à priori reason why a triangle has three sides, rather than two or four. There is an empirical reason why there are seven apples on this dish, rather than six or eight. But these reasons are not to be found in the nature of three or seven, but in the nature of triangles, or of the distribution of apples.

Now there are no non-quantitative considerations to determine the Quanta under this category. The only non-quantitative feature that the Quanta have at all is that each One is a separate and unique Quality. And this obviously can give no reason why some of the Ones should be conjoined in a particular Quantum and others left out. This could only be determined by some general quality, shared by some of the Ones, and not by Others. And this is a conception which the dialectic has not yet reached.

But, it may be objected, why should a reason be wanted at all? Why should it not be an ultimate fact—since some facts must be ultimate—that these seventeen Ones, for example, should be parts of the same Quantum, and that no others should be? This would give a definite Quantum.

I do not think this objection is valid. If this Quantum was an ultimate fact, it would imply that there was some difference between any One inside the Quantum and any One outside it, of a different nature from any difference which could occur between any two Ones inside the Quantum. A, inside the Quantum, cannot differ in the same way from B inside it and from C outside it. Now, with the category at present before us, it is impossible that there should be such a difference between differences. Each One differs from every other One precisely in the same way. Each is a separate numerical One, and each is a unique Quality. And there is no other way in which any One can differ from another One[1]. Thus, not only

---

[1] This argument assumes the principle of the Identity of Indiscernibles, since it would be invalid if Ones could differ in their relations without differing in their nature. But Hegel habitually assumes the truth of this principle. (Cp. Section 6.)

can no reason be given for stopping at one point rather than another, but to stop at one point rather than another would introduce a conception (that of different sorts of differences between Ones) positively incompatible with the present category.

60. Hegel expresses this by saying that, while each Quantum has its determination in another Quantum[1], and stops where the other begins, it is at the same time continuous with this other Quantum—the Ones are just the same on each side of the Limit, and there can be no reason why the Limit should not be put elsewhere, and so add to the Quantum or diminish it.   And so we come to

(c)   The Alteration of Quantum.

(*G. L.* 261.)   Why, it may be asked, did not this conception of the necessary variation of Quantity come before ?   Surely it is as true of an Extensive Quantum as of an Intensive Quantum that it is essentially alterable.

I think it is true that, if we had stopped at Extensive Quantum, without going on to Intensive, this conception of Alteration would have necessarily followed from Extensive Quantum.   But the more immediately obvious transition— and therefore the one to take first—was the transition to Intensive Quantum.   And, if Intensive Quantum was to come in at all, the transition to Alteration of Quantum comes better after it, for the necessity of that transition then becomes far more obvious.   As was said in the passage quoted above, it was developed in Extensive Magnitude, but finds its determinate being in Intensive Magnitude.

When we regard a Quantum as Extensive, we regard the plurality of Ones as the element which is logically prior, and the Quantum as a whole is regarded as dependent on the Ones. Now so long as we refer the Quantum to the Ones, there is a reason for the Quantum being the size it is, and no other, namely that it includes those Ones, and no others.   If we go further, and ask why those Ones and no others should be

---

[1] The transition from the Quantum is taken by Hegel as being *first* to an indefinite Quantity. (Cp. below, Section 61.) It would therefore have been better if he had said here that each Quantum was bounded by another *Quantity.*

included, no answer could be given, and the conception of Alteration would arise, but so long as we regard the Ones as ultimate in reference to the Quantum, the necessity of Alteration remains in the background.

But with Intensive Quantum it comes at once to the front. For then the unity of the Quantum is the prominent element. And therefore our question—why is it this Quantum, and not a larger or smaller one—cannot be referred back to the Ones which it contains. And therefore the necessity of Alteration, which is due to the impossibility of answering this question, follows more obviously and naturally from Intensive Quantum.

This is what Hegel means when he says (*G. L.* i. 253) that a determination of a Quantum through Number (which is a category previous to Intensive Quantum) does not need another Magnitude, because in Number Quantum has its externality, and its relation to another, inside itself. (If this passage seems to deny *all* tendency to Alteration in the case of an Extensive Quantum, we must remember the explicit assertion on page 261 that the difference in this respect between Extensive and Intensive is merely a matter of degree.) And again (*G. L.* i. 254) "Degree, therefore, which is simple and in itself, and so has its external Otherbeing no longer in itself, has that Otherbeing outside itself, and relates itself to it as to its determination."

61. We have now come to the end of Extensive and Intensive Quantum, and pass on to the third subdivision of Quantum, which is called

C.   *The Quantitative Infinity.*

(a)   *Its Notion.*

(*G. L.* i. 263.) The first subdivision of Quantitative Infinity, -is, as it should be, the restatement of the last subdivision of the preceding triad. The first movement of the Quantum when it passes its Limit is into a Quantity which is simply defined as not being that Quantum. So far, then, it is only Quantity, and no longer Quantum. And as Quantity is only bounded when it is Quantum, this Quantity has no boundaries at all. Thus it is infinite.

Hegel now proceeds to remark on the difference between the Qualitative Infinity, which was one of the triads in Being

Determinate, and that Quantitative Infinity with which we are
now dealing (*G. L.* i. 264). That which is Qualitatively determined is not *posited* as having the other in itself. Magnitudes,
on the other hand, are posited as being essentially Alterable—
as being, in Hegel's somewhat peculiar language, "unequal to
themselves and indifferent to themselves."

The difference is one which always arises between lower and
higher categories in Hegel's philosophy. The method of the
dialectic changes gradually as the dialectic process advances.
(Cp. *Enc.* 111, 161, 240.) It becomes more of a spontaneous
advance from category to category, and less of a breaking
down, by negative methods, of the resistance of categories
which oppose any movement beyond them. It is thus to be expected, since Quantity comes later than Quality in the process,
that the finite in Quantity should lead on to the infinite more
expressly and directly than the finite in Quality does.

The transition to the Infinite Quantitative Progress, which
now takes place, is analogous to the transition to the Infinite
Qualitative Progress. (Cp. above, Section 33.) The Quantum
is after all continuous with the indefinite Quantity into which
it has passed over. If it were not, it would not have passed
over into it. The passage has only taken place because both
terms are Quantities, only separated by a Limit to which it
is the nature of Quantity to be indifferent. But the Quantity
on the other side of the Limit will also be composed of Ones,
and thus the argument is again applicable which originally
transformed Quantity into Quantum. The Other Side (Jenseits)
of the original Quantum is now itself a Quantum. And therefore, like the original Quantum, it is essentially subject to
alteration, and will pass the Limit, only thereby to reach a
third Quantum, which will be suppressed in its turn, and so
on (*G. L.* i. 265)[1].

[1] The category of the Notion of Quantitative Infinity, which we have just
been considering, corresponds to the category in Quality called Infinity in
General, and the Quantitative Infinite Progress corresponds to the Reciprocal
Determination of the Finite and Infinite. We saw reason to think (Section 31)
that the stage of Infinity in General was a mistake, and that we should have
passed, in Quality, direct from Finitude to Reciprocal Determination of the
Finite and the Infinite.

I do not, however, think that the Notion of Quantitative Infinity is an
invalid category. The argument for the Infinity is quite different in the two

62. We now come to

(b) *The Quantitative Infinite Progress.*

(*G. L.* i. 264. *Enc.* 104.) At this point Hegel inserts an interesting note on the supposed sublimity of the sort of Infinite which is revealed in such a progress as this. Such an Infinite, he says, can produce nothing but weariness (*G. L.* i. 268. *Enc.* 104)[1]. This is extremely characteristic of Hegel. When he says that the true Infinite is not the unbounded, but the self-determined, he does not merely change the meaning of a word, but claims for the self-determined all the dignity which is commonly attributed to the unbounded. It is, perhaps, to his deep conviction that true greatness lies in self-limitation, and not in the absence of limitation, that we are to ascribe much of the special reverence which he shows for the ideas of the Greeks, as well as his low opinion of the Romanticism of his own age and country.

We must not forget, however, that Hegel never says that the False Infinite of an Infinite Series is necessarily contradictory, though he does say it is worthless and tedious. But in the present case there is a contradiction, as there was with the Infinite Series in Quality. We had reached the idea of a Quantum, and a Quantum has to be definite. But it can only be definite by having a certain Limit, and by keeping within it. We have seen, however, that any Quantum necessarily passes its Limit, and overflows into a fresh Quantum. It is not, therefore, determined in Magnitude. But it is of

---

cases, and here it seems to be valid. If a Quantum passes its Limit, the first result of that is, as Hegel states it to be, that it becomes an unlimited Quantity. It is a fresh step in the argument to show that this Quantity must still be a Quantum and have a fresh Limit, and so on indefinitely. Thus the passage to the Infinite Progress in Quantity, unlike the passage to the Infinite Progress in Quality, does require a transition through a stage of absence of Limitation.

It was possibly the necessity for such a stage of absence of Limitation in Quantity, which misled Hegel into supposing that it was necessary in Quality as well.

[1] His expression in the *Encyclopaedia* is "welches Kant als schauderhaft bezeichnet, worin indess das eigentlich Schauderhafte nur die Langweiligkeit sein dürfte." In the first edition of his translation Prof. Wallace happily renders this: "which Kant describes as awful. The only really awful thing about it is the awful wearisomeness." The second edition is, I think, less successful.

the essence of Quantum to be determined, and the dialectic
will not permit us to reject the idea of Quantum altogether.
In this case, therefore, a contradiction arises.

63. To this argument an objection might be raised. Let
us take the Quantum as enlarged till it includes the whole
Quantity of Ones. Will it not then be determined, since it
is impossible for it to increase beyond this point? It will not,
indeed, have a Limit, in the technical Hegelian sense, but it
will have a fixed Magnitude, and this is all that is wanted.

Hegel does not seem to have considered this point. As I
said above (Section 54), he would probably have considered
that an infinite Quantity of Ones would have no Number, and
no definite Magnitude, and he apparently ignored the possibility
of the Ones being finite in number. But this possibility, as we
saw above, cannot justifiably be ignored.

It does not, however, remove the contradiction. And this
for two reasons. In the first place, the category of Quantum
arose from the fact that Quantity, in virtue of its characteristic
of Discreteness, could be divided at any point—we could make
a Quantum wherever we liked by dividing Quantity. Now if
the only way in which we can get a Quantity of a fixed
Magnitude is by including all the Ones, then there will only
be one such fixed Magnitude, and it will not arise by dividing
the total Quantity, but by including it all.   This is not a
Quantum. For a Quantum is made by dividing the total
Quantity, and has always, therefore, other Quanta beyond it.
The fixed Magnitude of the whole of Quantity, then, would not
be a Quantum, and thus the contradiction would still remain—
that it has been proved that there must be determined Quanta,
and that no Quantum can be determined.

In the second place, a Quantum would not be determined
by the fact that it could increase no further. For its instability
works both ways. There is no more reason why it should not
be smaller than it is, than why it should not be larger than it
is. (Hegel only speaks of the indeterminateness in the one
direction, but his arguments apply equally to the other.) Thus,
suppose a Quantum could contain all the Ones, the process of
Alteration would take place with it as much as with any other,
though it could only take place in one direction.

64. How is the contradiction to be avoided? In a very similar way to that in which the same difficulty was met in the case of Qualitative Infinity. That which is outside any Quantum is another Quantum. If we try to find the determination of any Quantum in itself exclusively, then we find that its Limit continually alters, and that the task is endless. But the case is changed if we fully accept the relation of each Quantum to the other which is outside it. No Quantum can determine itself as against another Quantum. But two Quanta can reciprocally determine one another. There is no reason why 7 Ones should not change to 8, or 17 Ones to 16, if we take 7 Ones and 17 Ones as isolated facts, each of which must be determined by itself, or not at all. But if we take these Quanta as related to one another, then there is a reason why 7 Ones should not become 8—for then the Quantum would bear a different relation to the 17 Ones. And there is a corresponding reason why 17 Ones should not become 16. Thus the Quanta have now some real self-determination, though it is slight; A cannot become greater or less, because it would thereby change its relation to B. And its relation to B is what it is, not only because B is B, but because A is A. With this partial self-determination we reach

(c)   *The Infinity of Quantum*

(*G. L.* i. 279.   *Enc.* 105) by which is meant the true Infinity of self-determination, as opposed to the False Infinity of an unending progress.

65. It will be noticed that there is a difference between the Quantitative Infinite Progress and the earlier Qualitative Infinite Progress. In Quality the Something finds its nature only in another Something, which in turn finds its nature in a third, and so on. The Somethings themselves do not change, but fresh Somethings are continually reached in the vain search for a final determination. In Quantity, however, the Infinite Progress is not a Progress of an Infinity of Quanta, but of a single Quantum, which endlessly increases in size as it successively overleaps every Limit.

In Quality no change of anything was possible. The nature of reality was not yet sufficiently complex to allow anything

to become different in one respect while remaining the same
in others.   If a thing is not completely the same it has utterly
vanished.   It is impossible, therefore, for a Something to change,
and the Infinite Progress can only take place by adding fresh
Somethings.

In Quantity, however, change is possible.   The gradual
addition of fresh Ones to a Quantum affords a changing
element, while the Ones previously in it afford the permanent
element, without which there can be no change.

With this stage of the dialectic the idea of Quality becomes
more prominent again.   Not only are the Ones each a separate
Quality, as they have been all along, but in each Quantum,
also, a Qualitative nature begins to develope (*G. L.* i. 281.
Enc. 105).   This is most clearly stated in the *Encyclopaedia.*
" That the Quantum in its independent character is external
to itself, is what constitutes its Quality.   In that externality
it is itself and referred connectively to itself.   There is a union
in it of externality, *i.e.* the Quantitative, and of independency
(Being-for-Self)—the Qualitative."   The essential character of
Quantity was its instability.   Now this characteristic begins
to disappear.   The Quantum can no longer alter without any
effect on anything but its own Magnitude.   For it is now in
relation to some other Quantum, and it cannot alter unless
either that other Quantum, or the relation, alters simulta-
neously.   This is the first step (though as yet a very small one)
towards bringing back, on a higher level, the fixity of Quality.
With it we pass out of Quantum to the third and last division
of Quantity, after some mathematical digressions occupying
nearly a. hundred pages.

III.   The Quantitative Ratio.

66.   (*G. L.* i. 379.   *Enc.* 105.)   The Ratio between two Quanta,
says Hegel, is itself a Quantum (*G. L.* i. 380).   And it is true
that it is a determinate number.   But it differs too much from
the Quanta, which it relates, to have any claim to the name of
Quantum.   For they are Quanta of Ones, while the Ratio is
not.   The Ratio between twelve existent Ones and six existent
Ones is certainly two, but it is not two existent Ones.   Hegel

does not seem to see this, and treats all three quantities here
as if they were simply terms in abstract arithmetic, in which he
is not justified.

67. The first and simplest form of Ratio is called

A. The Direct Ratio.

(*G. L.* i. 381.) The related Quanta are here taken as logically prior, and the Quantum which is their Ratio as logically
subsequent. Thus we get, for example, that the Ratio of 7
to 35 is 5. The Ratio is called the Exponent.

Now the Quantum which is the Ratio is no more determined by the two Quanta of which it is the Ratio than it is
by an infinite number of pairs of other Quanta. For example,
5 is equally the Ratio of 6 and 30, of 8 and 40, and so on.
It follows that the related Quanta can alter to any extent
absolutely, provided that they do not alter relatively. So long
as one remains five times the other they may both increase or
diminish indefinitely.

Nothing is stable but the Exponent. And therefore Hegel
finds it a defect in this category that the Exponent is not
sufficiently discriminated from the other Quanta. It cannot be
the largest of the three Quanta concerned, but it can be either
of the others. We have said that 7 and 35 stand to each other
in a Ratio expressed by 5. But we might just as well have
said that 5 and 35 stand to each other in a Ratio expressed
by 7 (*G. L.* i. 383).

It seems to me that this argument is defective because it
ignores the fact, pointed out above, that the Ratio is not a
Magnitude of the same sort as the Quanta of which it is a
Ratio. They are Quanta made up of existent Ones, using the
word One in the special sense in which the dialectic has
determined it. But the Ratio is not a Number of Ones, in
this sense, at all. Therefore the Ratio and the related Quantum
are not interchangeable in the way Hegel asserts.

68. It is on this supposed defect that the transition to
the next category is based. Since — this appears to be
Hegel's argument—the Exponent has the stability which the
other Quanta do not possess, it must be distinguishable from
them. But in Direct Ratio this is not the case, since the

Exponent is interchangeable with the related Quanta. We must therefore seek out another sort of Ratio, where the Exponent is marked out by the nature of the relation. Now, if we take three integral numbers, there is a relation between them which has the required definiteness. If one of them is the product of the other two, then it is the largest of the three that will be the product[1]. So we come to

B. The Inverse Ratio

(*G. L.* i. 384) where the Exponent is the product of the two related Quanta. It appears to be called Inverse because the increase of one of the related Quanta involves the diminution of the other.

69. The transition to the next category is extremely obscure. So far as I can understand it, it is as follows (*G. L.* i. 389). Either of the two related Quanta can increase, so long as the other diminishes, the only Limit of this process being that neither of the related Quanta can become larger than the Exponent. Thus either of the related Quanta is implicitly (an sich) the Exponent. Hegel calls this "the negation of the externality of the Exponent." This means, I believe, that there are no longer necessarily *three* Quanta, but only two, namely the Exponent, connected with one other Quantum, no longer by a third Quantum, but by some non-quantitative relation. And thus, says Hegel—without giving any further explanation—we reach

C. The Ratio of Powers.

(*G. L.* i. 389.) By this he appears to mean only the special relation which exists between two numbers, one of which is the square of the other. It is the square, as the result of the process, which is treated as the Exponent.

70. The transition appears very questionable. It may be admitted that the indefinite approximation of one of the related Quanta to the Exponent brings a Qualitative element into greater prominence, and that the Ratio of Powers has also a relatively prominent Qualitative element. But in other

---

[1] The related Quanta must be represented by integral numbers, since they consist of indivisible Ones. The product therefore must also be integral.

respects they are quite different conceptions. And Hegel gives us no reason for passing at this point from one partially-qualitative relation to another and distinct partially-qualitative relation. He is satisfied with showing that they are both partially-qualitative, which is clearly not sufficient.

It is difficult to see, too, why Hegel thought himself justified in considering only those cases where one Quantum was the square of the other, and in excluding cubes and other powers. If, however, he *had* considered those other powers, it would have become evident that the relation between the two Quanta was not yet one which could dispense with a third Quantum. For the question of the power to which one was to be raised to equal the other could only be answered by naming a third Quantum.

Hegel makes the transition to the next category as follows: " Quantity as such appears as opposed to Quality; but Quantity is itself *a* Quality, a determination in general which relates itself to itself, and which is separated from the other determination, from Quality as such. Yet it is not only *a* Quality, but the truth of Quality itself is Quantity: Quality has shown itself as going over into Quantity; Quantity, on the other hand, is in its truth that externality which is turned back on itself, which is not indifferent. So it is Quality itself, in such a way that outside this determination Quality as such is no longer anything....The Quantum now as indifferent or external determination (so that it is just as much transcended as such, and is the Quality, and is that, through which anything is what it is) is the truth of the Quantum—to be Measure " (*G. L.* i. 392).

71. We have now reached the end of Hegel's treatment of Quantitative Ratio. As we have seen, serious objections exist both to the transition from Direct to Inverse Ratio, and to the transition from Inverse Ratio to the Ratio of Powers. But, apart from these, there is a more general objection. The whole triad of Quantitative Ratio is a blind alley. It does not lead, as it professes to lead, to the category of Measure, and the chain of the dialectic cannot be continued through it.

The passage I have quoted above contains the transition from Quantity to Measure. We have therefore before us the way in which the inadequacies of Quantity are, according to

Hegel, to be transcended, and in which Quality is to be synthesised with Quantity in Measure. These objects would certainly have been attained if Hegel had succeeded in his attempt to demonstrate that Quantity is Quality. But it seems to me that he has not reached this result by Quantitative Ratio, and that therefore he has neither removed the inadequacies of Quantity, nor synthesised it with Quality.

As to the first. The special characteristic of Quantity was its instability. We saw, to begin with, that it was that which could alter, and yet remain the same. When we reached Alteration of Quantum, we found that it not only could alter, but must alter, and it was to remedy the contradictions thus caused that we were forced to resort to Quantitative Ratio.

Does Quantitative Ratio remove this indifference, even when taken in its highest form, the Ratio of Powers ? Let us pass over the difficulty that the power to which a number is to be raised can only be expressed in another number, which might be any other. Let us confine ourselves, as Hegel does, to squares, and ignore the quantitative nature of the index. Has this removed the instability ? If we take 49 Ones as a simple Quantum, it is under the necessity of changing continually. If we take it as the square of 7^1, has the necessity disappeared ?

Surely it has not. It is true that the Square cannot now change unless the Root changes as well. But the Root is also a Quantum, and so it also will be unstable, and the Square will be unstable with it. The first numbers the Square can change to are no longer 48 and 50 but 36 and 64. But the number of changes of the Square is unbounded except by the total number of Ones, and we have seen that this restriction does not remove the instability of Quantum. And therefore Quantitative Ratio has not removed the contradictions of Quantitative Infinity, nor has it enabled us to transcend the characteristic nature of Quantity. It is true that the Square and the Root are linked Quanta, but they are still Quanta.

Very closely connected with this is the second defect of the triad. It professes to lead us to Measure, and it must therefore

---

[1] I do not recur here to the difficulty that 49 Ones (in the Hegelian sense) are neither the square of 7 Ones, nor of 7, nor of anything else. This is a fresh case of the mistake mentioned above (Section 66).

bring back Quality. In the passage quoted above (*G. L.* i. 392)
Hegel says that it has done this. Quantity " is Quality itself,
in such a way that outside this determination Quality as such
is no longer anything." That is to say, he holds that we have
here reached a Synthesis of Quality and Quantity. Now it is
true that the introduction of related Quanta has introduced a
certain Qualitative element into Quantity. The movements of
each separate Quantum are no longer completely arbitrary and
unconditioned, and every restriction on the movement means
some departure from the typical idea of Quantity. But this
does not amount to what Hegel claims to have reached—the
complete absorption of Quantity. We have got a Quantity,
which is more like a Quality than before, but which is still
essentially a Quantity and not a Quality. The test of this is
the instability, and the Infinite Progress to which the instability gives rise. Till we have got rid of this, we have not
transcended Quantity. For the instability is, as we have seen,
the special characteristic of Quantity. Thus we have not
reached a point at which Quantity is transcended, and therefore
united with Quality. The category at which we stand is still
essentially Quantitative, and does not combine Quantity with
Quality. And as Measure certainly has to combine Quantity
with Quality, we have not yet got a valid transition to
Measure.

72. What then is to be done ? We saw reason to think
that the transition from Quantum to Quantitative Ratio is
valid, and I believe that it is possible to recast the triad of
Quantitative Ratio in such a way as to make a valid transition
to Measure. The Thesis of my proposed triad would be the
restatement of the general idea of Quantitative Ratio, as it
had been arrived at in the previous category of Infinity of
Quantum. It might be called *Quantitative Ratio as such,* or
again *Quantitative Ratio in general* (überhaupt), either of which
would be in accordance with Hegel's terminology.

The inadequacy of this Thesis would lie in the fact that a
Quantum is not fully determined by its Ratio to another unless
that other Quantum is determined. Nor can the two Quanta
mutually determine one another by their Ratio, for, as we have
seen, two Quanta can vary and yet preserve the same Ratio to

one another. The second Quantum, then, must be determined
by its Ratio to a third, with regard to which the same question
will arise, and so on continually. This Infinite Series forms
the Antithesis of our triad, and might be called the *Infinite
Series of Ratios.*

It will be noticed that this Infinite Series resembles the
Infinite Series of Quality rather than the Infinite Series of
Quantity. For the Ratios do not continually alter, as the
Quanta did in the Series of Quantity. The Infinity comes
in through the necessity of going to fresh Ratios to determine
those already existing.

Here, as in the two previous cases, the Infinite Series
involves a contradiction. The original Quantum is determined.
But it can only be determined by a Ratio to a Quantum
which is determined otherwise than by a Ratio. But no such
Quantum is to be found. Therefore the original Quantum is
not determined, and we have a contradiction.

We must pass on, then, to a fresh category, which will
remove this contradiction, and will form the Synthesis of
Quantitative Ratio. We have seen that Quantity, however
developed, can never, while it remains only Quantity, get
rid of the inadequacy which has shown itself once more in
the Infinite Series of Ratios. Now the ground of this inadequacy was the necessary instability of all Quanta. And
this instability, we saw, proceeded from the fact that the
differences between all Ones were so similar that no reason
could be assigned why a Quantum should stop at any particular
limit rather than another. (Cp. above, Section 59.)

The only way of escaping from our difficulty, therefore,
will be to reject this similarity of the differences between the
Ones, and to find a state of things in which the natures of the
Ones shall link some of them more closely together in a group
from which others are excluded. And this can be done only
if there are Qualities each of which belongs to several Ones,
but not to all, so that each of these forms a bond which binds
those Ones which have it into a group from which those which
do not have it are excluded.

The instability of Quanta would thus be arrested. For
there would be a reason why the Quantum should not increase

beyond a certain Limit.   Every Quantum is a Quantum of
Ones which have a certain common Quality, and beyond a
certain Limit there would be no more Ones with that Quality.
The Ones outside it would have some other Quality.

We have now reached a category which transcends the inadequacy of Quantitative Ratio, and also of Quantity generally,
and so reaches the category of Measure as defined by Hegel
(*G. L.* i. 392) in the passage quoted above.   Our argument
avoids Hegel's error of ignoring the difference between a
Quantum of Ones and a Quantum (if that name is appropriate
to it) which is a Ratio between Quanta.

73.   The treatment of Quantity in the *Encyclopaedia* is
practically the same as in the *Greater Logic*, except in one
point.   In the *Greater Logic*, as we have seen, Extensive and
Intensive Magnitudes, and the Infinite Progress all fall within
the second subdivision, while the third subdivision is completely taken up by Ratio.   In the *Encyclopaedia*, the second
subdivision (named, as in the *Greater Logic*, Quantum) deals
with Extensive Magnitude only.   The third subdivision is
called Degree, and contains Intensive Magnitude, the Infinite
Progress, and Ratio.   This arrangement shows more clearly
that an advance is made in passing from Extensive to Intensive
Magnitude, but otherwise it seems inferior to the order of the
Greater Logic.   For Intensive Magnitude seems more closely connected with Extensive Magnitude than it is with Ratio.   And,
again, the Infinite Progress makes manifest the characteristic
contradiction inherent in all Quantity.   It would seem, therefore,
more appropriately placed in the second subdivision, which is
the Antithesis of the triad of Quantity, than in the third,
which is the Synthesis.

CHAPTER IV

MEASURE

74. Measure (Das Maass) is divided by Hegel in the following manner:

I. The Specific Quantity. (Die specifische Quantität.)

A. The Specific Quantum. (Das specifische Quantum.)

B. Specifying Measure. (Specifirendes Maass.)
   (*a*) The Rule. (Die Regel.)
   (*b*) The Specifying Measure. (Das specifirende Maass.)
   (*c*) Relation of both Sides as Qualities. (Verhältniss beider Seiten als Qualitäten.)

C. Being for Self in Measure. (Das Fürsichsein im Maasse.)

II. Real Measure. (Das reale Maass.)

A. The Relation of Stable Measures. (Das Verhältniss selbstständigen Maasse.)
   (*a*) Union of two Measures. (Verbindung zweier Maasse.)
   (*b*) Measure as a Series of Measure Relations. (Das Maass als Reihe von Maassverhältnissen.)
   (*c*) Elective Affinity. (Wahlverwandtschaft.)

B. Nodal Line of Measure Relations. (Knotenlinie von Maassverhältnissen.)

C. The Measureless. (Das Maasslose.)

III. The Becoming of Essence. (Das Werden des Wesens.)

A. The Absolute Indifference. (Die absolute Indifferenz.)

B. Indifference as Inverse Relation of its Factors. (Die Indifferenz als umgekehrtes Verhältniss ihrer Factoren.)

C. Transition to Essence. (Uebergang in das Wesen.)

It should be noticed that the title of Specifying Measure is borne both by I. B., and by its second subdivision, I. B. (b).

75. It seems to me that the whole of Hegel's treatment of Measure is invalid. He has no right to the fundamental conception of Measure—the conception with which he begins, and which, in a modified form, persists till we reach Essence. If this is so, of course, all the categories of Measure must be abandoned, and the transition from Quantity to Essence, if it can be made at all, must be made in some other way. I should depart too largely from the object of a commentary if I attempted, in this book, so large a reconstruction. But it is necessary, before considering Hegel's treatment in detail, to substantiate my general criticism of the validity of Measure.

The categories of Quantity ended with the result that every Quantitative difference must involve a Qualitative difference. Every Quantum, consequently, must have a common Quality. And since each of the Ones, of which every Quantum is composed, has its own separate and unique Quality, it follows that each One must have at least two Qualities—its unique Quality and another which it shares with other Ones which are united with it in a Quantum.

I maintained in the last chapter that Hegel's treatment of Quantitative Ratio failed to justify this result, and also that it could be demonstrated another way. But whether Hegel did or not fail to demonstrate the result, I do not think it can be doubted that this is the result which he believed himself to have demonstrated, and that it is, therefore, the only basis which he was justified in taking for the categories of Measure.

His argument all through Quantitative Ratio was directed to show that the Quanta which were thus related had also a Qualitative aspect. His final words are "The Quantum now as indifferent or external determination (so that it is just as much transcended as such, and is the Quality, and is that, through which anything is what it is) is the truth of the Quantum—to be Measure" (*G. L.* i. 392). And again in the *Encyclopaedia*, "Measure is the Qualitative Quantum, in the first place as immediate—a Quantum to which a Determinate Being or a Quality is attached" (*Enc.* 107).

76. This is the last conception of Quantity, and ought to be the first of Measure. At any rate Hegel has no right to go beyond it without justifying the transition by an argument. But directly he begins to deal with Specific Quantum—the first of the categories of Measure, he suddenly assumes that he has reached an entirely different conception. "The Quantum as Measure has ceased to be a limit which is no limit; it is now the determination of the nature of the fact[1] such that this nature is destroyed, if it is increased or diminished beyond this Quantum" (*G. L.* i. 403). The conception here is that which is involved in the changes, for example, of water into a solid, a liquid, and a gas, according to its varying temperature.

It is clear that this is quite a different conception from that of Qualities common to all the members of a Quantum. It is a more complicated conception. For it involves that each One to which it applies should have at least two Qualities which *can* be common to it with other Ones. Of these Qualities one—the temperature, in our example—varies in Quantity, but remains the Quality of all the Ones included under this Measure. The second Quality in each case is common to those of the Ones for which the first Quality falls within certain Quantitative limits. Thus all water whose temperature exceeds a certain limit has the second common Quality of being gaseous. Now the conception at the end of Quantitative Ratio only involved the existence, in each One, of *one* Quality common to it with other Ones.

And, in the second place, the relations of Quality and

---

[1] The original is "Die Bestimmung der Sache." On the whole, I think "nature of the fact" fairly represents Sache in this passage.

Quantity to one another are quite different in the old conception and in the new conception. In the old conception Quantity came in as the number of Ones which had the same Quality. Here it comes in as a Quantity, not *of* Ones, but *in* each One. It is a Quantity of a Quality of the One.

The old conception, then, at the end of Quantitative Ratio, is quite different from the new one with which Hegel starts in Specific Quantum. And the latter could only be legitimately reached from the former by a fresh step of the dialectic, the necessity of which would have to be demonstrated. But Hegel offers no demonstration of the transition, and, indeed, fails to see that there is any difference between the conceptions. He treats them as if they were identical, and as if he was only using the final result of one section as the starting point of the next—which is what *should* happen according to the dialectic method, but which is not what has happened here.

77. How he fell into so serious a mistake is a difficult question. The new conception, it is true, resembles the old in so far that they each involve both Quantity and Quality, and that in the new conception also Quantity is limited by Quality[1], though the Quantity limited is not, as the dialectic requires here, a Quantum of Ones. Again, the new conception is compatible with the old, though it is not identical with it or deduced from it. If the Ones A, B, C, have the common Quality x, and the Ones D, E, F, the common Quality y, the old conception would apply to them. And it would be possible that the one group were x because they had a quality z with a certain intensity, and that the other group were y because they had the Quality z with a different intensity. In this case the new conception would apply also.

These circumstances might have led Hegel to confuse the two conceptions. Or, again, it is possible that Hegel started with a presupposition that Measure (in the sense of the new conception) was probably the Synthesis of Quality and Quantity. This would be natural enough, since it does involve them both, and involves them in a form which is frequently present to us in empirical experiences. If he started with such a presup-

[1] If, *e.g.*, certain water has the Quality of being fluid, the Quantity of its temperature is fixed by that fact.

position he might more easily fail to see that he had not deduced his new conception of Measure from the previous categories.

Passing to the consideration of the categories of Measure in detail, we have first

I.   THE SPECIFIC QUANTITY.

A.   *The Specific Quantum.*

78. (*G. L.* i. 403.) This category is naturally the expression of the new conception of Measure in its simplest form. The Ones have each two Qualities such that if the first varies in Quantity beyond certain limits, the second Quality is changed for another. (The first Quality might be called the permanent Quality, the second and its successors the varying Qualities.)

This category is pronounced inadequate by Hegel because the union of Quality and Quantity is only apparent, and it does not, therefore, really remove the difficulty which called it into being. So long as the Quantitative change keeps within the limits of the Quality—as when fluid water becomes colder without freezing, or hotter without boiling, we get the Quantity changing while the Quality remains the same. The two sides thus remain isolated, and there is nothing which checks the inherent instability of Quantity. Now the whole object of our transition to Measure was just to check this instability.

At intervals, no doubt, the Quantitative change is accompanied by a Qualitative change. Water passes from a liquid state into the form of ice or steam. But here, also, the changes of Quantity and Quality are not really connected For a Qualitative change is always instantaneous, in the strictest sense of the word.

This may at first sight appear to be inconsistent with our experience. But when we say that a Qualitative change can be gradual, we mean one of two things. We may mean that the different parts of a whole undergo the change successively, as when a kettle full of water is gradually converted into steam. This, of course, is compatible with the change being instantaneous for each part.

Or we may mean that the change from the quality A to the quality B is not instantaneous, because there are intermediate

qualitative changes. Ice does not pass instantaneously into
steam, for it must first become water. And a process which
appeared to go directly from A to B may be found, on closer
investigation, to go through the forms X Y, and Z, before it
reaches B.

But however many stages may be intercalated before B, it
is certain that, when the quality A changes, it must do so
instantaneously. For if A changes, it must change into something which, whatever its positive nature, can be correctly
described as not-A. And, by the law of Excluded Middle, the
quality must either be A and not not-A (when the change will
not have begun) or else not-A and not A (when the change will
be completed). The change, therefore, is instantaneous ($G. L.$ i.
405. $Enc.$ 108).

Quantity, then, can change without Quality changing, and
all changes of Quality take place while the Quantitative change
is infinitely small. The two terms are thus, in Hegel's opinion,
not really united. It is this defect, he tells us, which is at the
root of the old difficulty as to the point at which a head, whose
hairs are being pulled out one by one, becomes bald. To say
that the absence of one hair can make a head bald, which was
not bald before, seems absurd. Yet, if one hair never made the
difference, we come to the equally absurd conclusion that a head
with no hair on it could not be called bald ($G. L.$ i. 406. $Enc.$ 108).

79. Hegel's conclusion is that the Measure now becomes
double. We have (1) the actually existing Quantity of the
permanent Quality, (2) the other Quantity of the permanent
Quality which, if reached, would involve the change of one
varying Quality into another. The second Quantity forms the
limit within which the first can vary, while it is itself fixed.
This limitation Hegel expresses by saying that it specifies the
first Quantity, and so we reach

B. Specifying Measure.

($G. L.$ i. 407.) This transition seems to me erroneous. We
have not really got a new category at all. Two Quantities were
involved in the idea of Measure from the beginning—the
Quantity which exists, and the other which marks the point of
transition into a fresh Quality. If a basin of water is fluid,

rather than gaseous, because its temperature is 60°, this involves the conception of a further temperature at which it would become gaseous. Thus Specifying Measure takes us no further than Specific Quantum. It is neither a development of the difficulty involved in the transition from Specific Quantum, nor a solution of that difficulty, and it has no right to be the next category to it. Hegel calls its first subdivision

(a) The Rule.

(G. L. i. 408.) This, he tells us, is identical with the general idea of Specifying Measure. The defect of the category is that the Rule—that is, the limiting Quantity, is merely arbitrary. And as this is inconsistent with the nature of Measure, which is not merely arbitrary, the category is inadequate.

But why are we to suppose that the Quantity taken for the Rule is merely arbitrary? Hegel's example is a linear foot, and this, no doubt, is arbitrary. We might just as well measure length by ells or by metres as by feet. But the example is not fair. Measures of length are used for the measurement of space. And the conception of space makes abstraction of all Qualitative differences. We measure the Quantity of space, and the Quantity only, regardless of the Quality of the matter which fills that space. Any Rule here must be purely arbitrary, for it concerns Quantity only, and all limits of Quantity, taken by itself, are purely arbitrary. But the dialectic has now passed beyond mere Quantity to Measure, where a change of Quantity brings about a change of Quality. And here the Rule is no longer arbitrary. The Rules of the temperature of liquid water are 32° and 212° Fahrenheit, and these are not arbitrary, but grounded in the nature of the subject-matter. (It is arbitrary, no doubt, to call them 32° and 212°, rather than 0° and 100°, or any other numbers. But it is not arbitrary that the limits to the heat of liquid water are these temperatures and not others.)

80. Hegel endeavours to remove the defect of this category by passing on to

(b) The Specifying Measure

(in the narrower sense) (G. L. i. 408). Here the something (Etwas) which is the Measure receives an alteration of the amount of its Quality from outside. It reacts against this, and receives it in a way of its own, so that the resulting Quantum of the Quality, as reproduced in the Something, is not the same Quantum as in the external source of the alteration, but is increased or diminished through the effect of a Qualitative difference in the Something.

The introduction of such a category at this point seems very extraordinary, but Hegel's language places it, I think, beyond doubt. The description of the category will bear no other meaning, and the nature of the other categories, which immediately follow, supports the same interpretation. And his example is also quite clear. Material objects he tells us (*G. L.* i. 410) have specific temperatures, which cause the changes of temperature which they receive from outside to be different in them from what they are in the medium from which they are received.

81. This transition appears to me to be quite illegitimate, since it introduces an entirely new conception of Measure without deducing it from the conception previously established.

Hegel does not even say that it *is* changed. But the change is very great. We started with a conception of Measure, according to which the continuous change of Quantity involved at certain points a sudden change of Quality. There was only one Quantitative series involved, and there was a Qualitative series. Here, on the other hand, we suddenly find ourselves with a new conception. We have now two Quantities in different Somethings (in the example, the temperature of the medium, and the temperature of the object). The first of these determines the other. We have also two Qualities (in the example, heat, and that Quality in the object which causes its heat to be more or less than that of the medium. But there is no Qualitative series, for neither Quality is conceived as necessarily changing into another Quality.

This category is not in any sense implied in the previous category of Rule. It simply ignores it. The difficulty in Rule, according to Hegel, was to find for the Quantitative changes of any particular Quality, a limit which should not be arbitrary. But in the new category the Qualities never change into other Qualities at all, and even the imperfect check on the Quantitative changes has been swept away.

Again, in this category we have two objects connected with each other—the original object and a second one.   (In the example which Hegel gives, the first object is that with a specific temperature, the second object is the medium.)   Before this, the Measure of each object was stated without reference to any other object.   The introduction of this new element ought to be justified as an inevitable consequence of the preceding category.   But, so far as I can see, Hegel makes no attempt whatever to do this.

Moreover this category, as stated by Hegel, includes the idea of Cause.   This is not the case with previous categories.   In Quantitative Ratio the Quantities implied one another, but did not cause one another.   But here we are told ($G. L.$ i. 408) that the Something experiences an " external alteration " of the amount of its Quality.   This is nothing but Causality.   It may be doubted, indeed, whether it does not involve more than Hegel's category of Causality, but it certainly could not be introduced without including that category, and if the dialectic is right in introducing Cause for the first time towards the end of Essence, it cannot be right here.

If what I have said is correct, the dialectic at this point is vitiated by two errors—there was no adequate ground for condemning Rule as inadequate, and there has been an unjustified change in the meaning of Measure[1].   I shall now only expound Hegel's arguments, without further criticism, until we reach the Nodal Series of Measure-Relations, at which point, as will be seen, the effects of the second error are eliminated.

82.   So far only one of the two objects has been considered as having a Quality which affects the Quantity of its other Quality.   In Hegel's example, the object which receives heat from the medium is considered as having its specific temperature, while no specific temperature is attributed to the medium.   But now Hegel points out that each object must have a similar Quality.   In each the Quantity of the quantified Quality will be dependent on the nature of the object ($G. L.$ i. 411).   The

---

[1] The error in the transition from Specific Quantum to Rule cannot be counted as a third, since the only error there is in supposing that a transition has taken place at all.

medium, for example, is either air or something else, which must have a specific nature of its own. We thus reach

(c) *Relation of both Sides as Qualities.*

(*G. L.* i. 411.) Here the two sides have each (*a*) a Quality, which it possesses in a certain (*b*) Quantity. And each of them has (*c*) a second Quality, which determines the magnitude of *b* in it. Now as the two *b*'s are each a Quantity, their relation to each other can be expressed by a third Quantity (*G. L.* i. 412). And, as the nature of the two *c*'s is just to determine the different amounts of the two *b*'s, this third Quantity expresses also the relation of the two *c*'s (*G. L.* i. 417, 418).

83. This third Quantity is the Measure of the two sides— it is the Quantity which expresses their relation. In Specifying Measure (in the narrower sense) one of the two sides was the Measure of the other, while in Relation of the two Sides as Qualities each was the other's Measure. Now that they are united into a whole which has a Measure, we pass out of Specifying Measure (in the wider sense) and reach the third division of Specific Quantity, which Hegel calls

C. *Being for Self in Measure.*

(*G. L.* i. 417.) The name is apparently due to the fact that we have passed from finding the Measure of anything outside it to finding it within itself. For the two Somethings which have the common Measure may be considered, Hegel tells us (*G. L.* i. 421) as a single Something, which may also be called a Thing. (I shall call them Things, in what follows, to distinguish them from their constituent Somethings. But of course Hegel does not mean that we have yet reached the conception of a Thing, properly so called, which does not come till half-way through Essence.)

84. This Measure, he says, must be considered as realised Measure, since both its sides are Measures (*G. L.* i. 430). Thus we reach the second of the three divisions of Measure

II. Real Measure.

(*G. L.* i. 421.) This Real Measure relates itself to another Real Measure (*G. L.* i. 422). This gives us

A.   The Relation of Stable Measures.

(*G. L.* i. 423.)   Why it should relate itself to another Real Measure, Hegel does not, so far as I can see, explain.

It should be noted that we have by this time relations of three degrees of complexity.   (1) In each Something we have relations of Quality and Quantity.   (2) The Somethings are related to one another by a Common Real Measure, which unites the Somethings into a Thing.   (3) The Real Measures, or Things, we have just been told, are in relation to one another.

85.   This last relation will be, in the first place, immediate (though between terms which are no longer immediate, but stable), thus we get

(a)   Union of two Measures.

(*G. L.* i. 423.)   Hegel's treatment of this is very extraordinary. He starts with considering the union as a relation between the two Things.   And this is all that he seems justified in deducing from the previous position—if he is justified in deducing even so much.   But suddenly (*G. L.* i. 425) he tells us that the two Things "in Beziehung stehen und in Verbindung treten."   And from this point he speaks of the actual chemical combination of chemical elements.

Now the fact of chemical combination, which Hegel brings in here, involves, according to his own subsequent statement, the category of Chemism, which occurs in the middle of the categories of the Notion.   If Hegel is right in postponing the category of Chemism till the Notion, he cannot be right in introducing here a category under which he professes to explain chemical combination.

And this is not all.   Hegel does not merely introduce into this category the pure idea which is implied in, and specially characteristic of, the facts of chemistry.   He also introduces empirical chemical details, which could not form part of the dialectic process of pure thought at any stage, and he introduces them as part of the argument.

86.   We read that, while in such combinations the weight of the whole is equal to the weights of the parts (*G. L.* i. 425), the volume of the whole is not equal to the volume of the parts, but is generally less ʹ(*G. L.* i. 426). This is stated, not as an illustration only, which might have been legitimate, but as the ground of the transition to the next category. For he says (*G. L.* i. 426) that the Measure itself of the new combination is thus shown to be variable, and that therefore even so-called Stable Measures have shown themselves not to be stable. We must therefore try to find the determination of the combination in other Measure relations. And this is the way in which he reaches

(b)   *Measure as a Series of Measure Relations.*

(*G. L.* i. 426.) Here each of the Things regains the stability it has lost. It regains it, because it can combine not only with one other, but with any one of many others. Its capability of each of the changes which it could undergo in combining with any of these others is a permanent characteristic of its nature. This gives it stability. When M changes as it combines with N, it keeps a permanent nature throughout, for it remains that Thing which would undergo another definite change in combining with O, another with P, and so on. It has a nature beyond and unaffected by that change which it is actually undergoing, and so remains the same.

87. But in its union with each of the other Things with which it can unite, it does not merge its unity in something which remains unaffected. The other side is also altered, and they combine to form something new. The union is thus an "exclusive" unity (ausschliessende Einheit) (*G. L.* i. 429, 430). By this Hegel appears to mean that neither side is merely passive, awaiting any other Thing that may come to it, but that both sides express their nature in the union, since neither of them would suffer precisely that change, except in combining with the other. Thus we get

(c)   *Elective Affinity.*

(*G. L.* i. 430.) In connexion with this Hegel introduces a digression on some chemical theories of his time. It does not, however, profess to be part of the main argument.

88. We now come to a very remarkable transition. Each Thing which is formed by Elective Affinity has in it an element of Separability (Trennbarkeit) due to the fact that each of its constituents *can* enter into other relations (*G. L.* i. 446). It may be convenient to distinguish these constituents as Elementary Things, and their combinations as Compound Things. It must be remembered that, as was pointed out above (Section 83), even the Elementary Things are compounded of Somethings.

From this we proceed to a passage which I do not venture to paraphrase. " The exclusive Measure according to this more exact determination is external to itself in its Being for Self. It repels itself from itself, and posits itself both as a merely quantitative other, and also as another relation, such that it is also another Measure; and is determined as a unity which specifies itself, and which produces relations of Measure in itself. These relations are distinguished from the kind of affinities mentioned above, in which one stable object relates itself to stable objects of a different quality, and to a series of such objects. These relations occur in one and the same Sub-stratum, inside the same moments of neutrality. The Measure determines itself as repelling itself to other relations which are only quantitatively different, but which form at the same time *Affinities and Measures*, alternating with such as remain only quantitative differences. They form in this way a *Nodal Line* of Measures on a scale of more and less " (*G. L.* i. 446, 447). Thus we get

B. *Nodal Line of Measure Relations.*

(*G. L.* i. 445.) With regard to this category we have to remark three things. In the first place, we have suddenly returned to that conception of Measure which the dialectic suddenly aban-doned at Specifying Measure (in the narrower sense, I. B, (*b*), not I. B). We had started with the conception of Measure as the relation between a Quantity and a Quality, which Quality was such that, when the Quantity altered beyond certain limits, it changed into another Quality. At that point Hegel substituted the entirely different conception of a relation between two

Somethings, each with one Quantity and at least two Qualities.
And now, when the Somethings have developed into a Thing
formed by the union of Somethings, we find in this Thing the
old conception of Measure. The Elementary Thing, as its
Quantity changes, dissolves the connexion which made it part
of one Compound Thing, and forms another connexion, which
makes it part of another Compound Thing. And this is a
Qualitative change in the Elementary Thing. Once more the
Measure of the object is in itself.

That this is the right interpretation seems to follow from
the passage quoted above, and also from the next sentences
(*G. L.* i. 447). "Such a Being for Self, since it is at the same
time essentially a relation of Quanta, is open to externality and
the alteration of Quantum. It has an extent within which it
remains indifferent (gleichgültig) to this alteration, and within
which it does not alter its Quality. But a point comes in this
alteration of the Quantitative, at which the Quality is altered,
and the Quantum shows itself as specifying, so that the altered
quantitative relation is transformed into a new Quality, a new
Something."

The second point to be noticed is that, in spite of the categories which have intervened, we return to the old conception
in a form no higher than that in which we left it, so that, even
if the intervening categories had been legitimately deduced, we
should have gained nothing by them. It is true that the substratum which undergoes the changes of Quantity and Quality
is now a more complex unit, but this does not make the problem
of the relation of the changes a more complex problem, nor does
it advance it nearer to a solution. When we consider the
treatment in the *Encyclopaedia*, we shall see that the category
of the Nodal Line can be reached directly from the category of
Specific Quantum.

89. The third point to be noticed is that the transition
from the category of Elective Affinity to that of Nodal Line is
illegitimate. Let us grant that the Elementary Things which
are combined by Elective Affinity into Compound Things retain,
within these latter, a certain separability, due to the fact that
they could combine otherwise than as they do. But what
follows from this?

All that can properly be deduced is that the Elements in a Compound can separate, and then combine again, either with one another, in which case the same Compound would be formed again, or with other Elements, thus forming fresh Compounds. But Hegel asserts that the dissolution of the Compound would only take place after there had been certain Quantitative changes in its Elements—changes which did not dissolve the Compound till they had exceeded certain limits. This does not seem justifiable. Elective Affinity caused the Elements to combine in certain proportions. So long as these proportions were observed, the Combinations would not be broken up. But if the proportionate Quantities were altered in the least, it would follow from Hegel's previous account that the Compound might be instantly destroyed. There is nothing to permit him to treat the nature of the Compound as being variable within limits.

90. Thus both the departure, in Specifying Measure, from the previous conception of Measure, and the return to it at this point are illegitimate. Hegel's next category is

C. The Measureless.

(*G. L.* i. 452.) When the Quantitative change has gone beyond its limit, and a Qualitative change has come about, the new Quality is at first to be considered as the Measureless. The Measure of the original Quality is that it cannot go beyond certain Quantitative bounds. Of the new Quality we only know, so far, that it has gone beyond these bounds. It is therefore, so far, the Measureless.

The category, however, contains more than this, so that the name is not very appropriate. The new Quality, Hegel continues, is itself a Measure. It has its Quantitative bounds which it cannot pass. When the Quantity exceeds these fresh bounds, yet a fresh Measureless is created. And so we get an Infinite Series. It is this Infinite Series which seems to be the most characteristic feature of the category.

In this way, we are told, "the first immediate connexion between Quality and Quantity, in which Measure in general consists, is turned back on itself, and is itself posited"

(*G. L.* i. 453). The Quantity changes till it brings about a new Quality. The Quality in its turn has a new Quantity of its own, which varies till it once more changes into Quality, and so on indefinitely.

Quantities and Qualities are, then, neither of them stable. Yet something must be stable, for we could not say that Quality *A* had changed into Quality *B*, unless something was identical in *A* and *B*. Otherwise there would be no reason to suppose that it was *A*, rather than anything else, which had changed into *B*.

What is constant then? Hegel answers that it is the substratum. The conception of substratum, he reminds us, has already been introduced. "What is before us is one and the same fact (Sache), which is posited as ground of its difference, and as persisting. This separation of Being from its determination has already begun in Quantum in general; Something has magnitude, in so far as it is indifferent to its determination as Being (seiende Bestimmtheit)" (*G. L.* i. 453).

It should be noticed that Hegel does not say that *this* Infinite Series is contradictory. As I said above (Section 33) he never does assert that Infinite Series as such are contradictory, but only that some of them are. His position here is that the Infinite Series would be impossible unless there were something stable underlying it, and that therefore we must conclude that something stable does underlie it.

It must also be noticed that it would have been equally necessary that something stable should underlie the series, if it were not infinite but finite. Any series of Qualitative changes would require the substratum, whatever the length of the series. The transition, therefore, would not be invalidated, if it could be shown that the series here was not, as Hegel holds it to be, infinite.

91. The substratum is stable, then, and the lesson of the ceaseless oscillation—first the change of the Quantity of a Quality, then the change of the Quality, and so on without end—is that the substratum is indifferent to its determinations. Since they change, while it remains unchanged, they can have no effect on it whatever. Thus we reach (*G. L.* i. 456)

III. THE BECOMING OF ESSENCE.

A. *The Absolute Indifference*[1].

92. But, after all, the Indifference cannot be absolute. That which is indifferent is a substratum. It could not be a substratum, unless there was the series of changes to which it is a substratum, and therefore they have an influence on it. "It is just the externality and its disappearance which determines the unity of Being to be indifferent and is thus within that unity of Being, which therefore ceases to be merely substratum" (*G. L.* i. 456). Thus we get

B. *Indifference as Inverse Relation of its Factors*

(*G. L.* i. 457), the characteristic of which is that the Quantities of the different Qualities vary inversely, so that the sum of them is always the same.

This category seems indefensible. The Quantities, we are told, are "variable, indifferent, greater or smaller against one another" (*G. L.* i. 457). And the substratum is the sum of them and a "fixed Measure" (same page). The increase or decrease of one side must be simultaneous, therefore, with the increase or decrease of the other. But this is impossible, for the sides are the Qualities of the substratum, and the different Qualities of the substratum are alternative and not compatible. The increase or decrease of Quantity produces one Quality and destroys another. The whole point of that earlier conception of Measure, to which we returned in the category of the Nodal Line, was that a reality had one Quality or another, according to the Quantity. If the Qualities of the series became compatible, we should not only have removed the Absolute Indifference in which Hegel finds a contradiction, but we should have removed all Indifference altogether. For the Indifference arose solely from the permanence of the substratum among the variations of the Quality series, and would cease if the variations were abandoned.

---

[1] Since the Measureless and Absolute Indifference are undivided categories, and are respectively Synthesis and new Thesis, the second would naturally be only a repetition of the first, which is not the case. This seems to indicate that the category of the Measureless was really considered by Hegel as subdivided— the Infinite Series forming a separate stage from the Measureless in the stricter sense.

Now it is clear from the title of this category, and from the treatment of the early categories of Essence, that the Indifference of the substratum is not considered to be yet removed.

93. After these considerations Hegel's transition from this category need not, perhaps, be examined in detail. He argues that the Qualities are not independent of each other, since that would make the Indifference an empty name. Each of them has, therefore, only reality in its quantitative relation to the other, and each, therefore, can only reach as far as the other (*G. L.* i. 460). It is impossible for either to gain at the expense of the other, and so the Inverse Relation breaks down, and we are driven back to Indifference in the form of a " contradiction which transcends itself" (*G. L.* i. 461). In other words, the external is not absolutely unreal, but is not real in its own right. It is the appearance of a reality which is not itself. So we reach (after a digression on Centripetal and Centrifugal Force) the last category of Measure

C.   Transition to Essence.

(*G. L.* i. 466.) In reaching this category we have already reached the fundamental characteristic of Essence. This consists in the assertion of the duplicity of reality—its possession of an external and an internal nature, capable of distinction from each other, but not indifferent to each other. And this is the conception which we have now reached.

This conception is rendered necessary by Qualitative change. All change requires some distinction in the nature of that which changes. For if the nature of reality were all of one piece, then each thing must be completely the same as something else, or completely different from it. Thus, under the categories of Quality, no change is possible. With the categories of Quantity, it is possible to have Quantitative change. For there each One has its own Quality, and is also part of a Quantum, and so the same One can be part of Quanta of varying sizes, and the Quanta can change. A Quantum, for example, can change into a larger Quantum, and the necessary identity in difference is found in the fact that certain Ones form part of both Quanta.

But now that we have Qualitative change, the duplicity of nature must not be merely between Quality and Quantity, but

must be found within Quality.   If that which has Quality A is so
to change as to have Quality B, there must be a unity in the thing
which persists through this change.   At the present stage of
the dialectic this can only be a permanent Quality X, and so we
have the two strata of Essence.

94. The treatment in the *Encyclopaedia* is very different
from that in the *Greater Logic*.   In the first place, it is much
simpler.   In the *Greater Logic* there were thirteen undivided
categories.   In the *Encyclopaedia* Hegel gives no divisions at
all.   This gives indeed an appearance of greater simplicity than
really exists, for by observing the course of the argument we can
see that it really does form a triad, the three categories of which
may be called Specific Quantum, The Measureless, and The Becoming of Essence.   Still, there are only three divisions instead
of thirteen.   The difference is accounted for by the fact that
Becoming of Essence forms only one undivided category, instead
of three, as in the *Greater Logic*, and by the omission of the
seven categories, from Rule to the Nodal Line inclusive, which
only bring the dialectic back to the point of Specific Quantum
again.   Also the *Encyclopaedia* treats under the head of the
Measureless what is divided in the *Greater Logic* into the Nodal
Line and the Measureless.

The *Encyclopaedia* then starts (*Enc.* 107) with the simple
conception of Measure, as it is found in the *Greater Logic*, to
which we may give the name of Specific Quantum, as in the
earlier work.   Hegel then discusses, as in the *Greater Logic*, the
contrast between the continuous change of Quantity and the
instantaneous changes of Quality, and the sophisms which are
based on it (*Enc.* 108)[1].   Then comes the transition to the
Measureless, which here, as in the *Greater Logic*, he seems to
connect in some especial manner with the contrast just mentioned between the methods of change in Quantity and Quality.

How it should be connected with this contrast is not very
plain, nor does this seem necessary for the transition.   The
category of Specific Quantum gives us the result that, if any

[1] In the *Encyclopaedia* Hegel seems to use Rule to indicate a Measure in
which the Quantity does not pass the limits which involve a change of Quality
(*Enc.* 108).   This is different from the use of Rule in the *Greater Logic* (cp.
above, Section 79).

thing has the Quality A within certain Quantitative limits, it will also have the Quality M. This inevitably raises the question of the result which will follow if the Quantity of A passes the limits within which it determines the presence of M. "Quantity...is not only capable of alteration, *i.e.* of increase or diminution : it is naturally and necessarily a tendency to exceed itself" (*Enc.* 109). And this is sufficient to take us over to the next category.

In the first place, all that is said is that the object will no longer have the Quality M. It is therefore the Measureless— since Measure consisted in the relation between the permanent Quality A and the variable Quality. But M will be replaced by a fresh Quality N—solidity, *e.g.*, by fluidity, when heat has passed the melting-point. From this Hegel proceeds to the Infinite Series in the same way as in the *Greater Logic* (*Enc.* 109).

The transition from the Infinite Series to Becoming of Essence (*Enc.* 111) is the same as in the *Greater Logic*, except that the intermediate forms of Absolute Indifference and Indifference as Inverse Relation are omitted, and the transition made direct to the fully developed conception which, in the *Greater Logic*, forms the third subdivision.

The treatment in the *Encyclopaedia* is superior to the other in avoiding the unjustified and useless loop which stretches from Rule to Elective Affinity in the *Greater Logic*. The absence of Indifference as Inverse Relation is also an improvement. On the other hand, the transition from the Infinite Series in the category of the Measureless direct to Essence seems somewhat abrupt, and inferior to the path taken by the *Greater Logic* through Absolute Indifference.

But the vital defect of the *Greater Logic* is not removed in the *Encyclopaedia*. This is the substitution for the conception of Measure, reached at the end of Quantity, of another conception of Measure—undeduced and unjustified. This invalidates the chain of reasoning in both books, and if the broken links are to be replaced it must be by something which is not to be found in Hegel's own work.

CHAPTER V

ESSENCE AS REFLECTION INTO ITSELF

95. Essence is divided in the *Greater Logic* into Essence as Reflection into Self, Appearance, and Actuality. In the two first of these the difference between the *Greater Logic* and the *Encyclopaedia* is more marked than elsewhere in the process. Categories which are found in one of these two secondary divisions in the *Greater Logic* are transferred to the other in the *Encyclopaedia*—a change which has no parallel in any other part of the dialectic. For this reason I shall postpone any reference to the *Encyclopaedia* till the end of Chapter VI.

Essence as Reflection into itself (Das Wesen als Reflexion in ihm selbst) is divided as follows:

I. Show. (Der Schein.)

    A. The Essential and Unessential. (Das Wesentliche und Unwesentliche.)

    B. Show. (Der Schein.)

    C. Reflection. (Die Reflexion.)

        (*a*) Positing Reflection. (Die setzende Reflexion.)

        (*b*) External Reflection. (Die äussere Reflexion.)

        (*c*) Determining Reflection. (Die bestimmende Reflexion.)

II. The Essentialities or Determinations of Reflection. (Die Wesenheiten oder Reflexions-Bestimmungen.)

    A. Identity. (Die Identität.)

B.   Difference.   (Der Unterschied.)

(*a*)   Absolute Difference.   (Der absolute Unterschied.)

(*b*)   Variety.   (Die Verschiedenheit.)

(*c*)   Opposition.   (Der Gegensatz.)

C.   Contradiction.   (Der Widerspruch.)

III.   Ground.   (Der Grund.)

A.   Absolute Ground.   (Der absolute Grund.)

(*a*)   Form and Essence.   (Form und Wesen.)

(*b*)   Form and Matter.   (Form und Materie.)

(*c*)   Form and Content.   (Form und Inhalt.)

B.   Determined Ground.   (Der bestimmte Grund.)

(*a*)   Formal Ground.   (Der formelle Grund.)

(*b*)   Real Ground.   (Der reale Grund.)

(*c*)   Complete Ground.   (Der vollständige Grund.)

C.   Condition.   (Die Bedingung.)

(*a*)   The Relatively Unconditioned.   (Das relative Unbedingte.)

(*b*)   The Absolutely Unconditioned.   (Das absolute Unbedingte.)

(*c*)   Transition of the Fact into Existence.   (Hervorgang der Sache in die Existenz.)

The term Show is used ambiguously—both as the title of I., and as the title of I. B.

96.   At the end of the Doctrine of Being the conclusion was reached that there was a Qualitative substratum to the changes of Quantity and Quality. At first this substratum was regarded as entirely indifferent to the changes, but this view was discovered to be untenable, and it was then that the conception of Essence was reached. " At this point " Hegel says (*G. L.* i. 468), " Being in general, and Being as the immediacy of separate determinations and as Being *an sich* has vanished. The Unity is Being, immediately posited Totality, in such a way that this is only simple relation to self, mediated by the transcending of this positing. This positing and this immediate Being are themselves only a moment in its repulsion, and its original stability and identity with itself only exists as the resulting and infinite coming together with itself. In this way Being is determined to Essence—that Being which, through the transcending of Being, is simple Being-with-itself."

The language of this passage is rather difficult, but the meaning is not, I think, doubtful. Things are no longer simple in their nature. The nature of each thing has two sides. That which previously seemed to be the whole nature of the thing is now only a moment in a more complex whole. The other element, to which it is related, is called the substratum by Hegel—a natural metaphor, since it is the element which the dialectic process reaches after the other. It is this element to which he gives the general name of Essence, the first element being called Appearance.

97. Both these names have some erroneous suggestions about them. That the first element should be called Appearance might lead us to suppose that the distinction between it and Essence was that the Essence is the real nature of the thing, and the Appearance the partially erroneous representation of the thing to some conscious subject. But this would be a complete mistake. Hegel justly says that the categories of his dialectic are objective in the sense that they deal with what the reality is, and not with what it is thought to be. Unlike Kant's categories, they do not refer to our knowledge of the reality, but to the reality which is known. And therefore, when Hegel speaks of the Appearance of a thing, he means a part of its own nature, not of the knowledge of it in us.

If we avoid this mistake, we may fall into another. We may be led by the names Appearance and Essence to suppose that the Essence represents a truer way of looking at the reality than the Appearance does. This would certainly be suggested by the English adjectives apparent and essential, though the suggestion is perhaps not so strong in German. And this view would be supported by the fact that the first two categories of Essence, in the *Greater Logic*, treat the Appearance as less real than the Essence[1]. But in the other categories this is not so.

---

[1] I shall try to show later that the categories in which the Appearance is treated as unreal are unjustified, and that their omission in the *Encyclopaedia* was an inprovement. (See Section 103.)

The Appearance there is as real as the Essence, and it is as essential (in the ordinary English use of the word) to the Essence, as the Essence is to it.

The reason for calling this side Appearance is, I think, as follows. It is real, but it has not the exclusive reality which was attributed to it in the earlier categories of Being, when it was taken as the only nature of reality. Its true position, as now determined, gives it a less important function than that with which it started. And it is to express this, I believe, that Hegel gave it a name which, as contrasted with Essence, suggests subordination and diminished reality. The name cannot, however, be regarded as fortunate.

98. Hegel speaks of the Appearance as being immediate. This cannot mean that which is immediately known, for that would bring in the subjectivity which has already been said to be foreign to the dialectic. Nor can it mean literally that which is not mediated, since Appearance is mediated by Essence. It means, I conceive, that the Appearance corresponds to the nature of reality as seen in the categories of Being, when there was no internal mediation, because there was no internal diversity. It is not what is immediate, but what had previously been supposed to be so. The element of Essence would not be called immediate for this reason, since from the first point at which it is reached, it is seen to be in relation to the other side.

99. The name of Essence is not more fortunate than that of Appearance. In the first place, as has already been said, it suggests, when contrasted with Appearance, that one side of the relation is more real than the other. And in the second place it is ambiguous. Hegel uses it to designate one side of the relation. But he also uses it for the relation of the two sides, as when he speaks of the categories of Essence. It is sometimes difficult to see whether he is using it in the former sense or the latter, and it is desirable to find another name to designate the side of the relation which is not Appearance, so that we can confine Essence to its other meaning—the view of reality as consisting of the two related sides. The name of Inner, which would perhaps be the most natural, is unavailable, since Hegel uses it for a special category further on. I propose to use the word Substratum, which has already been used by Hegel of this

side (*G. L.* i. 453). The Appearance side can then be called
Surface, which will avoid the ambiguity arising from the fact
that the second division of Essence is called Appearance.

At this point we may notice Hegel's remark (*G. L.* ii. 5) that
Essence has the same characteristic, in the dialectic as a whole,
which Quantity has in the Doctrine of Being—the characteristic
of indifference to its boundaries. It is, as we shall see, impossible to keep Substratum and Surface separate. Whatever is
found in the one cannot be excluded from the other. But this
leads only to an oscillation between these two sides, and not to
an unending process in a straight line, such as we found in
Quantity.

100. Hegel tells us that while the form of the process is, in
Being "an Other and transition into an Other," it becomes in
Essence, "showing, or reflection in the opposite" (*Enc.* 240).
The transformation of form is, however, continuous throughout
the dialectic, and no sudden change must be expected at this
point[1].

I. SHOW.

A. *The Essential and Unessential.*

(*G. L.* ii. 8.) The first category of Essence ought to have the
same content as the last category of Measure. But its content
is, in fact, very different, and this constitutes a serious defect in
the argument.

At the end of Measure the Substratum was clearly the more
persistent Quality which only varied Quantitatively while the
other Qualities came and went. This was a perfectly definite
Quality with a determined nature of its own. Moreover, it
would seem that there were many such Substrata. For each
Nodal Line would have such a Substratum of its own, and there
is nothing to suggest the view that the whole of the universe
could be reduced to a single Nodal line.

But now, without any deduction or justification, the Substratum assumes a perfectly different nature. We are told
(*G. L.* ii. 4) that it is "an undetermined simple unity." And
the whole of the treatment of the three categories of Show[2]

---

[1] Cp. my *Studies in the Hegelian Dialectic*, Chapter IV.

[2] Show in the wider sense, whose three categories are the Essential and
Unessential, Show in the narrower sense, and Reflection.

supports this. This is very different from the definite Quality
at the end of Measure. From the new position it follows that
the whole universe has only one Substratum, since there can be
no plurality in what is undetermined. And this also is supported by the treatment of these three categories.

It is possible that this flaw in the process might be removed
by avoiding an earlier flaw. We saw, at the beginning of the
last Chapter, that Hegel starts Measure with a conception which
is unduly specialized and complex as compared with the conception which he had reached at the end of Quantity. I think
that it might be maintained that if he had kept, as he ought,
to the broader and simpler conception of Measure, it would have
developed in such a way as to enable him to reach legitimately
the wide conception of Substratum which, as it is, he reaches
illegitimately. But to work this out would take us too far from
what Hegel actually does say.

101. There is another point to be discussed with relation
to the starting-point in Essence. The Surface is conceived as a
plurality, and not merely as a plurality of qualities inhering in
a single subject, but as a plurality of subjects. These subjects
have been with us ever since the category of Quality (Quality
in the narrower sense, the Antithesis in the triad of Being
Determinate as such). At first they were called Somethings,
and afterwards Ones. At present Hegel gives them no special
name. A name is desirable, and I propose to call them at once
by the name of things. It may be objected that Hegel uses the
name of Thing for a special category later on. But his introduction of it there for the first time only means that there for the
first time the Thing forms the Substratum. It does not mean
that this is the first time that the conception of thing enters
into the dialectic at all. I shall therefore use the name from
this point[1].

There is, then, a plurality of things in the Surface at this
point. All Hegel's treatment implies this, and the transition
from the category of Identity to that of Diversity rests on it
explicitly. Now how is this assertion of a plurality to be

---

[1] To distinguish this more general use of the word thing from that in which
it refers to Hegel's categories of Thing, I shall use a capital initial only when
the special categories are spoken of.

justified ? There is, I think, not much doubt about the answer Hegel would make. There was, he would say, a demonstrated plurality in the categories of Being, which arose, as has been said, in the category of Quality, and continued to the end of Measure. Now that which was Being has become the Surface side in Essence, and therefore the plurality is legitimately transferred to the Surface.

But there seems to me a defect in this argument. In the Second Chapter we considered whether Hegel was justified in making his transition from one existent to a plurality of existents (Section 25). And the result at which we arrived was that he was justified because an isolated existent could only have a definite nature by having a plurality of qualities, and because the dialectic had not at that point reached the notion of one subject with a plurality of qualities. But now the case is different. We have been led on by the dialectic to the view that one subject can have a plurality of qualities. In that case I cannot see that anything that Hegel has said excludes the possibility of an existent having a definite nature although it should be the sole existent, and undifferentiated into parts. And if such a sole and undifferentiated existent could have a definite nature then nothing that Hegel has said excludes the possibility that nothing exists but one single undifferentiated unit. (I use undifferentiated to denote that which has no plurality of parts, though it may have a plurality of qualities.) If this is so, then Hegel is not justified in taking the Surface as consisting of a plurality of things.

102. The supposition that there is no plurality of things is doubtless wild enough. For it does not mean that the universe is one as well as many, or even that it is more truly one than many. Both these propositions would be compatible with a plurality of things. The only alternative which is incompatible with a plurality of things is the view that there is no differentiation at all—no plurality except a plurality of qualities of the same subject.

Such a view is incompatible with any reality of Space or Time, since the parts of Space and Time would give such a differentiation. And it is also incompatible with the existence of any belief, volition, or emotion, all of which are internally differentiated.

Moreover, there is certainly an appearance of differentiation in the universe as we perceive it. And if this is condemned as an illusion, the illusion will have to be itself part of the universe. And it is not easy to see how it is to be that without introducing differentiation into the universe.

But although there may be very good reasons of this sort for rejecting the view that the existent is completely undifferentiated, they are not such as the dialectic can appeal to. The dialectic has to deduce all its results from the category of Being without the introduction of any fresh *data*. If it is to exclude the hypothesis of an undifferentiated existent, it must be either because that hypothesis is self-contradictory, or because it is incompatible with some of the results reached by the dialectic process. It might be possible to show that it is to be rejected for one or other of these reasons, but I cannot see that Hegel has shown it. Here, too, therefore, we must regard the transition to Essence as erroneous.

103. We have then, in the present category, a Surface of a plurality of things with common qualities, and a Substratum which is "an undetermined simple unity." From this Hegel proceeds as follows: "that the Essence becomes a merely Essential, as opposed to an Unessential, comes about through this, that the Essence is only taken as transcended Being or Being Determinate. The Essence is in this way only the First, or the negation, which is determination, through which the Being becomes merely Being Determinate, or the Being Determinate becomes merely an Other. But the Essence is the absolute negativity of Being, it is Being itself, but determined not merely as an Other, but as the Being which has transcended itself both as immediate Being, and also as the immediate negation, as the negation which is linked to an Otherbeing. The Being or Being Determinate has in this not preserved itself as something Other than the Essence is. And the immediacy which is still distinguished from the Essence is not merely an unessential Being Determinate (unwesentliches Dasein) but is the immediate which is null (nichtig) in and for itself: it is only an Unessence (Unwesen), only Show " (*G. L.* ii. 9).

This argument seems to me to be mistaken. No doubt the
Being has not preserved itself as an element completely
separated from the Substratum of which it now forms the
Surface. But the proper conclusion from this is merely that
which has already been reached in reaching Essence—namely
that the two are related as sides or aspects of the same reality.
To infer that, because the Surface is nothing apart from its
Substratum, therefore it is null and an " Unessence " in its
relation to its Substratum, is surely erroneous.

If this is so, the transition to Show must be rejected. But
in rejecting the *Greater Logic* here we do not part company
altogether with Hegel, for in the *Encyclopaedia* the Surface
is never treated as null. The three categories of the triad of
Show—Essential and Unessential, Show, and Reflection, find no
place in the *Encyclopaedia*, where the Doctrine of Essence
starts with the category of Identity. In this the later work
seems to me to be much superior to the earlier.

B. *Show.*

104. (*G. L.* ii. 9.) The translation I have adopted for
Schein is scarcely satisfactory, but I can find no better.
Appearance is not available, as it is wanted to translate
Erscheinung. Nor would Appearance emphasise with suffi-
cient strength the total nullity of the Surface at this point.

This category must not be confounded with Absolute Indifference, which occurred towards the end of Measure. In
Absolute Indifference it was not the reality of either side of the
relation which was denied, but the relation itself was expressed
in such a way as to be rather the denial of relation. Here, on
the contrary, it is one side of the relation which is denied all
reality.

The position of this category—that the Surface is merely
nothing—is one which is easily seen to be untenable. If the
category were correct, the Substratum would have no Surface.
In that case it would not be a Substratum, and we should have
no Essence-relation at all. We should have fallen back on the
simpler conception of reality which was found in the Doctrine
of Being, and which the course of the dialectic has already
compelled us to abandon.

The Show *is*, then, and yet the Show is nothing. It is nothing and yet something. And this is impossible. Hegel aptly instances the attempt of the Sceptic to treat everything as devoid of all reality, and Fichte's endeavour to consider as merely negative the "Anstoss" which in the long run determines the Ego (*G. L.* ii. 11. His further examples from Leibniz and Kant might perhaps be criticised as misrepresentations).

Since this category is untenable, we must proceed further. We must do this, Hegel tells us, by perceiving that the Show is a moment of the Essence, and not something distinct from it (*G. L.* ii. 12). It is clear that he must mean, not merely that the Show is a moment of the Essence-relation, which it has been all along, but that it is a moment of the Essence-side of that relation. The Show is, then, an element in its Substratum. Thus Hegel is able to admit that all the reality is in the Substratum (the result which he thought he had arrived at in the category of the Essential and Unessential), while avoiding the impossible position of denying all reality to the Surface.

105. We reach here, then, a new category, in which the Essence-relation is between the whole nature of the Substratum and a part of that nature. To this Hegel gives the name of

C. Reflection

(*G. L.* ii. 14), which is, in the first place,

(a) Positing Reflection.

(*G. L.* ii. 16.) Noël remarks (*La Logique de Hegel*, p. 63) that in Ground "for the first time the Essence appears as substratum of the mediation." I cannot regard this as correct. The Essence-side of the relation seems to me to be a true Substratum in the two first categories of Essence, and to become so again in Diversity—if not in Identity. But, with regard to Reflection and its subdivisions, it is, I think, true that the Essence-side is not properly a Substratum. It does here, as Noël says (*loc. cit.*), "confound itself with the very movement of reflection." For the Surface is here, as we have seen, actually part of the Essence-side. The whole of the relation of the two sides falls within one of them.

At this point, therefore, the name of Substratum, which I have adopted for the Essence-side of the relation, is unsuitable, since it suggests that the Surface is outside it. But it would be difficult to find another which was not already claimed by Hegel for use elsewhere. And, when we have passed beyond the three categories of Reflection, Substratum will again be an appropriate term.

Hegel says of the category of Positing Reflection that it is "a movement from nothing to nothing," and again that it is "transition as transcending of transition" (*G. L.* ii. 16). The immediacy of the Surface is "only the negative of itself, only this—not to be immediacy," for it is only a moment of the Substratum. But again Reflection is "the transcending of the negation of itself, it is coming together with self; in this way it transcends its positing, and since it is, in its positing, the transcending of positing, it is presupposition (Voraussetzen)" (*G. L.* ii. 17). In other words, in this category the immediate element loses its immediacy, because it is only a moment of the non-immediate element, the Substratum. But the Substratum has now nothing outside itself, and is therefore itself immediate. As the negation of itself, the immediate ceased to be immediate. But the Reflection is "the transcending of the negation of itself" and thus immediacy is restored.

106. The first form in which it is restored is, according to Hegel,

(b) *External Reflection*

(*G. L.* ii. 19), in which the Reflection *finds* an immediate element which exists independently of it—which is, in Hegel's language, presupposed (vorausgesetzt), not posited (gesetzt).

107. But this, the argument continues, is an untenable position. The two are not really external to one another, but depend on each other for their existence. For Reflection is clearly dependent on the Immediate. Without an Immediate, it would be unable to perform its work of mediation. The Immediate, again, without the Reflection, would be the *mere* Immediate of Being over again. This, of course, it is not. But for the difference it depends on Reflection. Thus the connexion between the two sides is essential to them. This gives us

(c)   *Determining Reflection*

(*G. L.* ii. 23), in which we see that the Immediate is really the " absolutely mediated "—that is to say, the self-mediated, that which is mediated, not by anything outside it, but by a process within itself. That which is absolutely mediated has the same character of stability as the Immediate, since it does not refer to anything outside itself. Thus the new category synthesizes the two former. Like Positing Reflection, it places the mediation within that which is mediated. But, like External Reflection, it provides a real Immediate for mediation. The Surface no longer falls within the Substratum, as in Positing Reflection, nor is it something independent of the Substratum, as in External Reflection. The Surface and Substratum are now two moments, neither of which falls within the other, but both of which as moments in the same reality, are intrinsically united, and not independent of each other.

It seems to me that Hegel would have done better if he had suppressed Positing and External Reflection altogether, and had taken what he now calls Determining Reflection as the undivided category of Reflection. For the conception of Determining Reflection is really much simpler than that of Positing Reflection, and it would have been more convincing to reach it directly from Show (which it would have synthesized with Essential and Unessential), than first to proceed to Positing Reflection and then to reach Determining Reflection through it.

This would avoid, also, the transition from Positing Reflection to External Reflection, which seems to me fallacious. No doubt, as Hegel points out, the Substratum, if it absorbed the Surface, would be immediate, but it is very difficult to see how we could possibly pass, as Hegel apparently does, to the position that it has an immediate reality external to it.

II. The Essentialities or Determinations of Reflection.

108. (*G. L.* ii. 26.) Hegel accounts for the name as follows : " The Reflection is determined Reflection ; and so the Essence is determined Essence, or it is Essentiality (Wesenheit)" (*G. L.* ii. 26). But this does not help us to see why these, rather than the other categories of Essence, should be distinguished by a title so specially connected with Essence.

A. Identity.

(*G. L.* ii. 30.) This category is a restatement of the last. If anything is self-mediated, then that which is found on one side of the relation has exactly the same content as that which is found on the other side. Surface and Substratum reflect each other perfectly. If we start from an immediately given *A*, and endeavour to understand it by determining its Essence, the result which we get at this point will be " *A* is *A*."

Before this point we could not have reached the category of Identity. So long as we had not passed beyond the Doctrine of Being, it would have been impossible to assert Identity as a category. For no category of the dialectic is a tautology. And consequently the Identity asserted must be an Identity between what can be distinguished, from another point of view, as not identical. Now this would be impossible among the categories of Being. For there we find no difference *within* the subject. And, if we predicate anything of it besides itself, our judgment will not be one of identity. The category of Identity only becomes possible when the division of form between Substratum and Surface enables us to put the same content on each side of the judgment, while at the same time keeping a distinction in form.

109. We must now consider Hegel's treatment of the logical law of Identity, $A = A$, or, as he also expresses it, " Everything is identical with itself (Alles ist sich selbst gleich)." In the first place, in his general discussion of the Essentialities, he asks (*G. L.* ii. 27) why this law (which also, as he points out, takes the form of the Law of Contradiction, *A* is not not-A), and the Law of Excluded Middle, should be considered as universal laws of thought, to the exclusion of others. All the other categories, he reminds us, are also predicates of all things (" von Allem," *G. L.* ii. 28). Such laws as " Everything is," " Everything has Determinate Being" are just as true as the laws of thought in formal logic. In the case of the higher categories, it is not surprising that they have not formed the basis for generally recognised laws of thought, as the validity of the higher categories is not so immediately obvious—is, indeed, often not to be seen at all without the aid of the dialectic. But this cannot be said of the categories of Being—especially of the earlier among them.

In answer to this question Hegel points out (*G. L.* ii. 28) that in Being the Antithesis of each Thesis is its direct opposite. If we attempted to base a universal law on each category, these laws would directly contradict one another. By the side of the law that "Everything is," we should find, based on the category of Nothing, the law that "Everything is nothing[1]." It would be quite clear then that each of these laws could not be absolutely true, since they contradict one another, and therefore they would not be taken by formal logic as universal laws of thought, to all of which it must ascribe absolute truth.

With the categories of Essence the case is different, owing to the gradual modification in form of the dialectic process. Difference is not so directly opposed to Identity, as Nothing is to Being. As we shall see, the Difference is added to the Identity, and does not replace it. And therefore no law formed out of Difference can be obviously and directly incompatible with the law of Identity, and thereby challenge the absolute truth of the latter.

I do not, however, see that the difference in question, though it certainly exists, can be accepted as the reason why previous thinkers did not make " universal laws of thought" out of the categories of Being. For the necessity of proceeding from the Thesis to the Antithesis is Hegel's own discovery. The founders of formal logic would not have been deterred from making " Everything is " into a universal law of thought by its

---

[1] Hegel does not specify what the laws of Being and Nothing would be, but only says that they would be directly opposed to one another.

obvious incompatibility with "Everything is nothing." For the latter would have seemed simply false to them, and to everyone else who had not accepted or anticipated the first triad of Hegel's dialectic.

110. We must look for another way out of the difficulty. And I believe that this is to be found in the fact that the Law of Identity is not specially connected with Hegel's category of Identity at all, and therefore gives us no reason to expect that similar laws will be connected with the other categories.

The category of Identity is, as we have seen, the assertion of an Identity of content in the Surface and Substratum of existent things. This, of course, narrows its field. Not to speak of non-existent realities, if such there are, it is clear that the category cannot be applied either to qualities or relations, since it is not qualities or relations which have Surfaces and Substrata, but only things. And, again, it cannot be applied to a Surface or Substratum. For, if so, there would have to be, within that Surface or Substratum, a division into a fresh Surface and Substratum, and this is not Hegel's view.

On the other hand, the Law of Identity can be applied to any subject whatever. We can say just as well that a quality is a quality, or that a Substratum is a Substratum, as we can say that a thing is a thing. Since the law and the category have such difference in their application the law cannot be founded on the category.

And, again, the truth of the category of Identity is by no means a tautology. When we bring a thing under this category we assert that its nature has the two sides of Surface and Substratum, and that the content of these two sides is the same. And both these propositions are very far from being tautologies.

It is different with the Law of Identity. In the sense in which that asserts A to be A, the proposition is a complete tautology. Its truth rests, not on identity in difference, but on the absence of all difference. If any difference existed between the A of the subject and the A of the predicate, the assertion of their identity would be a proposition which might be true, and which, true or false, would have some interest. But it would not be the Law of Identity of formal logic. And it is this Law of Identity of which Hegel speaks here.

Later on (*G. L.* ii. 35) he admits the tautologous character of
the Law of Identity. Such propositions as " a plant is a plant,"
he says, are simply useless and wearisome. They would be
universally admitted to be true, and universally admitted to say
nothing. This is sufficient to show that the Law of Identity is
not based on Hegel's category of Identity. The statements that
the nature of a plant has a Surface and a Substratum, and that
the content of these is identical, certainly tells us something,
whether it be false or true.

The connexion, then, between the logical Law of Identity
and Hegel's category of Identity is so slight that we need not
be surprised at the absence of similar Laws corresponding to the
earlier categories.

In his criticism of the Law of Identity Hegel, I think, goes
too far when he says that its truth is incompatible with the
existence of Difference (*G. L.* ii. 29, " If everything is identical
with itself, it is not different, not opposed, and has no Ground."
Again, *G. L.* ii. 37, " The Law of Identity or Contradiction,
since its object is only to express abstract Identity as the truth
in opposition to Difference, is no law of thought, but rather the
opposite of such a law "). That A is A would surely be quite
consistent with the facts that A is not B, that A and C are
polar opposites, and that A and D have a Ground E.

111. From the category of Identity Hegel passes on as
follows. " The Identity is the Reflection into itself, which is
only this as being inner Repulsion (Abstossen), and this Repulsion exists as Reflection into itself, Repulsion which immediately
takes itself back into itself. It is thus Identity as the Difference which is identical with itself. But the Difference is only
identical with itself in so far as it is not the Identity, but
absolute Not-Identity. Not-Identity, however, is absolute in so
far as it contains nothing of the Other, but only itself, that is to
say, in so far as it is absolute Identity with itself " (*G. L.* ii. 32).

We have already discussed the fact that Hegel starts the
categories of Essence with a Surface containing a plurality of
things (Section 101). This has not so far involved a corresponding plurality in the Substratum. For, till the transition to
Determining Reflection, there was nothing in the relation of
Surface to Substratum which should prevent an undifferentiated

Substratum from having a differentiated Surface, and we could not argue from the differentiation of the Surface to a differentiation of Substratum. But in Determining Reflection, and its restatement as Identity, the Surface and the Substratum are identical in their content. And therefore the Substratum, like the Surface, is differentiated.

It is in this way that Identity, as Hegel says, involves Differentiation. Things are different on the Surface, and if the Substratum in each thing is identical with the Surface, then it must be different from the Substratum of every other thing. Since the conception of Difference is thus carried into the Substratum, we reach

B. Difference.

(a) Absolute Difference.

(*G. L.* ii. 37.) Difference is at first simple (einfach) (*G. L.* ii. 38). The Difference between two things is only that they *are* different. If one is *A*, the other is not-*A*. By this Hegel cannot mean that the second is a mere negation of the first, for the second must also be identical with itself, and therefore must be as positive as the first. What he means is that the *element of Difference* between them lies simply in the fact that the second element, *B*, is not-*A*. If we had begun with *B*, then the difference would consist in *A* being not-*B*.

He goes on to say that we have here the Difference of Reflection and not the Otherbeing of Determinate Being. In the Otherbeing of Determinate Being, the things are conceived primarily as isolated, and only secondarily as related. But now that we have reached Essence, the connection with others is seen to be a fundamental part of the nature of each thing.

There is no Difference without Identity, and no Identity without Difference. Identity, Hegel says, may thus be considered as a whole of which Difference and itself are moments. And Difference may be considered as a whole of which Identity and itself are moments (*G. L.* ii. 38). (This seems to be only an unnecessarily paradoxical way of expressing the fact that Identity involves itself and Difference, and that Difference involves itself and Identity.) This, he continues, "must be regarded as the essential nature of Reflection, and as the deter-

mined fundamental ground of all acting and self-movement."
It is, indeed, a rudimentary form of the principle of the mutual
implication of Unity and Differentiation, the establishment of
which may perhaps be maintained to be the supreme result of
the whole dialectic.

(b)   Variety.

112. (*G. L.* ii. 39.) The deduction of this category (*G. L.*
ii. 39—41) is extremely obscure. Hegel says that from
Absolute Difference arise two forms, "Reflection into self as
such, and Determination as negation, or the Posited. The
Posited is the Reflection which is external to self" (*G. L.* ii. 40).
Of these the first is primarily Identity, and the second is
primarily Difference (*G. L.* ii. 40). So far this seems only a
repetition of what was said before. The Reflection into self is
the Identity which includes itself and Difference, while the
External Reflection is the Difference which includes itself and
Identity. Hegel's statement that they are indifferent (gleichgültig) to one another is also explicable. Identity and
Difference, pure and simple, were not indifferent to one another.
Each was the other's complement. But if Identity is taken as
including itself and Difference, or Difference is taken as including itself and Identity, each of them is a stable whole,
since it includes its complement. And therefore they may be
taken as indifferent to one another.

Things are Various, he continues, when they are indifferent
in their connexion with each other. For, when they are
indifferent to each other, it is because the Difference between
them is seen to involve the Identity of each. *A* and *B* are
indifferent, when *B*'s difference from *A* lies in the fact that it is
B (and not in the merely negative consideration that it is not
A), and when *A*'s difference from *B* lies in the fact that it is *A*.
And it is this—the difference of positive from positive—that he
calls Variety, as distinguished from Absolute Difference, which
is the difference of a positive from its mere negation. And
since Reflection in self gives us indifference, he says (*G. L.* ii. 41)
that it gives us Variety.

But now Hegel goes on to a further argument which appears
to me fallacious. "The External Reflection on the other hand

is the determined Difference" of the two moments "not as absolute Reflection in self but as Determination, against which the Reflection in self is indifferent; its two moments, the Identity and the Difference itself, are thus externally posited, and are not Determinations which are in and for themselves. Now this external Identity is Likeness (Gleichheit) and the external Difference is Unlikeness. Likeness is indeed Identity, but only what is posited, an Identity which is not in and for itself. In the same way, Unlikeness is Difference, but as an external Difference, which is not in and for itself the Difference of the Unlike" (*G. L.* ii. 41).

But Likeness cannot be reduced to a sort of Identity. For the Identity of which Hegel speaks—the Identity of the previous category—is a relation which falls entirely within some particular thing. *A* is identical with itself because it has the same content in Surface and Substratum. And this cannot possibly become the Likeness of which Hegel speaks, which is a relation between different things.

It is true that, if things are like one another, they will have some identical quality. But then the identity is of the quality, while the identity of which Hegel has been speaking is an identity of a thing. And the identity of a quality cannot be an instance of Hegel's category of Identity, since that only applies where there is a Substratum and Surface with an identical content, and it is only things, and not qualities, which Hegel regards as having Surfaces and Substrata.

113. It seems to me that it is necessary to reconstruct part of Hegel's argument, though it is only the latter part which will need altering. The transition will start, as it does with Hegel, from the fact that Identity implies Difference, and Difference Identity. Then that *A* should be not-*B*, not-*C*, etc., is implied in its being *A*. And again that *B* should be not-*A* is implied in its being *B*. Thus *A* differs from *B* now because *B* is *B*, since its being not-*A* is seen to be a moment of its nature as *B*.

We have thus got two of Hegel's steps towards Variety. The things are (*a*) indifferent to each other. For their connexion is now through their positive qualities on both sides, which have other meanings than merely to express their Difference, though they do express it. And the things are (*b*) Unlike.

For they have positive qualities, which are different in each of them. And so we get Unlikeness, a name which Hegel does not give to the difference between a term and its mere negation, such as A and not-A.

On both these points we have followed Hegel's argument, except that we have not distinguished between the two forms in which the unity of Identity and Difference can be put, which seems to be irrelevant here. But there remains the third point. The Various things must be determined by Likeness as well as by Unlikeness.

Some Likenesses exist wherever there are common Qualities, and we found in the categories of Measure that each thing had at least two qualities in common with others. But the break of continuity which we found to exist at the beginning of Essence renders it doubtful how far we are entitled to rely on this now. And, at any rate, it would not be sufficient. For the Likenesses to be found in Measure group things in one order only. No cross-groupings are possible by means of them, unless a thing (or, as it was there called, a One) should belong to two different Measure-series, which is not apparently contemplated by Hegel. Now the Likenesses in the category of Variety are clearly more complicated than this. For when the Likenesses turn into Grounds, we shall find that Hegel tells us that A can be connected with B and not with C, or with C and not with B, according to the Ground chosen. It is clear, then, that the category of Variety requires that A shall have one Likeness to B, and a different Likeness to C.

Can we prove that this must be the case? I think we can. Take any group of things, M, N, O, which is less than the whole universe[1]. There will therefore be one or more things outside this group. If we call one of these Z, it is clear that the individuals in the group M, N, O, have each the quality of not being Z—or, if you prefer it, of being not-Z. And this constitutes a Likeness between them.

We can go further. For any group of things we can find, not only a Likeness, but a Likeness shared by no others. Let

---

[1] All the things in the universe have likewise a common Likeness. For of all of them it may be said that they are things, besides various other statements which are true of all of them.

M, N, O, X, Y, Z, stand for a complete list of existent things. Then take the group M, N, O. Each of these has the quality of not being either X, Y, or Z, which constitutes a Likeness between them. And no other group can have this Likeness, for no other group can be formed (except one included in the group M, N, O) which does not include either X, Y or Z. And the same principle will apply, however great the number of things in the universe may be.

114. Thus we should be entitled to predicate Likenesses, as well as Unlikenesses, of the various things. But to do so in this manner would raise an important question which Hegel never considers. It will be noticed that the only qualities which have been deduced by my argument are the qualities which arise from the relation of Difference which has already been proved to exist between all things. The argument therefore rests on the principle that every relation determines a quality in each related thing. If Smith is taller than Brown, then "to be taller than Brown" is a quality of Smith, and "to be shorter than Smith" a quality of Brown. This principle, as I mentioned in Chapter I. (Section 6), is accepted by Hegel.

But when this principle is accepted, the question arises whether all qualities arise out of relations in this way, or whether there are some which do not. (These latter might be called for distinction ultimate qualities.) To this question there can, I think, be no doubt that Hegel's answer would be that there were such ultimate qualities. The Qualities mentioned in the Doctrine of Being certainly did not depend on relations, though relations depended on them, and nothing in the subsequent transitions has removed these Qualities from our view of the nature of things.

These ultimate qualities differ in such an important way from the qualities determined by relation, that it would be very desirable to know something about them as distinguished from the others. Hegel unquestionably held, when dealing with Measure, that each thing had at least two ultimate qualities which *could* be common to it with other things, without being common to all things. And he probably went further, and held that every thing possessed some qualities which *were* common to it and to some other things. But does this hold now that we

have passed out of Measure ?   It is clear that things have still
ultimate qualities.   It is clear, from what has been said above,
that everything has still qualities which are common to it with
some other things, without being common to it with all other
things.   But are any of these common qualities ultimate
qualities ?   On this point the dialectic tells us nothing.

115.   Hegel discusses here Leibniz's principle of the Identity of Indiscernibles (*G. L.* ii. 44).   The reasons by which he
accounts for the supposed connexion of the Law of Identity
with his category of Identity (cp. above, Section 109) would
suggest that a similar Law might be found in connexion with
the category of Difference, and he seems to regard the principle
of the Identity of Indiscernibles as holding this place.   But the
analogy is very slight.   The Law of Identity, Hegel tells us,
was universally admitted, was a mere tautology, and fell within
formal logic.   Now the principle of the Identity of Indiscernibles
is by no means universally admitted, is certainly not a mere
tautology, and does not come within the sphere of formal logic.

116.   We now proceed to the transition to the next category.
Hegel says (*G. L.* ii. 44) " the Various is the Difference which
is merely posited, the Difference which is no Difference."   And
he goes on to say that the transition is due to the Indifference
(Gleichgültigkeit) of Variety.

What is meant by this ?   I conceive that he means that in
this category there is no special connexion of any thing with
any other thing.   The relation may fairly be said to be one of
Indifference, if no thing has any connexion with one other
except that which it has with all others.   And this Indifference,
I conceive, arises as follows.   We are now dealing with Likenesses and Unlikenesses.   But every thing is, as we have seen,
Unlike every other thing.   And it is also Like every other
thing, for in any possible group we can, as we have seen, find a
common quality.   Thus under this category everything has
exactly the same relation to everything else.   For it is both Like
and Unlike everything else.

It may naturally be objected to this that the relations are
not precisely similar. A may be both like and unlike B and C,
but it will be like B because they both have the quality x,
unlike because A has and B has not the quality y.   With C, on

the other hand, it may be the quality m which makes the likeness, and the quality n the unlikeness.

The answer to this, I believe, would be that our present
category makes the Substratum of things to be simply their
Likeness and Unlikeness, and that therefore the relations recognised by it are just the same although they may be founded on
different qualities. A is like B in respect of x, like C in respect
of m, but all that this category deals with is the abstract relation
of Likeness. And this is the same in the case of A and B as it
is in the case of A and C.

The possession of a common quality is not, for Hegel, a
direct determination of the nature of things till we reach the
categories of the Notion. It is this, I believe, which is indicated
by the fact that he then for the first time calls them Universals,
and says that they constitute the nature of the things. Before
the Notion is reached a community of quality only affects the
nature of a thing by putting it into, or taking it out of, a group
with another thing. In Quantity and Measure this did not
produce Indifference, because the common qualities there per-
mitted only one system of grouping (cp. above, Section 113).
But in Variety, where everything is like and unlike everything
else, the Indifference arises.

The Indifference is a defect which makes the category
untenable. We passed from Being to Essence because the
existence of a plurality completely ungrouped and unorganised
was impossible, and because its grouping required the duplicity
of nature which comes in Essence. But it is evident that
Essence cannot fulfil its task if all that the Substratum does is
to give a' relation which links everything to everything else in
exactly the same manner. It gives no reason why A should be
linked with B rather than with C, or with C rather than with
B. And, ever since Undivided Quantity passed into Quantum, we
have seen that such preferential linkings must exist.

Hegel maintains that we can only escape this difficulty by
finding a Likeness and Unlikeness which are not indifferent to
each other. Now if A and B have a particular Unlikeness which
depends on their having a particular Likeness, then the indifference, he holds, has broken down. A and B are not simply
Like and Unlike. Their Unlikeness depends on their Likeness.

And, if A can only enter into this particular relation to B, and to nothing else, then A and B are specially connected. Now this happens in cases of what is called polar opposition. Such is the case where A and B have both a temperature, and A is hot and B is cold. And again we have it when A and B are movements on the meridian of Greenwich, and A is a movement North, and B a movement South, or when A and B are sums of money, and I owe A and am owed B. Thus Hegel passes to a category which he calls

(c) *Opposition.*

(*G. L.* ii. 47.) This is a synthesis of Absolute Difference and Variety. As in Variety, the differences are positive on each side, but, as in Absolute Difference, the differences lie in characteristics which are in a definite negative relation to one another, and are not simply not the same.

117. Hegel says (*G. L.* ii. 48) that the Likeness is the Positive here, and the Unlikeness the Negative. I must own myself entirely unable to understand what he means by this. The whole course of the argument seems to show that the Likeness consists in the common character shared by two opposites, and that each of these opposites can be taken either as Positive or Negative.

He then recapitulates (*G. L.* ii. 49, 50) the three elements which make up the Positive and Negative. The first is that in which they are merely moments of the Opposition. In the second, each side has both elements in it—the elements of Positive and Negative—and they thus become indifferent towards one another. In the third, they are essentially connected, and yet at the same time have each a positive nature.

This recapitulation must not be mistaken for a subordinate triad within Opposition. In the first place, its terms are not marked off from each other in the text by separate headings, or provided with names of their own, which always happens with distinct categories. In the second place, it is obviously a recapitulation, since the *last* stage of the three is just the idea which we gained on passing from Variety to Opposition—that of two things, different in their positive nature, and yet each determining the other as its negative. The two earlier stages—

those dealing with a mere difference and with indifferent diversity—had been transcended before we came to Opposition at all, and could not return in it, since they are incompatible with the principle of Opposition.   They are, as Hegel calls them, "determinations which constitute Positive and Negative," but not forms of the category which contains Positive and Negative.

The transition to the next category (*G. L.* ii. 57) is as follows: Each extreme, he says, "has indifferent stability for itself through the fact that it has the relation to its other moment in itself (an ihm selbst).   Thus it is the whole Opposition contained in itself.   As this whole, each is mediated with itself through its Other, and continues its Other.   But it is also mediated with self through the Not-Being of its Other; thus it is a unity for itself, and excludes its other from it."   As thus it includes and excludes the Other in the same respect (Rücksicht), and therefore is only stable in so far as it excludes its own stability from itself, it involves a contradiction.

Is the category of Opposition valid?   I do not think that it is.   The Indifference of Variety was really a defect, and had to be transcended.   But all that is needed for this purpose is that some Likeness shall be taken as specially fundamental—the conception which is introduced afterwards in Ground.   If this were done, the Indifference would be removed, since things which had the same Ground would be specially linked together. And we have no right to introduce into the new category more than is necessary to remove the contradiction of the one below it.   Now Opposition, involving as it does a special relation of the Unlikeness between two things to the Likeness between them, is a more complicated idea than Ground, and we ought not to have introduced it when Ground would suffice—to say nothing of the incorrectness of reaching Ground (as Hegel does) *after* the more complex conception of Opposition has been transcended.

Moreover, if we could have accepted the transition which Hegel makes into Opposition, we should still have to reject the transition by which he passes out of it.   The contradiction which he finds here rests on a mistake.   The stability of the Extremes of an Opposition rest, no doubt, on their relation to one another, and this very stability excludes them from one

another. But there is no contradiction here. There is simply
the truth, which the dialectic gave us as long ago as Being for
Self, that a thing is determined to be itself by the fact of not
being other things.

I think, therefore, that the category of Opposition is not to
be justified, and that the transition should run from Variety
direct to Ground[1]. The insertion of Opposition may be due to
the tendency to which we have to ascribe so much of what is
weakest in the dialectic—the tendency to bring in irrelevant
conceptions which play a large part in empirical science, or
in the history of philosophy. Polarity is, of course, a very important conception for science. And—a still more important
consideration—it was the central conception of the philosophy
which Schelling had constructed, and from which Hegel had
found his way to his own system. It is not wonderful therefore
that Hegel should have unconsciously deflected the course of
the dialectic to include it.

118.   We now pass to a category which Hegel calls

C. Contradiction.

(*G. L.* ii. 57.) In giving it this name, however, he seems to
confuse the category with the transition to it. The contradiction
just stated is the reason why we must pass on from Opposition
to another category, but it cannot be the category itself. How
could we pass to a conception which, as we get to it, we know
to be contradictory ? The whole point of the dialectic method
is that the perception of a contradiction is a reason for
abandoning the category which we find contradictory. Moreover
the category now before us is the Synthesis of Identity and
Difference. And it is especially clear that a category cannot be
accepted as a reconciliation of others where it is seen to be itself
contradictory.

Hegel's transition *from* his category of Contradiction is to be
found on p. 61. " The exclusive Reflection of the stable
Opposition makes it a Negative, something only posited. So
it "—the Reflection—" degrades its previous stable Determinations, the Positive and the Negative, to the level of being *only*

---

[1] Though not, as I shall explain later on, to the same subdivision of
Ground which comes first in the *Greater Logic* (cp. below, Section 131.)

Determinations, and since the Position (Gesetzsein) has been made Position in this way, it has gone back into unity with itself. It is simple Essence, but Essence as Ground."

119. It seems to me that we can do justice to Hegel's argument here by taking the contradiction (which he makes the category of Contradiction) as the transition into a category constituted in the way described in this passage. The conception of Ground will thus be reached in II. C., instead of at the beginning of III., where Hegel puts it.

The contradiction which, if Hegel is right, is found in Opposition is now removed by taking the terms as each possessing its own Substratum—no longer merely sharing one with its Opposite—but a Substratum which is clearly recognised as something with both positive and negative nature. As Hegel says, " Ground is Essence as positive Identity with itself, which, however, at the same time relates itself to itself as negativity, and thus determines itself and makes itself exclusive (ausgeschlossenen) Position ; but this Position is the whole stable Essence, and the Essence is Ground, which in its negation is identical with itself and positive " (*G. L.* ii. 62).

For this category, to which the name of Contradiction is clearly inapplicable, I should suggest the name of Stable Essentiality. It bears a marked resemblance to Identity, for in it, as in Identity, each part of the Surface has its own Substratum, which belongs to it, and to no other. This contrasts with the categories of Difference in each of which the Substratum of each thing consisted in its relation to others.

But the difference between this category and Identity must not be overlooked. In the new category the Substratum is not merely the nature of the thing, but that nature recognised as essentially different from the nature of the other things round it. In the category of Identity, Difference has not yet been recognised. When it is recognised, we have passed on to the category of Difference. But in Stable Essentiality the Substratum includes in it, as an essential element, the fact of its difference from other Substrata. It is therefore, as its position in the process requires it to be, the Synthesis of Identity and Difference.

And this involves another change from Identity. The

Substratum and Surface in Identity were seen to be identical, except in the form of being Surface and Substratum. Here, on the other hand, there is a further difference between Surface and Substratum. For the Substratum includes in itself its determination as different from the other Substratum—to which nothing corresponds in the merely immediate reality of the Surface.

120.   At this point (*G. L.* ii. 66) Hegel inserts a Note on the Law of Excluded Middle, which he regards as specially connected with the category of Opposition. He remarks that there is one thing which is neither $+A$ nor $-A$, namely A itself, which enters into both. No doubt this is true, and we might add that all the indefinite number of things in the universe of which A cannot be predicated are neither $+A$ nor $-A$. If A is Seven, for example, Courage is neither $+A$ nor $-A$. But the Law of Excluded Middle says nothing of $+A$ and $-A$, but of A and not-A, which is very different (Hegel states the Law correctly at the beginning of his Note, but, towards the end, suddenly substitutes $-A$ for not-A, without any warning or explanation). Now with regard to A and not-A, it is quite true that everything must be one or the other. Courage, for example, is not-Seven. And the law is true of A itself. For, although it is neither $+A$ nor $-A$, yet it is A, and it is not not-A.

121.   We now pass (*G. L.* ii. 73) to

III.   GROUND.

A.   *Absolute Ground.*

(*a*)   *Form and Essence.*

(*G. L.* ii. 77.) Here the Substratum of each part of the Surface belongs to that part of the Surface alone. But it is distinguished from it as being explicitly determined by the negative relation to its surroundings, which is not the case with the Surface.

122.   But, again, we cannot keep these relations out of the Surface. If the Surface is to be anything definite at all, it must have in it the negative relation of one thing to another, without which nothing can be definite. And thus, as Hegel says (*G. L.* ii. 79), "everything definite belongs to the Form."

The Substratum is left behind as an empty shell. "The Essence is according to this moment the Undetermined, for which the Form is an Other. So the Essence is not" (*i.e.* is no longer) "the absolute Reflection in itself, but is determined as formless Identity; it is Matter" (*G. L.* ii. 82). So we get

(*b*) *Form and Matter.*

(*G. L.* ii. 82.) Matter here is much more indefinite than the Matter of Materialism, or of physical science. For that is conceived as having a definite nature while here all the definite nature has been absorbed by the Form, leaving the Matter as an undetermined and undifferentiated basis for the Form.

It is, however, impossible that Matter, taken in this sense, should be the Substratum of anything. For, with no definite nature, it can have no definite relation to anything. It is clear then that it cannot be in the very definite relation to the Surface of being its Substratum, without which the Surface would be inexplicable.

123. We must therefore conceive the Matter as having Form as a moment of itself—as being formed Matter. But again, the Form, since it has, according to the argument which produced the category of Form and Matter, everything in it, must have the Matter as a moment in itself (*G. L.* ii. 86). Thus both sides—Substratum and Surface—have the same nature, and we come to

(*c*) *Form and Content.*

(*G. L.* ii. 88.) In this category, says Hegel (*G. L.* ii. 89), we reach Determined Ground. It might be objected to this that the Ground is to be conceived rather as determining than as determined. But it must be remembered that Ground, like Essence, is used by Hegel both as the name of a relation and as the name of one term of that relation. It is, I think, rather the Ground-relation than the Ground-element of that relation of which he speaks here. And this relation may properly be called at this point determined, because here, for the first time in Ground, the nature of the two sides is explicitly identical, and there is therefore nothing on either side which is not related to its correlate on the other.

B.   *Determined Ground.*

(a)   *Formal Ground.*

124. (*G. L.* ii. 90.) This is simply the restatement of Form
and Content. The Ground of the whole nature of the thing is
its whole nature. The explanation is thus perfectly complete.
A B C is the Ground of *A B C*. Such an explanation leaves out
nothing, assumes nothing, and explains nothing. It is for this
reason that it is called Formal.

It is worth while to compare this category with two previous
categories which resemble it to some extent—Identity, and Form
and Essence. Form and Essence is distinguished from it by not
possessing the same absolute likeness of the two terms which is
found in Formal Ground. The Substratum in Form and Essence
has, as we saw, a more explicit reference to other reality than is
found in the Surface.

But the resemblance between Identity and Formal Ground
is closer, for in neither of them is any difference to be found
between Surface and Substratum, beyond the fact that they are
Surface and Substratum. The distinction between the categories
is that, when we come to Formal Ground, the advancing process
has determined each thing as explicitly possessing differences
from other things, and similarities with them. The question is
no longer a vague " What?" but a more definite "Why this and
not that ? " In the category of Identity we merely tried, in a
quite undetermined manner, to explain the thing. Here we
have the definite problems to answer which are presented by a
thing, each of whose similarities and differences is a special
problem. In Identity, it is to be remembered, there was not
yet a plurality of characteristics for each thing. That came in
for the first time in Variety.

The inadequacy of Formal Ground is clear. If the Surface
was sufficient to explain itself, we should not want the Essence-
relation at all. And since it is not sufficient to explain itself,
we shall not gain anything by formally offering its own nature
as its explanation. We must therefore look elsewhere for a new
category, to avoid the contradiction of positing as an explanation
that which can explain nothing.

125. How do we proceed ? Hegel says (*G. L.* ii. 97) " The side of Ground has shown itself to be something posited, and the side of the Grounded has shown itself to be itself Ground; each is in itself this identity of the whole. Since, however, they belong at the same time to the Form, and constitute its determined Difference, each of them is *in its own Determinateness* the identity of the whole with itself. Each has thus a separate content as against the other. Or—to consider it from the side of Content—since it," the Content, " is Identity as the Ground-relation with itself, it has essentially within itself this difference of Form, and is as Ground something different from what it is as Grounded.

" From this fact, that the Ground and the Grounded have a different content, it follows that the Ground-relation has ceased to be formal. The return into the Ground, and the advance to it from what is posited is no longer a tautology; the Ground has become real (ist realisirt). We demand therefore, when a Ground is enquired for, that the Ground shall have a different determination of content from that for whose Ground enquiry was made."

The truth contained in this, I think, is that however much the argument may require us to think of the two sides as exactly similar, still, if we keep to the Ground-relation at all, we must conceive the two sides as more or less different. The Ground is that to which we refer in order to explain the Grounded, and a thing cannot be explained by a mere repetition of itself. Thus " the Determinateness of the two sides "—that is, the fact that one is Ground and the other is Grounded—requires a difference in what is contained in each of them.

Hegel's language, however, is misleading. It suggests that the relation between the Ground and the Grounded not only *requires* a difference between what they contain, but also *produces* such a difference. In other words, it suggests that the Formal Ground turns into the Real Ground—that the Formal Ground which appeared at first sight to have both sides identical, turns out on further consideration to show some difference between the two.

This is not what really happens. What does happen is that the category of Formal Ground has broken down, because the characteristics implied by the Formality are contrary to those

implied by the Ground. We have therefore to look for a
category in which this contradiction shall be removed, and in
which Ground shall be so expressed that the required difference
in the content of the two sides shall be possible. And when
Hegel developes the idea of his new category we see that in the
new category the Ground is part of the nature of the thing and
no longer the whole nature. It is not therefore the same
Ground as before, looked at in a different manner, but a different
Ground. It is called

(b) Real Ground.

(<i>G. L.</i> ii. 96.) Its advance on the last category consists in
the Surface—the Grounded—having more in it than there is in
the Substratum—the Ground. The Grounded is "the unity of
a double content" (<i>G. L.</i> ii. 97), of which one side is also to be
found in the Ground, and the other is not. The difference has
to be made somehow, and therefore one side must have more in
it than the other. The reason why the excess is to be found on
the side of the Grounded is not given by Hegel. I conceive it
to be that we always start from the Surface, as that which now
represents the stratum of the reality which was first determined.
The Substratum is what is required to explain this. It is
possible, therefore, that we should determine a Substratum
which only explains part of the Surface, if all of the Substratum
does explain part of the Surface. But if the Substratum contained more than the Surface, so that there was an element in
the Substratum which did not explain the Surface, how could
we ever show the existence of that element? For it is not
part of the <i>datum</i> to be explained (since it is not part of the
Surface), and it is not part of the explanation. The only
alternative, then, is to take the Surface as having more in it
than the Substratum.

The ungrounded element in the Grounded has a merely
immediate connexion with the other element. The unity of
the double content "is, as unity of the different, their negative
unity, but since the Content-determinations are indifferent
towards one another, it is only their empty relation, without
Content in itself, and is not their mediation; it is a One or
Something as their external junction" (<i>G. L.</i> ii. 97).

Thus Something, as the explanation of the union of the two

elements—or rather, as the assertion of it as an ultimate fact—
is itself to be considered a Ground of a different sort. "The
two relations, the essential Content, as the simple immediate
Identity of Ground and Grounded, and then the Something, as
the relation of the separated Content, are two separate Grounds[1]"
(*G. L.* ii. 99).

126. It may be remarked of a Real Ground, though Hegel
does not mention the fact, that it may be shared by two or
more things. For the nature of several things may be in part
similar, and the Real Ground only explains part of a thing, so
that it may in this way explain several similar things. But it
is also the case, as Hegel points out in a Note (*G. L.* ii. 101),
that a thing can have more than one Real Ground. (This is
distinct from the fact that both the Real Ground and the
Something may be considered as Grounds.) For the special
characteristic of any Real Ground is that it does not contain
so much as is contained by the Grounded, and out of the
remainder of the content of the Grounded, other Real Grounds
may be made. This, as Hegel points out, gives a chance to
Sophistry (*G. L.* ii. 103). To refer a thing to part of its content
as its Real Ground implies that that part is the true significance
of the thing—that which is, even in ordinary language, called
essential to it. This can, by a selection of characteristics for
that purpose, be used to disguise truth. Thus it would be
sophistical to take as the Ground of highway robbery that it
diverted wealth from a richer man for the benefit of a poorer
man. For that would imply that the resemblance of highway
robbery to voluntary charity or to the imposition of a poor rate,
was more important than its difference from them.

127. This possibility of different Real Grounds for the
same thing shows the defect of the category. It does not serve,
as it professes to do, as a basis for the Surface of which it is a
Ground. It does serve as a basis, no doubt, for that part of the
Surface which has the same content as itself—but if we stopped
there we should have got back into Formal Ground. And the
other element is merely immediately connected with the

---

[1] The last word of this extract is in the original Grundlage, not Grund (as
in the other places where I have used Ground in translating). But later on Hegel
gives the name of Grund to both the Real Ground and the Something.

actually Grounded element—so that this other element is not Grounded at all. Either no Ground, or the Formal Ground, which has already been abandoned—this is obviously an impossible position for a category of Ground. The solution is offered by the possibility, already noticed, of considering the Something, in which the Grounded and not-Grounded elements meet, as a Ground of their union. We thus reach

(c) Complete Ground.

(*G. L.* ii. 103.) On the one hand we have the Real Ground connected with the corresponding element in the Surface. On the other hand we have the new connexion between that element and the other element in the Surface. (For the sake of distinction we might call this second element the Supplementary Ground.) Hegel calls this category the Complete Ground because it contains both the Formal and the Real. The Real Ground remains, and in the Supplementary Ground we have the Formal Ground back again, in the sense that in the Supplementary Ground whatever is in the Grounded is also found in the Ground. If the Grounded is *ABC*, and the Real Ground is *A*, then the Supplementary Ground is the assertion of the connexion of *A* with *BC*. It thus accounts for the whole of the Grounded (*G. L.* ii. 104).

128. The elements of the Surface are not yet on an equality. If *A* is the Real Ground, then the element *A* in the Surface is grounded in a sense in which the other elements are not. And thus the elements *BC* are considered as less fundamental to the nature of the thing, but equally necessary. That is to say they are Conditions. Thus we pass to the last division of Ground,

C. Condition.

(a) The Relatively Unconditioned.

(*G. L.* ii. 107.) This new category is a transformation of the Supplementary Ground, the Real Ground being maintained within Condition as it was within Complete Ground. The Supplementary Ground, as has been said, was Formal. It explained *ABC* by asserting that *A* was connected with *BC*. The two sides being thus alike, the difference vanishes, and, instead of the connexion of A with BC being referred to a Ground which only repeats it, it is simply taken as an immediate fact. Condition is what was a form of Ground, but is so no longer. "The Condition stands over against the Ground-relation. The Something has a Ground besides its Condition" (*G. L.* ii. 109).

We may ask why the Ground-form should collapse here because of the identity of the two sides, though it did not do so in the category of Formal Ground. The answer, I think, is that there was then another way of avoiding the tautology, namely the recourse to Real Ground, and that this did not involve the collapse of the Ground-form. This alternative is not available here, for the Supplementary Ground has been required just because Real Ground, by itself, has been shown to be untenable.

But although Hegel's position may be correct, his terminology seems to me to be misleading. He first calls the connexion of A with BC a new sort of Ground, by the side of Real Ground, and then ceases to call this by the name of Ground, though the earlier Real Ground still persists. It would surely have been clearer, if the connexion of A with BC—something quite different from any previous Ground—had from the first been called Condition and not Ground. The category of Complete Ground might then have been called Conditional Real Ground, which would be a natural and appropriate name for the category whose restatement takes us into Condition.

129. The two elements in the Surface—the Condition-element and the Ground-element—are at first considered as related, but as being also on one side indifferent and unconditioned towards one another (*G. L.* ii. 109). It is because of this that the present category is called the Relatively Unconditioned.

But this involves a contradiction. "Each of the two sides is thus the contradiction between indifferent immediacy and essential mediation—both in one relation; or the contradiction between stable existence and the determination of only being a moment" (*G. L.* ii. 110). The same element in a thing cannot both be immediate and mediated by something else.

Moreover, Hegel continues (*G. L.* ii. 110), if the same thing could be both immediate and mediate, then, as immediate, it would be Being Determinate.   And Being Determinate, like all the other categories of Being, has been shown to lead up to Essence.   Thus the very conception by which the Immediacy is expressed has been shown to involve Mediation.

Thus we pass to

(b)   The Absolutely Unconditioned.

(*G. L.* ii. 110.)   The two elements have no longer any independence of one another.   The whole thing is a single unity, and, looked at as a single unity, it is Absolutely Unconditioned.   The elements indeed condition each other, but the whole has nothing determined as conditioning it.   The Absolutely Unconditioned "contains the two sides, the Condition and the Ground, as its moments within itself; it is the unity into which they have returned.   The two together make the Form or Positing of the Absolutely Unconditioned.   The Unconditioned Fact is the Condition of both, but the Absolute Condition, which is itself the Ground" (*G. L.* ii. 113).   It will be seen that the Absolutely Unconditioned is not equivalent to the Absolutely Undetermined, but means that we are no longer considering a reciprocal determination of separate elements.

(c)   Transition of the Fact into Existence.

130.   (*G. L.* ii. 114.)   Ground has now disappeared.   The Unconditioned Fact is its own Ground, and thus the two sides, Surface and Substratum, are identical, destroying the distinction which is essential to Ground.   The same situation arose previously in Formal Ground.   But there the distinction was restored by making the Ground correspond to part only of the Surface.   This, however, has now been shown to lead us back to the rejection of the distinction.   For the ungrounded parts of the Surface became Conditions, and these, with the grounded parts, have now fallen back into the unity, which is its own Ground, and which is therefore immediate.   "This immediacy, mediated through Ground and Condition, and identical with itself through the transcending of the mediation, is Existence" (*G. L.* ii. 118).   (It is not, of course, all mediation which is transcended, but the mediation through Ground and Condition, mentioned in the first part of the sentence.)

Existence is the first subdivision of Appearance, and in reaching it we pass out of Essence as Reflection into Self.

131. If the dialectic process were amended, as I suggested, by passing straight from Variety to Ground, the transition should be, I think, direct to Real Ground, since this would remove the Indifference, which was the defect of Variety, by making one Likeness between any two things (the Likeness selected as the Ground) of special significance and importance. From this the argument would proceed to Condition, as it does with Hegel, and from Condition a valid transition could be made to the categories of Form and Essence, Form and Matter, and Form and Content, with which Ground would close. Thus Formal Ground, which is identical with Form and Content, would follow Real Ground instead of preceding it. This would resemble the treatment in the *Encyclopaedia*, where, though Ground is not explicitly divided at all, the course of the argument begins with Real Ground and then passes through Formal Ground to Existence.

The difference is not so great as might be supposed. Formal and Real Ground are complementary conceptions. The defects of either would drive us to the other, unless the other had already been proved untenable. In that case we are driven to a new conception. Thus a transition from Real to Formal and a transition from Formal to Real would be in themselves equally valid. Which is correct would depend on which conception the dialectic ought to reach first.

CHAPTER VI

APPEARANCE

132. Appearance (Die Erscheinung) is divided as follows :

I. Existence. (Die Existenz.)

   A. The Thing and its Properties. (Das Ding und seine Eigenschaften.)

     (a) The Thing in itself and Existence. (Ding an sich und Existenz.)

     (b) Property. (Die Eigenschaft.)

     (c) The Reciprocal Action of Things. (Die Wechselwirkung der Dinge.)

   B. The Constitution of the Thing out of Matters. (Das Bestehen des Dings aus Materien.)

   C. The Dissolution of the Thing. (Die Auflösung des Dings.)

II. Appearance. (Die Erscheinung.)

   A. The Law of Appearance. (Das Gesetz der Erscheinung.)

   B. The World of Appearance and the World in itself. (Die erscheinende und die an-sich-seiende Welt.)

   C. The Dissolution of Appearance. (Die Auflösung der Erscheinung.)

III. Essential Relation. (Das wesentliche Verhältniss.)

   A. The Relation of Whole and Parts. (Das Verhältniss des Ganzen und der Theile.)

   B. The Relation of Force and its Manifestation. (Das Verhältniss der Kraft und ihrer Aeusserung.)

     (a) The Conditionedness of Force. (Das Bedingtsein der Kraft.)

     (b) The Solicitation of Force. (Die Sollicitation der Kraft.)

     (c) The Infinity of Force. (Die Unendlichkeit der Kraft.)

   C. The Relation of Inner and Outer. (Verhältniss des Innern und Aeussern.)

It will be seen that Appearance is used ambiguously, as the name of the whole secondary division, which we are here considering, and also as the name of its second tertiary division.

I. EXISTENCE.

133. (*G. L.* ii. 120.) Hegel, as we saw in the last chapter, defines Existence as "an Immediacy, mediated through Ground and Condition, and identical with itself through the transcending of the mediation" (*G. L.* ii. 118). This goes too far, if we take it literally. If Existence were really constituted by transcending mediation, and so was identical with itself, there would be no more difference, here or in any subsequent category, between Surface and Substratum. But such a distinction exists, as we shall see, throughout all the categories of Appearance. We must therefore regard this definition as exaggerated.

On the next page we find a more moderate statement. "The doctrine of Being contains the first proposition : Being is Essence. The second proposition : Essence is Being, constitutes the content of the first division of the doctrine of Essence. But this Being, to which Essence has determined itself, is Essential Being (das wesentliche Sein), Existence, that which has emerged from negativity and inwardness" (*G. L.* ii. 119).

Here the meaning does not appear to be that Existence is completely immediate, but that its immediacy is greater than that of the categories in the first division of Essence. And this is correct. The typical conception in Existence is that of the Thing and its Properties, and the relation between a Thing and its Properties is, I think, to be considered as closer than that between a Ground and the thing which is Grounded.

Now if the connexion is closer, the category may be called more immediate. The Surface is always immediate; immediacy is its distinguishing characteristic. The Surface, however, has to be referred for explanation to a Substratum. In so far as this Substratum is distantly and negatively related to the Surface, the reality as a whole will not be immediate. In so far as the relation is close and positive, and the immediate Surface expresses the nature of the Substratum, the reality as a whole is to be looked on as immediate.

To this extent, therefore, Hegel would be right in asserting the greater Immediacy of Essence. But I think he goes further. The extreme expressions, indeed, which indicate absence of all mediation, cannot be taken literally. It is evident he does not mean them literally, since, as has been said, each of the categories of Existence is described by him as having both a Surface and a Substratum. But when this correction has been made, there remain so many expressions emphasising the immediacy of Existence, that it seems difficult to deny that he maintained some sudden and exceptional increase in immediacy at this point—perhaps, indeed, an increase which was not maintained in subsequent categories.

Here, I think, he is wrong. Existence is more immediate than Ground, but, so far as I can see, only in the same way in which Ground is more immediate than Essentialities, and Essentialities than Show. In the same way, Appearance (the tertiary division) seems to me more immediate than Existence, and Essential Relation, again, more immediate than Appearance. If the Thing is more closely connected with its Properties than the Ground is with the Grounded, the Law again is more closely connected with its examples, than the Thing is with its Properties. Hegel's emphasis on the immediacy of Existence must thus, I think, be considered excessive.

134. The first subdivision of Existence is

A. *The Thing and its Properties.*

(*G. L.* ii. 124.) The different elements of the Fact were
Conditions of one another. Thus a fresh unity is substituted
for the unity of Ground, which has disappeared. The various
elements were directly connected among themselves. They
belong to this Fact, and not to another. They are thus
mediated by their relation to this unity. The Substratum is
now the union of various elements of the Surface, instead of
being, as in Ground, one of those elements. Thus we get the
category of the Thing and its Properties.

It will be observed that there is no new element introduced
here into our conception. Both Things and Properties had
been already recognised. The Properties which we have here
are only the Qualities, which we have had previously, under
another name. And a Thing, for Hegel, is that which has
Qualities or Properties. Thus the dialectic has been considering things ever since it reached, at the end of Quantity,
the conception of a subject with a plurality of Qualities.
Hegel has not given them the name of Things before this
point, but the conception of a thing is the conception which
he has previously employed.

In what way, then, is this a new category? It is a new
category because a different element is selected for the
Substratum. The conception which runs all through Essence
is that the explanation of reality lies in the relation between
one element of it and the rest. In Ground the element which
formed the Substratum was a Quality. Now that we have
been driven beyond the category of Ground, we find that in
abandoning it we have emphasised another principle of unity.
If the multiplicity of the surface can be united by the fact
that different things have a common Ground, it can also be
united by the fact that different Qualities belong to the same
thing. And as the first relation has proved inadequate as an
explanation, we proceed to the second. It is the union of
different Qualities in the same thing which is now the Essence-
relation. Hegel now, as we said above, uses the name of Thing
for the first time. The word Property, I think, is used with

this slight difference from Quality, that two Things would not be said to have the same Property, though they might have similar Properties, while Qualities can be said to be common to two things. This individualising of the Property is necessary when, as is the case here, the vital point is its connexion with this particular Thing. We shall see that it is again transcended when we pass to the category of the Constitution of the Thing out of Matters.

135. The connexion between the Thing and its Properties is first taken as merely immediate. Thus we have

(a) The Thing in itself and Existence

(*G. L.* ii. 125), where Existence denotes the Properties—the Surface-element. The externality of the relation consists in the fact that, although the general nature of the Thing in itself requires it to have *some* Existence, yet there is nothing in its nature which requires it to have that particular Existence rather than any other. It " is not the Ground of the unessential Determinate Being, it is the unmoved, undetermined unity " (*G. L.* ii. 126). He continues, " Therefore the Reflection also, as Determinate Being mediated through another, falls outside the Thing in itself. The latter must have no definite multiplicity in itself; and so receives it first when it is brought in by external Reflection; while it remains indifferent to the multiplicity. (The thing in itself has colour first in the eye...&c., &c.)"

In this last sentence Hegel appears to regard his Thing in itself as equivalent to Kant's. This comes out more clearly on p. 131. "In so far as the Thing in itself is posited as the undetermined, all determination falls outside it, in a reflection which is strange to it, and against which it is indifferent. For Transcendental Idealism this external reflection is Consciousness." And he then proceeds to point out Kant's error in taking the conception of the Thing in itself as absolutely valid.

It seems to me, however, that this identification is erroneous. Kant's Thing in itself differs from Hegel's in two important respects. In the first place, Hegel's Thing in itself does possess the characteristics which form its Existence, however imperfectly it possesses them. They are the Surface of which it is the Substratum. They can be predicated of it, and there is nothing else of which they can be predicated. In the second place, Hegel's Thing in itself can have no characteristics except in this imperfect way. Its fundamental nature is to be indifferent to all characteristics which belong to it.

In neither of these points does Kant's Thing in itself resemble it. In the first place, the phenomenal qualities are not, for Kant, the characteristics of the Thing in itself at all. They may be partly caused by it (inconsistent as this is with other parts of the theory) but they are not its characteristics. It may be due to the Kantian Thing in itself, on Kant's theory, that I have a sensation of green. But to say that the Thing in itself *was* green, would be simply a mistake. In the second place, Kant does not exclude the possibility of the Thing in itself having characteristics, which not only belong to it, but express its nature, so that they would be what Hegel calls Properties, and the Thing in itself would not be what Hegel calls a Thing in itself. Such properties of the Kantian Thing in itself cannot, indeed, be known by the Pure Reason. But the Pure Reason, according to Kant, expressly recognises their possibility, and when we come to the Practical Reason we find that some of them are pronounced to be actual.

136. We now pass to Hegel's demonstration of the inadequacy of this category. There are, he tells us (*G. L.* ii. 127), a multiplicity of Things in themselves. And it is clear that this follows from the multiplicity of things which, as we saw, Hegel started with at the beginning of the doctrine of Essence. The Things in themselves are simply these things transferred to the Substratum side of the relation.

The various Things in themselves are connected by their respective Existences (*G. L.* ii. 127). It is clear that it is only through these that they could enter into any relations, since the nature of the Thing in itself, as distinguished from its Existence, excludes any relations.

But Things in themselves, as distinct from their respective Existences, are not in any way different from one another (*G. L.* ii. 128). They can only be distinguished by their characteristics, and these all fall within their Existence. Apart from that, all that can be said of any Thing in itself is that it is a Thing in itself which stands in an external and indifferent relation to *some* Existence. And as much as this can be said of any other Thing in itself.

So far the argument seems clear. But now Hegel continues: "The two Things in themselves, which ought to form the extremes of the relation, do in fact (since they are to have no definiteness as against one another) *fall together into one*; there is only one Thing in itself, which in the external relation relates itself to itself, and it is its own relation to itself, as if to another, which makes its definiteness. This definiteness of the Thing in itself is the Property of the Thing" (*G. L.* ii. 128).

But it is not evident why that which was merely Existence, when it related two Things in themselves, should now, when the two Things in themselves have become one, have ceased to be external and indifferent to the Substratum, so as to turn itself into Property, and the Things in themselves into Things. Hegel gives no reason why the connexion should be less external and indifferent when it is with one Thing than when it is with two.

Again, if all Things in themselves, which are connected by their Existence, run together into one, then in the end there will be only one Thing in itself. For all the Things in themselves are taken by Hegel as connected by their Existences. And as this fusing of the Things in themselves forms the transition to Things with Properties, then all reality would consist of only one Thing with Properties. But Hegel's treatment of the next category involves that there are many Things, and not only one. And he explicitly asserts this plurality (cp. *G. L.* ii. 133: "The Thing in itself is therefore a Thing which has Properties, and there are therefore many Things, which separate themselves from one another through themselves, and not through an alien aspect ").

Hegel's demonstration of the transition does not, therefore, seem satisfactory. But we can see that the transition is necessary. The conception of the Thing in itself was that its Properties, although they were its Properties, did not affect it, or form part of its nature. And this is impossible. A Property is a Quality. And the Qualities of anything are just what constitute its nature. If they could be different without producing any difference in the Thing, they would not be its Qualities. And if the Qualities of the Thing were not part of its nature, it could have no nature at all, for nothing but the Qualities of anything can form part of its nature. Thus it would have no nature, and, consequently, no reality.

We must, therefore, abandon the isolation of the Thing from its Properties which was the characteristic of the Thing in itself, and thus we pass to (*G. L.* ii. 129)

(*b*) *Property.*

137. Here the nature of the Thing is seen to consist in its Properties. It might seem that we had returned to such a tautology as is found in Formal Ground. But each of the Properties, taken by itself, is not identical with the nature of the Thing. The nature of the Thing consists in having all its Properties and uniting them. It is this element of union in the Substratum which keeps the category from being tautological.

The Things are now in a living connexion with each other, and not in the merely external connexion which existed between Things in themselves (*G. L.* ii. 133). As with the Things in themselves, so the present Things also are connected by means of their Surface element, but while the Things in themselves were only externally connected with their own Existence, and consequently only externally connected with one another, here the connexion expresses their own nature. So we reach

(*c*) *The Reciprocal Action of Things.*

(*G. L.* ii. 132.) Things, as we have seen, are connected with one another through their Properties. But the only connexion that has been demonstrated is that through the similarity of Properties. Hegel, however, seems to think that there is more. For he says (*G. L.* ii. 129) that the Properties *are* " determined relations to an Other," which is very different from saying that they *produce* relations of Likeness.

He also says (*G. L.* ii. 129) that " a Thing has the Property to produce (bewirken) this or that in its Other." This looks as if we had already arrived at Causality, and Hegel's distinction

between Causality and his present position is not very
clear. ("The Thing is here still only the quiescent (ruhige)
Thing of many Properties; it is not yet determined as actual
Cause; it is still only the Reflection of its determinations *an
sich*, not yet itself the positing Reflection of them" (*G. L.*
ii. 130).)

138. Having reached this result he goes on to argue that
"the Property is this Reciprocal Action itself, and the Thing
is nothing outside it. ...Thinghood is thus degraded to the form
of undetermined Identity with itself which has its Essentiality
only in its Property" (*G. L.* ii. 133). His conclusion is "The
Property, which had to constitute the relation of the stable
extremes, is now therefore itself that which is stable. The
Things on the other hand are the Unessential" (*G. L.* ii. 134).
Thus the Properties are now the Substratum, and the Things
the Surface. But it is not clear why all this should follow
from the connexion of Things by their Properties. Even if the
Properties could be reduced, as he supposes, to the Reciprocal
Action of the Things, the Things are as essential to the
Reciprocal Action as the Action can be to the Things, and
nothing has been introduced by which the Things should
become unessential, relatively to the Properties.

Hegel confuses the transition by mentioning, as if it were
relevant here, the ambiguity of Things. "A book is a Thing,
and each of its leaves is a Thing, and likewise every fragment
of its leaves, and so on infinitely" (*G. L.* ii. 133). This is
quite true, but, if it were brought in here, the next category
could not follow. For, as we have just seen, that category
takes the Properties as stable instead of the Things. But such
an ambiguity of Things as that of the book and its leaves,
makes the Properties as unstable as the Things. "I am cold,"
as written here, may be taken as one sentence, as three words,
as seven letters, or as an indefinite number of fragments of
letters. But the Properties will vary in each case. For
example, the sentence has, among its Properties, truth or
falsehood. The three words, taken separately, cannot be true
or false, but they each possess the Property of having a
meaning. The separate letters, again, have no meaning. The
ambiguity of Things which Hegel mentions here does not

really come in until the category of Whole and Parts at the earliest.

The name of the present category also seems unfortunate. For the new conception in it is not the Reciprocal Action of Things, which, if Hegel's argument were right, would have been reached in the category of Property, but the transfer of stability from the Things to the Properties.

The name of Property now becomes inappropriate to such stable existences. Hegel calls them Matters. Thus we reach

B. The Constitution of the Thing out of Matters

(*G. L.* ii. 135), which may be called, for brevity, the category of Matters and Things. Matters correspond to Qualities, rather than to Properties, since the same Matter is to be found in many Things (*G. L.* ii. 135), while Things had similar Properties, but did not share the same Property. An identical Quality might form two separate though similar Properties, for they would be distinguished by the fact that it was the nature of one to belong to one Thing, and of the second to belong to another Thing. But Matters have to be determined independently of the Things which they constitute, for it is the Matters, not the Things, which are stable. And thus what was two similar Properties in the last category, is here replaced by a single Matter.

The Things, though now subordinate in importance, still remain. The Thing is now defined by enumeration of the Matters which constitute it. It is simply made up of its constituent Matters. It is a mere "Also" ("Auch," *G. L.* ii. 138.) There is Matter *A, and* Matter *B,* and the simple juxtaposition of these *is* the Thing.

139. Hegel now finds a contradiction in this category, on the ground, apparently, that if the Matters are really united by the Thing they will have to exist "in one another's pores." (This is clearly only a metaphor, but what is meant by it is very difficult to see.) In that case they will not be as stable as the nature of Matters requires. On the other hand, if they are *not* really united by the Thing—if the Thing is a mere Also—it will not be a true Thing at all (*G. L.* ii. 139, 140).

This argument leads him to

C. The Dissolution of the Thing.

(*G.L.*ii.138.) The name is somewhat misleading, for the Thing
is in no greater difficulties than the Matters. But what Hegel
appears to mean is that this category marks the break down of
the attempt to explain the universe by the correlative conceptions of Thing on one side and of Properties or Matter on
the other. It might more appropriately be called the Dissolution of Existence, in the sense in which Hegel uses Existence.

We have the Things still, and we have their Qualities or
Properties. But the attempt to account for the facts by taking
either the Things or the Qualities as the Substratum has broken
down. We want a principle which will determine certain
Qualities to be found together in one Thing, and each of these
Qualities to be also found in other Things. It must be something which underlies both the Things and Qualities—which
will be a Substratum while Things and Qualities are in the
Surface. And we find what we want in the conception of
Law. Such and such Qualities are grouped in a Thing, or a
Thing has such and such Qualities in its nature, according to
Laws. Things are no longer explained by Qualities, or Qualities
by Things[1], but the Laws explain both of them. Law is the
characteristic idea of the second subdivision of Appearance—
the subdivision which is also, in a narrower sense, called
Appearance, and to this we now pass.

140. Looking back on the categories of Existence, the
transition from the Thing in itself to Property must be
pronounced inevitable, even if we see cause to reject Hegel's
account of it. As to the transitions which led us from
Property to Matters and Thing, they must, I think, be rejected.
For even if Hegel had been right in taking the Properties of
Things as Relations between them, I cannot see how this would
entitle him to abandon the conception of Things and Properties
for that of Matters and Things.

But I believe it would be easy to show that the conception

---

[1] It will be remembered that Matters are only Qualities taken as the Essence
of Things, while Properties are Qualities of which Things are taken as the
Essence.

of Matters and Things possesses *equal* validity with that of Things and Properties (though not, as Hegel maintains, *greater* validity). And from the category which would be formed by the recognition of the validity of both conceptions, I believe we could pass to Law by a process not unlike that which Hegel does adopt.

II. APPEARANCE.

141. (*G. L.* ii. 144.) The name is, as I have pointed out, ambiguous, and it seems to have no very definite connexion with the particular categories which are found in this division. Its first subdivision is

A. *The Law of Appearance.*

(*G. L.* ii. 146.) The transition to this category from the last has been already discussed. The change is that the categories of Thing could only account for the grouping of the Surface-elements by making those groupings ultimate and essential to the elements grouped. Here the groupings are accounted for by something other than themselves, which leaves them only a subordinate and conditioned position.

Hegel now proceeds to point out three defects in this category. In the first place, the Law does not account for the whole of the nature of the Surface. "The Appearance has also another content against the content of the Law. This other content is indeed unessential, and a return into the content of the Law, but for the Law it is a First, not posited by the Law; it is therefore a content externally connected with the Law" (*G. L.* ii. 151). If, for example, we endeavour to explain the fall of a leaf by the Law of Gravitation, the explanation is only partial. The shape of the leaf, the currents in the air, and other considerations will affect its course. Nor would it have fallen at all, if it had not been heavier than the air. That it is heavier is a fact, not a Law. Or if its greater weight could be traced to another law, we may then ask why this Law should be applicable to the leaf, and not to hydrogen. And the answer must finally be found in a fact which is not a Law.

The second defect in the category of Law is that the additional content, whose existence constitutes the first defect, is related to the content of the Law in a negative manner. The Law is unchanging (ruhig) (*G. L.* ii. 151). The other content is changing (unruhig). I do not believe that Hegel means that some Laws (it would not be true of all) deal with changes of what is subject to them, while the Laws themselves are unchanging. I believe him to mean that the additional content, besides being indifferent to the Law, is different in different cases, in all of which the Law is the same. A leaf and a stone both obey the Law of Gravitation in falling to the earth. But the additional element in the two cases is very different. Hegel is, however, rather obscure here.

The third defect is the absence of any inherent connexion between the circumstances linked together in the Law itself. Why should one body attract another? And why should the relation between the distance of the bodies and the force of the attraction be what it is, and not something else? This may be explained by another Law. But then a similar question will arise about this second Law. Eventually we must come to a conjunction which is ultimate and inexplicable (*G. L.* ii. 152).

142. The first two defects are due to that part of the content of the Surface which is not accounted for by the Law. But this content is not intrinsically different from the part which the Law does account for. If one can be accounted for, so can the other (*G. L.* ii. 153). This can be done by making the Law more precise. Instead of referring the fall of the leaf and the rise of the tides to the same Law of Gravitation, we can find for each a separate and more detailed Law of the action of gravitation under particular circumstances, which will leave much less of the content of the Surface unaccounted for. Still, however, a general Law of tides will leave outside of itself many aspects of the rise of the tide at a particular time and place. To remedy this we must make the Law still more particular. And so we shall go on, till the Law covers all the circumstances of the particular case. But by doing so it will have ceased to be a Law, for it will have no generality. It will not explain the case by connecting it with others. It

will simply restate it. Thus we pass, when this is applied to
the whole of the Surface of the universe, to

B. *The World of Appearance and the World in itself.*

(*G. L.* ii. 153.) Here the Substratum is merely the restatement of the Surface, or, to put it more accurately, the Surface
is the reflection of the Substratum.

Hegel appears to think that this cures the third defect which
he finds in Law, as well as the other two. He says that the
two sides of the Law now involve one another, because each is
determined as being different from the other, and so involves
the other (*G. L.* ii. 154). But I cannot see that they do this
more than they did before. The Law is changed into the World
in itself. The connexion between two classes of particulars
which we found in the Law is replaced (since generality is now
sacrificed for the sake of completeness) by a connexion between
two particulars in the World in itself. But the two particulars
are no more inherently connected than the two classes were.

It seems to me, indeed, that Hegel was wrong in counting
this third characteristic of Law as a defect which has to be
transcended here. We find just the same immediate ultimate
conjunction far higher up in the dialectic in the Syllogisms of
Necessity. And there it is not regarded as a defect to be transcended, but, on the contrary, as a truth the explicit recognition
of which is itself an advance. The characteristic inadequacy of
the present category of Law—the one which we must transcend as we pass out of it—seems to me to be contained in the
first and second defects given by Hegel. And these, as we
have seen, *are* transcended in the World of Appearance.

Hegel regards these two worlds as having their corresponding contents related to each other as polar opposites. The
North Pole in the World of Appearance is "in and for itself"
the South Pole. Evil and unhappiness in the World of Appearance are "in and for themselves" good and happiness (*G. L.*
ii. 158. The phrase used here is "an und für sich," and not, as
in the title of the category, "an sich").

I must confess myself at a loss to understand this. The two
Worlds are, of course, distinguished as Surface and Substratum.
But why should this make any difference in their contents,

except that of being Surface and Substratum respectively?
And what, on this view, would correspond, in the World in
itself, to those characteristics of the World of Appearance which
are not one of a pair of polar opposites ?

143. Since the two sides are now perfectly alike except for
a distinction of form (for Hegel does not regard the polar opposition of the two Worlds as more than this, and, if we reject the
polar opposition, it is still clearer that there is only a formal
difference) the category breaks down. In referring the World
of Appearance to the World in itself we are only referring it to
itself. The only difference is the difference of form, and that is
simply the affirmation of the fact that one is referred to the
other. Now to refer anything to itself as its own Substratum
is obviously useless. If it does explain itself, there could be no
need for a reference to a Substratum at all. If it does not
explain itself, such a Substratum can never explain it. So we
reach (*G. L.* ii. 158)

C. The Dissolution of Appearance.

Once more, as previously in Identity and in Formal Ground,
we find the conception of Essence reduced to a tautology, owing
to the identity of content in Surface and Substratum. What
is to be done ? We cannot, as we did in the case of Identity,
supplement *A*'s identity with itself by means of its difference
from *B*, for here the identical content covers the whole of the
universe. Nor can we, as with Formal Ground, avoid the
difficulty by ascribing to the World in itself only part of the
content of the World of Appearance. For that had already
been done in Law, and it was the inadequacy of this which
drove us on to the category of the two Worlds.

144. Only one alternative remains. We must abandon the
attempt—hitherto characteristic of the categories of Essence—
to explain the content of the Surface by means of the content
of the Substratum. The explanation of the Surface is now to
be found, not in the content of the Substratum, but in its own
relation to the Substratum—a relation which no less explains
the Substratum (*G. L.* ii. 160). Thus the tautology has
vanished. The Surface is no longer explained by the content
of a Substratum which has the same content as itself. It is

explained by the fact that this content is found in two aspects —Surface and Substratum.   And the fact of the relation of the two aspects is of course not identical with either aspect.   This is the positive significance of our present category, and this takes us out of Appearance, in the narrower sense, into the last subdivision of Appearance, in the wider sense (*G. L.* ii. 161).

III.   ESSENTIAL RELATION.
A.   The Relation of Whole and Parts.

(*G. L.* ii. 162.)   Hegel shows us with sufficient clearness the transition to Essential Relation as a whole, but he is not explicit as to the transition to Whole and Parts.   It is clear that this category falls properly within Essential Relation.   The identity of content between Whole and Parts is manifest; the cardinal fact about them is that they are equal to one another. And tautology has disappeared, for we do not attempt here to explain the nature of the Parts by the nature of the Whole, but by the relation of the form of the Parts to the form of the Whole.   But why is this the first subdivision of Essential Relation, and why do we proceed to it direct from the Dissolution of Appearance ?

The reason, I think, is as follows.   The Surface has always been a multiplicity throughout Essence.   On the other hand, the Substratum has always presented itself as a unity, not always as an undivided unity, but always as something which did unify the multiplicity of the Surface.   The only exceptions have been the limiting cases in which the Substratum became identical in nature with the Surface.   And this always involved a break down through tautology.

Whenever the Substratum has not been impotent from tautology it has unified.   Now that we have seen that the two sides of the Essence-relation have the same content, and only differ in form, what we require is a difference of form such that the one side is a unity and the other a multiplicity, while the content of each is the same.   And this just gives us the conception of the Substratum as a Whole, and of the Surface as its Parts. All that is existent forms a single Whole consisting of Parts.

145.   If we look more closely at this category, we see that the statement that the Whole is equal to its Parts is only true if the Parts are conceived as taken together. The Whole is not equal to all its Parts in the sense in which the original resembles all its copies—it is not equal to each of them. It is only equal to them as taken together—taken as a unity. But the unity of the Parts *is* the Whole. And thus we have come round to the tautology that the Whole is equal to the Whole (*G. L.* ii. 166).

In the same way the Parts are not equal to the Whole as a Whole. If the Parts are taken as separate (and, if not, they would *be* the Whole) then the Whole has to be taken as divided in order to equal them, since it is not, as a Whole, equal to each of the separate Parts. But the Whole as divided *is* the Parts. Once more we reach a tautology—the Parts are equal to the Parts (*G. L.* ii. 167).

The reason of this is the indifference of the relation between the forms of Whole and Part. Under this category there is no necessity to take what is taken as Many as also One, nor to take what is taken as One as also Many. And so we can only say that the One is the Many if it is the Many—*i.e.* that the Many is the Many, and, in the same way, that the One is the One. The One could as well be undivided, and the Many as well un-united. Since the undivided One is not a Whole, and the un-united Many are not Parts, we may say that if anything is merely a Whole, it is quite indifferent to its nature whether it is a Whole or not, and if any aggregate of things are merely Parts, it is quite indifferent to their nature whether they are Parts or not.

The category has thus broken down. Instead of the significant assertion that the Whole equals the Parts, we have the two tautologies that the Whole equals the Whole, and the Parts the Parts. Now our present position permits and requires that the content of the Substratum and of the Surface shall be identical, but this is only possible because the difference between them, which is still essential, is transferred to the form. If the difference of forms goes too, the tautology that results involves as complete a failure as previous tautologies. Indeed, the failure is more obvious, for the category has developed into two separate and unconnected tautologies. Thus all connexion between the Substratum and the Surface is denied. All that

we can say is that the Substratum is the Substratum, and the
Surface is the Surface.

And even the tautologies destroy themselves. As Hegel
points out (*G. L.* ii. 167) the Whole, when taken out of all
connexion with the Parts, ceases to be a Whole at all, and
becomes an abstract identity; and the Parts, taken out of all
connexion with the Whole, cease to be Parts, and become an
unconnected manifold.

146. The category has broken down on account of the
merely indifferent connexion of Whole and Parts. It is true
that, as we have just seen, a Whole is not a Whole unless it
has Parts. But when we bring a unity under the conception
of Whole, we imply that it is indifferent to it whether it has
Parts (and so is a Whole), or not. The indifference to the
correlative form makes the form with which we start itself
indifferent to the content it is imposed on.

It is this indifference which produced the tautologies, for,
since there was no inherent connexion between the two forms,
the equality could only be asserted by eliminating the difference of form. It is necessary, therefore, to regard the unity of
the Substratum as a form which cannot exist except in company with the other form of the variety of the Surface, and the
variety of the Surface, again, as a form which can only exist in
company with the unity of the Substratum. Whatever exists
in the one form must also exist in the other (*G. L.* ii. 168). So
we reach

B. *The Relation of Force and its Manifestation.*

(*G. L.* ii. 170.) This category seems to imply by its name
much more than has been reached in this deduction. But if we
take Hegel's definition of Force and Manifestation we shall find
that it contains no more than the deduction justifies. "The
Relation of Force is the higher return into itself, in which the
unity of the Whole, which determines the relation of the stable
Other-Being, ceases to be external and indifferent to this
multiplicity" (*G. L.* ii. 170). As elsewhere in the dialectic,
the name taken from a conception used in empirical science
does not indicate that the category has all the content to be
found in that empirical conception. It only implies that the

category finds in that conception its clearest empirical embodiment.

In the first place, says Hegel, Force has its Surface-moment in the form of an existent Something.   This gives us

(a)   The Conditionedness of Force.

(*G. L.* ii. 171.)   This Something, he tells us, is to be conceived as a Thing or Matter separate from the Force (*G. L.* ii. 171).

147.   But, as he remarks at once, the immediate existence is not, in Force, something outside it, but a moment in its own nature.   "The Thing, in which the Force is supposed to be (sein sollte), has here no more meaning....And the Force is thus not merely a determined Matter; such stability has long ago passed over into Positing and Appearance" (*G. L.* ii. 172).

Force has its immediate existence as an element in its own nature.   That which exists in the form of Force must also exist in the form of Manifestation.   Since the immediacy here "has determined itself as the negative unity which relates itself to itself, it is itself Force" (*G. L.* ii. 173).   The Surface and the Substratum are both Forces.   "The relation" of each to the other "is not the passivity of a process of determination, so that thereby something Other came into it; but the Impulse (Anstoss) only solicits (sollicitirt) them" (*G. L.* ii. 174).   From this Hegel calls the new category (*G. L.* ii. 173)

(b)   The Solicitation of Force.

148.   Solicitation is the determination exercised by each Force on the other.   (The two Forces are the original Force of the Substratum, and the Force of the Surface, which was originally Manifestation.)   But since this is so, each "only solicits in so far as it is solicited to solicit."   And each "is only solicited in so far as it has solicited the other to solicit it" (*G. L.* ii. 175).   Thus neither side has any immediacy as against the other, and all that is real is the unity of the two (*G. L.* ii. 176).   This gives us

(c)   The Infinity of Force.

(*G. L.* ii. 176.)   This is so called because Force is no longer limited either by a Thing on which it acts, or by another Force

outside it. The Force and its Manifestation have nothing independent of one another, even in form. The Force is thus
completely self-determined, that is, in Hegel's language, it is
infinite. From this Hegel proceeds to make the transition to
the next category of Inner and Outer.

149. I believe that the subdivisions of Force and Manifestation are not only unnecessary, but positively erroneous. The
Thesis seems to me unjustified, since it involves a degree of
independence between the Force and the Manifestation which
is quite inconsistent with the general idea of Force and Manifestation. The Force, as Hegel has told us (*G. L.* ii. 170,
quoted above, Section 146), is not external or indifferent to its
Manifestation. But in this category of the Conditionedness of
Force he makes the Manifestation "an existent Something."
Not only is this too independent to be reconciled with the
general conception he has given of Force, but it would even
involve a retrogression beyond Whole and Parts. For in
Whole and Parts, though the forms of the two sides were
indifferent to each other, their content was the same. Here,
however, since the Something is conceived as a Thing, or as a
Matter, it seems inevitable that it should be conceived as having
to some degree a different content from the Force.

It seems curious that Hegel should have introduced this
Thesis at all, since he remarks, in the passage quoted above
(Section 147) from *G. L.* ii. 172 that it involves conceptions
which have been already transcended. It is probable that he
had unconsciously slipped from his own definition of Force to a
more common use of the same word. It would be by no means
unusual to speak of a heavy body as manifesting the force of
gravity, or of a man as manifesting the force of ambition. But
they could not be Manifestations of Forces in the Hegelian
sense, for they are very far from being mere forms of gravity or
ambition. It is this that Hegel seems to have forgotten.

Even if we grant the Thesis, can we defend the Antithesis?
If Force is found on both sides of the relation, can Force, as
Hegel has defined it, retain any meaning? Force is for Hegel
merely the name of a form, since the content is identical with
that of Manifestation. And this form is strictly correlative with
Manifestation. If we ask what is the distinction of the form of

Force from the form of Manifestation, I do not see that there is any possible answer, except that Force is the form of the Substratum, and that Manifestation is the form of the Surface, and, further, that Force is the unity, and Manifestation the plurality.   Now if Force has to be taken so widely as to include the Surface-form (which is the plurality) it has lost both its characteristics, and ought not to be called Force.   We cannot have Force without Manifestation, and, if both sides are Forces, there is no Manifestation left.

Here, once more, Hegel seems to have slipped into the ordinary use of Force, in a way which is inconsistent with his own definition.   In ordinary language Forces often mean, not moments, but stable realities, which can exist each for itself, and can stand in causal relations to one another.   But Force, as defined and demonstrated by Hegel, means the whole of the Substratum of any reality.   To reduce the Essence-relation to a relation between two Hegelian Forces is therefore impossible. For they cannot exist without their Manifestations, and such a relation has no place for Manifestations.

150.   I believe that these two categories are unnecessary as well as unjustifiable.   We can proceed without any subdivisions from the undivided category of Force and Manifestation to the category of Inner and Outer.   We saw that Force and Manifestation differ only in form, and that the two forms are not indifferent to each other, as they were in Whole and Parts, but depend on each other.   There can be no Force without Manifestation, nor any Manifestation without Force.   Consequently each of them is no longer related to anything merely external to it.   The Force is distinguished from the Manifestation, but the difference is not one immediately given to Force, but one which is found in the Force's own nature.   The difference is also to be found in the Manifestation's own nature.

And thus we reach at once what Hegel calls the Infinity of Force.   The Force is not limited by anything outside itself —not even a form.   For the form of Manifestation is posited in the very nature of Force.   Force, therefore, only limits itself, and is, in Hegelian language, Infinite.   (This state of things might as well be called Infinity of Manifestation.   For the form of Force is involved in the nature of Manifestation.)   The

Infinity of Force is not an advance on its original conception, as Hegel says that it is, but is its characteristic from the first. He only appears to advance to it because, as we have seen, he first illegitimately falls back.

151. From the Infinity of Force we can go on, with Hegel, to Inner and Outer. For now all difference between Surface and Substratum disappears. That difference, till Essential Relation was reached, had been a difference of content, so that, wherever the difference of content was eliminated, the category broke down from tautology. With Essential Relation the content of both sides was admitted to be the same, and the difference was confined to the form. But now even the difference in form has vanished. It is no longer the case that the universe can be taken under one form or under the other form, and that this duplicity of form can be relied on for an explanation. To get rid of the contradiction in the category of Whole and Parts, we had to say that the unity has ceased to be " external and indifferent to " the " multiplicity " (*G. L.* ii. 170). And thus the universe cannot be taken as One and again as Many and an explanation sought in the relation of these two forms. There is only one form in which it can be taken, in which it is both Many and One. When you take it as Force, you thereby take it as Manifestation. When you take it as Manifestation, you thereby take it as Force. The Surface is involved in the Substratum, and the Substratum in the Surface. " The Externality of Force is identical with its Internality " (*G. L.* ii. 177). With these words Hegel passes to

C. The Relation of Inner and Outer

(*G. L.* ii. 177), where the two sides are completely identical. There is no longer even a difference of form. " The Outer is not only equal to the Inner in respect to content, but both are only one Fact (Sache) " (*G. L.* ii. 178).

The name of the category may not seem very well chosen to express this absolute identity. The terms Inner and Outer are sometimes used to express a considerable difference between the two sides (cp. *Enc.* Section 140). Again, they are sometimes used to express a closer relation between the two sides, with very little difference. But, in ordinary language, they always imply some difference, whereas Hegel uses them to denote the absence of difference.

It would, however, have been difficult, if not impossible, to find a double name which would have been more appropriate. For when we are clear that we mean only a single reality, we do not naturally use a double name. Any other name, which consisted of two correlative terms, would have implied at least as much difference as Inner and Outer.

But why, it may be asked, does Hegel want a double name ? The Substance and the Substratum are now absolutely identical. Why, then, require a double name for what is essentially single ? The explanation is, I think, that Inner and Outer is the Synthesis of the previous categories, and that its double name has reference to those earlier stages. The identity of the Substratum and Surface is the result of a gradual and lengthy modification of the view that they are really different. The Synthesis states this in a way which sums up what has been gained, by mentioning the distinction only to deny it.

With the identity of Inner and Outer we pass from Appearance to Actuality—the third and last division of Essence.

Note on the Difference between the Greater Logic *and the* Encyclopaedia *in the first two divisions of Essence.*

152. I have postponed this question till now because, as I pointed out in Chapter V., some categories which are found in one division in the *Greater Logic* are found in the other in the *Encyclopaedia.*

The following table will show the different arrangements. For the sake of brevity I omit categories of the fifth order in the *Greater Logic*, except in the two cases where they correspond to categories in the *Encyclopaedia.*

Greater Logic.	*Encyclopaedia.*
ESSENCE AS REFLECTION INTO ITSELF.	ESSENCE AS GROUND OF EXISTENCE.
I. Show.	I. Pure Determinations of Reflection.
A. The Essential and Unessential.	A. Identity.

B. Show.

C. Reflection.

II. The Essentialities.
   A. Identity.
   B. Difference.
     (*a*) Absolute Difference.
     (*b*) Variety.
     (*c*) Opposition.
   C. Contradiction.

III. Ground.
   A. Absolute Ground.

     (*a*) Form and Essence.
     (*b*) Form and Matter.
     (*c*) Form and Content.
   B. Determined Ground.
   C. Condition.

APPEARANCE.

I. Existence.
   A. The Thing and its Pro-
      perties.
   B. The Constitution of the
      Thing out of Matters.
   C. The Dissolution of the
      Thing.

II. Appearance.
   A. The Law of Appearance.
   B. The World of Appearance
      and the World in itself.
   C. The Dissolution of Ap-
      pearance.

III. Essential Relation.
   A. The Relation of Whole
      and Parts.
   B. The Relation of Force and
      its Manifestation.
   C. The Relation of Inner and
      Outer.

B. Difference.
   (*a*) Diversity.
   (*b*) Likeness and Unlike-
      ness.
   (*c*) Positive and Negative.

C. Ground.

II. Existence.

III. The Thing.
   A. The Thing and its Pro-
      perties.

   B. The Thing and Matters.
   C. Matter and Form.

APPEARANCE.

I. The Phenomenal World.

II. Content and Form.

III. Relation.
   A. Whole and Part.

   B. Force and its Manifesta-
      tion.
   C. Inner and Outer.

153. Comparing these two tables, we find the following differences. (1) The whole triad of Show, which is a division of the third order in the *Greater Logic*, is absent in the *Encyclopaedia*; and the Essentialities, under a different name, are the first division of the third order in the *Encyclopaedia*, while in the *Greater Logic* they were the second division. (2) Contradiction is not found in the *Encyclopaedia*, and in its place among the Pure Determinations of Reflection we find Ground, which is here only an undivided category of the fourth order, while in the *Greater Logic* it was a category of the third order, and was itself divided, and again subdivided. The result of these two differences is that the whole content of the secondary division called, in the *Greater Logic*, Essence as Reflection into itself, is condensed, in the *Encyclopaedia*, into a single tertiary division.

The gap which is thus left for the *Encyclopaedia* is filled up by (3) transferring Existence from the second to the first of the secondary divisions; and by (4) dividing it into two, Existence and Thing being taken as two separate divisions of the third order, while in the *Greater Logic* Existence is the name for the division of the third order which contains the categories of Thing as its subdivisions.

This transference of Existence produces the result (5) that the Phenomenal World forms the first division within Appearance in the *Encyclopaedia*, although its significance is the same as that of Appearance (in the narrower sense) in the *Greater Logic*, which there forms the second division of Appearance in the wider sense.

The *Encyclopaedia* (6) takes, as the second division of Appearance, Content and Form, which is thus a division of the third order. In the *Greater Logic*, on the other hand, Form and Content is a division of the fifth order within Ground. We have now reached, in each Logic, to the categories of Relation, which are treated in the same way in both works.

In addition to these changes (7) Form and Matter is, in the *Greater Logic*, a division of the fifth order within Ground, while in the *Encyclopaedia* it is a division of the fourth order within Thing. Also (8) as was mentioned in Chapter V. (Section 131) the line of argument in the *Encyclopaedia* passes from Real to Formal Ground, while in the *Greater Logic* it passes from Formal to Real.

154. The first five of these changes place categories in different places in the chain, and make them of higher or lower orders than before, but do not invert their places. The changes of place are caused only by the omission of certain categories, and by the expansion and contraction of others. But the sixth and seventh do invert the order of categories. In the *Encyclopaedia* Form and Content comes after Existence, after Thing, and after the Phenomenal World, while it comes before the corresponding categories in the *Greater Logic*. Form and Matter is not so much displaced, but in the *Encyclopaedia* it comes after Existence, and as the last division of Thing, while in the *Greater Logic* it precedes both Thing and Existence.

The first of these differences—the omission of the categories of Show—appears to me an improvement for the reasons which I have given above (Section 103). With regard to Ground, I think, as I have also explained above (Section 131), that the line of argument adopted in the *Encyclopaedia* is better than that adopted in the *Greater Logic* in respect of the eighth of our differences—the order in which Formal Ground and Real Ground were taken. On the other hand the greater development given to Ground in the *Greater Logic*, and the number of subdivisions introduced (the second difference), seems to me to give it an advantage over the *Encyclopaedia*, where the treatment becomes obscure from its condensation.

The removal of Existence and Thing to the first section, which is the third difference, does not seem to have any great importance[1]. And the fourth change—the separation of Existence and Thing as separate categories—appears to be only a change in the use of names. In each Logic there is, between Ground and Thing, a stage where Ground and Consequent fall together. The only difference is that in the *Encyclopaedia* this is taken as a stage distinct both from Ground and Thing and called Existence, while in the *Greater Logic* it falls within Ground, and is called Transition of the Fact into Existence.

---

[1] Rosenkrenz, in his *Erläuterungen zu Hegel's Encyclopädie*, pp. 30, 31, finds a distinct change for the better in the arrangement of the *Encyclopaedia*, but I am not convinced by his argument.

Thus in the *Greater Logic* the name of Existence is left over as the general name for the categories of Thing.   The difference is thus simply verbal.

The fifth difference—that the Phenomenal World is a Thesis in the *Encyclopaedia,* while the corresponding category is an Antithesis in the *Greater Logic*—may also be dismissed as unimportant.   In respect of the sixth and seventh—those which concern Form and Content and Form and Matter, the *Greater Logic* appears to have the advantage.   It treats them as categories of Ground and places them next one another, while the *Encyclopaedia* puts them well after Ground, and inserts between them the category of the Phenomenal World.   Both these changes are for the worse.   Both Form and Matter and Form and Content are essentially categories of Ground—of the attempt, that is, to link things together by similarities.   (Form and Content is the collapse of Ground into tautology—the end to which it inevitably tends, and which proves its inadequacy.) And by placing them next one another there is a valid transition from one to the other.   In the *Encyclopaedia,* on the other hand, Hegel's attempt to pass from Thing and Matters to Matter and Form (*Enc.* Section 128), and, again, his attempt to pass from the Phenomenal World to Content and Form (*Enc.* Section 133), are unsatisfactory.

CHAPTER VII

ACTUALITY

155. Actuality (Wirklichkeit) is divided as follows:

I. The Absolute. (Das Absolute.)

    A. The Exposition of the Absolute. (Die Auslegung des Absolute.)

    B. The Absolute Attribute. (Das absolute Attribut.)

    C. The Modus of the Absolute. (Der Modus des Absolute.)

II. Actuality. (Die Wirklichkeit.)

    A. Contingency, or Formal Actuality, Possibility and Necessity. (Zufälligkeit, oder formelle Wirklichkeit, Möglichkeit und Nothwendigkeit.)

    B. Relative Necessity, or Real Actuality, Possibility and Necessity. (Relative Nothwendigkeit, oder reale Wirklichkeit, Möglichkeit und Nothwendigkeit.)

    C. Absolute Necessity. (Absolute Nothwendigkeit.)

III. The Absolute Relation. (Das absolute Verhältniss.)

    A. The Relation of Substantiality. (Verhältniss der Substantialität.)

    B. The Relation of Causality. (Verhältniss der Kausalität.)

      (a) Formal Causality. (Die formelle Kausalität.)

(b) Determined Causality. (Die bestimmte Kausalität.)

(c) Action and Reaction. (Wirkung und Gegenwirkung.)

C. Reciprocity. (Die Wechselwirkung.)

The only ambiguity in these titles is that Actuality is used to denote both the whole secondary division we are considering, and the second of the tertiary divisions contained in it.

Actuality is, I think, one of the parts of the *Greater Logic* which requires most amendment. In the first place, as I shall endeavour to show, the whole content of the first two subdivisions, the Absolute and Actuality, is erroneous, and should be removed. (In doing this, however, we should only be departing from the *Greater Logic* to follow the *Encyclopaedia*.) And, in the second place, the treatment of Causality presents very grave defects.

The transition which leads to Actuality asserts that Externality is identical with Internality (*G. L.* ii. 177). It is the stability and solidity given by this complete union which causes the present secondary division to be specially worthy of the name of Actuality. "In this identity of Appearance with the Inner or Essence, Essential Relation has determined itself to Actuality" (*G. L.* ii. 183).

I. THE ABSOLUTE.

A. *The Exposition of the Absolute.*

156. (*G. L.* ii. 186.) We have, says Hegel, the Inner, or Essence-element, and the Outer, or Being-element. "The Absolute itself is absolute unity of both" (*G. L.* ii. 186). "The determination of the Absolute is to be the absolute form, but not in the same way as Identity, whose moments are only simple determinations—but as an Identity, each of the moments of which is itself the totality, and is therefore indifferent towards the form, and is the complete content of the whole" (*G. L.* ii. 186). This is the restatement of Inner and Outer which is to be expected at this place, but there seems no particular reason

why it should be called the Absolute. On the next page, however, we find a very important statement—namely that the
conception of the Absolute is incompatible with a variety of
content. "The Absolute itself is the absolute Identity; this is
its determination, so that all multiplicity of the World in itself,
and of the World of Experience, or all multiplicity of the inner
and outer totality is transcended in it" (*G. L.* ii. 187).

This passage must, I think, be taken as meaning that in
this category not only has all difference between the Surface
and Substratum vanished, but all differences which previously
existed within the Surface, or within the Substratum, have also
vanished, leaving a unity quite free from difference. This is a
very important addition to the information about the category.
For the vertical difference, so to speak—the difference between
the immediate element and the deeper element which explains
it—might have vanished, and yet the horizontal differentiations
—the distinctions between one finite thing and another finite
thing—might have been preserved.

I do not think that there can be any doubt that Hegel
regarded both of them as eliminated here. The words quoted
above from p. 187 could not be made to apply to the difference
between the World in itself and the World of Appearance, or
between the Inner and the Outer. It is a multiplicity which
is here transcended, and not a mere duality, such as is the
difference between Surface and Substratum. And it falls within
the Surface, and within the Substratum, not between them.
This view is confirmed by the subsequent course of the argument in the triad which commences here, and is supported by
Hegel's choice of this place to discuss Spinoza's philosophy
(*G. L.* ii. 194).

157. We can now understand why Hegel gives this category
the name of the Absolute. The word is habitually used of the
universe viewed as a unity, and it forms a very appropriate
name for a category which denies everything except the
unity.

But the introduction of this fresh characteristic is illegitimate. The assertion of the unity between Surface and Substratum is justified, for it was demonstrated in the category of
Inner and Outer. But the removal of all multiplicity from the

Actuality thus formed has not been demonstrated at all.   And without the necessity of this transition being demonstrated, we have no right to go on to it.   It seems scarcely possible to suppose that Hegel has confused the two unities, and imagined that we are justified in denying all multiplicity in Actuality because the duality of Surface and Substratum has been transcended.   And yet it seems scarcely possible to explain in any other manner the introduction of the new characteristic without the least attempt at demonstration.

Hegel has proved, no doubt, that the Outer is now identical with the Inner.   And it may perhaps be said that, though this is not the same as the denial of all multiplicity, yet it involves it.   For, as against the Outer, the Inner was looked on as emphasising the unity of the content, while the Outer emphasised the multiplicity.   But the unity of Surface and Substratum has not been reached by explaining away the Surface and leaving the Substratum as the only reality.   The attempts of both sides to preserve their natures as they were when they were separate have been transcended.   The Inner has been identified with the Outer as much as the Outer with the Inner.   The result ought to be a category which combines harmoniously the multiplicity and the unity—such a category as we shall find later in Substance—not a category which ignores the multiplicity in favour of the unity.

The fact is that the conception which Hegel introduces here has been reached and transcended in the very earliest stages of Essence.   The Surface, in so far as it is real at all, is always taken by Hegel as a multiplicity.   And thus a category which denies the reality of multiplicity has to treat the Surface-element as completely unreal.

This is how Hegel does treat it here.   And by doing so he goes back to the category of Show.   (I do not mean the division of the third order, but the division of the fourth order, which forms the Antithesis of the division of the third order.)   The characteristic of Show was that the Substratum was everything and the Surface nothing.   And this is really Hegel's position with regard to the Absolute.   He asserts, indeed, that Surface and Substratum are identical, but, as we shall see, he admits that multiplicity still arises on the Surface, and has to be treated as unreal. Thus he falls back here into a position which he has already demonstrated to be inadequate, and replaced by something more adequate, and which he has therefore no right to introduce again here[1].

In so far as Spinoza's philosophy is appropriately treated under this category of the Absolute, it could be treated with equal fitness under the category of Show. It is only one side of Spinoza's thought—that which finds expression in the principle that all determination is negation—which exemplifies Hegel's category of the Absolute. And this is exactly the position of Show.

158. Leaving the question of the legitimacy of this category, we must now consider the transition to the next. We cannot after all get rid of the multiplicity. Since the Absolute "contains all difference and determination of form, or since it is the absolute form and reflection, the variety of content must also come forward in it" (*G. L.* ii. 187). The Absolute, that is, cannot preserve the purity of its unity by rejecting anything. It contains everything, including multiplicity. But the Absolute has been determined as this pure unity, and it follows that "the transparency of the finite, which allows only the Absolute to be seen through it, ends in entire disappearance (Verschwinden); for there is nothing in the finite, which could maintain for it a difference from the Absolute; it" (the finite) "is a medium that is absorbed by that which shines through it" (*G. L.* ii. 188). But such a disappearance cannot be complete. For, in order even to disappear, the finite must have some reality, and that is just what this category must refuse to it. The Absolute can destroy the finite, if it is assumed that the finite is there to destroy, but the fact that it should be there to destroy is incompatible with the supremacy of the Absolute. "Such a determination has not its beginning in the Absolute, but only its end" (*G. L.* ii. 189). And thus we are forced to the conclusion that the Absolute, which is a pure unity, cannot, after all, be the whole of reality. "That Absolute, which has its being only as absolute identity, is only the Absolute of an external reflection. It is therefore not the Absolute-Absolute, but the

---

[1] In several passages he actually gives the name of Show to the Surface-element of the Absolute, *e.g. G. L.* ii. 188 and 192.

Absolute in a determination, or it is an Attribute" (*G. L.* ii. 189).
So we reach (*G. L.* ii. 190)

B. *The Absolute Attribute.*

159. This transition seems to me not to be valid. For it
is a transition to a conception which is recognised, at the time
when we pass to it, to be a contradiction. The Absolute was to
be the sole reality. It is contradictory to take it as one side
only of the reality. It cannot be said that the conception of
the Absolute is so altered in the transition that there is no
longer a contradiction. The contradiction does remain, for it is
subsequently put forward as the ground of the transition to the
category of Modus.

Now it is illegitimate to pass to a category which is realised,
from the previous course of the argument, to be a contradiction.
The transitions of the dialectic are made to avoid contradictions,
and if we see that we create a new contradiction by going on,
there is no ground why we should go on at all. Of course each
category to which we go develops a contradiction, but as soon
as it does that, it is seen to be untenable. A category, which
was from the beginning seen to be contradictory, which we only
made by explicitly asserting the contradiction which makes it
necessary to leave it, can have no rightful place in the dialectic.

160. If, however, this category be once reached, the necessity
of advancing from it is obvious. If the Absolute is an Attribute,
it only expresses part of the nature of that of which it is an
Attribute. There must be other parts of that nature, which
are not expressed by the Absolute, and which are independent
of it. But this is impossible, for the Absolute has all along
been determined as the whole nature of reality, and if it can
only exist by the side of something which is not itself, it cannot
exist at all. " The Form therefore, whether taken as Outer or
Inner, through which the Absolute is an Attribute, is at the
same time posited as being something intrinsically null, an
external Show, or mere Manner (Art und Weise)" (*G. L.* ii. 191).
We thus reach

C. *The Modus of the Absolute.*

(*G. L.* ii. 191.) The meaning of this category is difficult to
grasp. Hegel says of it: " The true meaning of the Modus is

that it is the Absolute's own reflecting movement; a determination, but not one through which it becomes Another, but
only a determination of what it already is; the transparent
Externality which is the sign (das Zeigen) of itself; a movement out from itself, but so that this outward Being is as much
the internality itself" (*G. L.* ii. 193). This seems to indicate
that the category denotes a sort of logical movement, compar-
able to that found earlier in Reflection, by which the Absolute
determines, by its own nature, a multiplicity. But although
this seems to be the right interpretation, it is impossible to
explain why Hegel should have said that it was a mere " Art
und Weise," and how the name of Modus is appropriate to this
category.

Has the category been validly deduced? I do not think
that it has. For, if it is meant that the Absolute, while
remaining a pure unity, determines a multiplicity, the difficulty
remains the same as before. The multiplicity cannot be part
of the Absolute, if that is a pure unity. And yet there is
nothing outside the Absolute. (This difficulty did not occur in
the case of Reflection, because there the two sides of the relation
had not mutually exclusive qualities, such as pure unity and
multiplicity are here.)

If, indeed, we were to take the unity of the Absolute no
longer as a pure unity, but as a unity which contained multiplicity, and was all the more of a unity because it did so, we
should certainly have transcended the difficulty. But I cannot
find so advanced a conception as this in Hegel's words, nor does
the subsequent course of the dialectic suggest that it is reached
at this point.

The use of the names Attribute and Modus in connexion
with the Absolute seems suggested by Spinoza's terminology.
Hegel, however, uses the terms in a way quite different from
Spinoza's. For Hegel the Absolute is, in the Antithesis of this
triad, an Attribute of something, not, as with Spinoza, the
Substance to which all Attributes belong. And for Hegel
Attribute and Modus denote two different ways of looking at
the universe, of which the second transcends the first, while for
Spinoza the Attribute and the Modus have places in the same
theory of the universe as compatible elements.

161. We now pass to

II. ACTUALITY.

(*G. L.* ii. 199.) The last category has filled up the gulf which, in the category of the Absolute Attribute, had once more opened in reality. In the Absolute Attribute we had once more a Surface and a Substratum of different natures, but in Modus the separation is again transcended. The restored solidity of reality makes the name of Actuality appropriate. "The Actual is Manifestation, it does not enter the sphere of alteration by its externality, nor is it the appearance of itself in another, but it manifests itself; that is, in its externality it is itself, and is only itself in its externality, that is, in a determining movement which separates it from itself" (*G. L.* ii. 201).

It seems to me, however, that this conception of an Actuality which is itself in its externality, and only there, is just the conception which is reached in Inner and Outer, and that, after the triad of the Absolute, we have only come back to the place we started from. And it is to be noted that Hegel himself speaks of Actuality as "the immediate form-unity of Inner and Outer" (*G. L.* ii. 201. The context makes it clear that he is not speaking of the secondary division, but of the tertiary division which we are discussing here).

A.   Contingency, or Formal Actuality, Possibility and Necessity.

162. (*G. L.* ii. 202.) Here the first point is the introduction of Possibility. "Actuality is formal, in so much as it is, as first Actuality, only immediate unreflected Activity, and thus exists only in this determination of form, but not as a totality of form. It is thus nothing more than Being or Existence in general. But since it is essentially (wesentlich) not mere immediate Existence, but is the form-unity of Being in Self (Ansichsein) or Innerness, and Externality, it therefore contains immediately Being in Self or Possibility. What is Actual is Possible" (*G. L.* ii. 202).

The argument seems to be that in Actuality we once more look for a Substratum which shall explain the Actuality. We

find it in Possibility.   Accordingly Actuality, as opposed to
Possibility, becomes the Surface.

This seems unjustifiable.   Surely the result of the category
of Inner and Outer was that Surface and Substratum had
become permanently identical, and that it was impossible to
find the explanation of any part of immediate reality in a
Substratum which is in any way different from it.   Now
Possibility is, as Hegel fully recognises, something quite
different from the corresponding Actuality.   And so, in taking
Possibility as a Substratum, we have gone back to a position
already transcended—which is, of course, illegitimate.   The
only way to avoid this difficulty would be to show that
Actuality differed from Possibility in some subtle way which
had not been transcended in reaching Inner and Outer, and
which was not, therefore, denied in asserting the identity of
Inner and Outer.   Hegel does not make any such distinction,
nor does it seem possible that one could be made.   The
relations of Surface and Substratum were developed so carefully, and in so much detail, in the first two divisions of
Essence, that it would be improbable that any possible form
had not been considered.

At present the Possibility of each thing is looked for entirely
within itself.   Possibility due to the Actuality of something else is
not reached till we come to Relative Necessity.   Thus Possibility
can only mean here the absence of internal contradiction.   "A is
possible just means that A is A" ($G. L.$ ii. 203).   The only
difference, he goes on to say, between Possibility and Identity, is
that Possibility is only one side of the relation, while Identity is
both.   Possibility implies that there is something more—namely
Actuality.   It is "das Sollen der Totalität der Form" ($G. L.$ ii. 203).

It might be thought that Identity extended further than
Possibility.   A four-angled triangle is not formally Possible,
but it is true that a four-angled triangle is a four-angled
triangle.   But we must remember that Hegel's category of
Identity, as we have seen, has a much narrower scope than
the logical law of Identity.   The category applies only to
the existent, and, as nothing can exist which is not formally
Possible, Identity can only be rightly applied in cases where
Possibility can be applied also.

163. Hegel now asserts (*G. L.* ii. 204) that Possibility is in itself a contradiction, and therefore Impossibility. This is rather misleading. What he means, as he explains, is that Possibility is an Essence, a Substratum, which can only be if it is in relation to a Surface. Possibility taken without reference to an Actuality would be a contradiction, and so impossible. This is, no doubt, true, but it is only true in the same way that any other Substratum, in any of the previous categories of Essence, would be impossible without the corresponding Surface. Hegel's language suggests that Possibility passes into Impossibility as its contrary, which is not his meaning.

Since the content of the Possible, he continues, "is only a Possible, another which is the Opposite (Gegentheil) is just as Possible. A is A, in the same way $-A$ is $-A$" (*G. L.* ii. 204). Opposite is a rather ambiguous word. Hegel's example of $-A$ suggests that he means by Opposite a Material Contrary. But, as we saw in his treatment of the Law of Excluded Middle, he sometimes ignored the difference between not-A and $-A$. If in this passage he meant by $-A$ nothing more than not-A, his statement will be correct. If there is no internal contradiction in A, there can be none in not-A. The assertion of not-A is exactly equivalent to the denial of A. And if there is no internal contradiction in A when it is asserted there can be no internal contradiction in A when it is denied.

Thus we reach the conception of the Contingent, "an Actual, which is at the same time determined as only Possible, whose Other or Opposite is also possible" (*G. L.* ii. 205).

From the Contingent we proceed to the Necessary, as follows. The Contingent as such has no Ground. For the fact that it is Contingent means that its Opposite might have taken its place, and that there is no reason why it has not done so (*G. L.* ii. 205). But, again, it must have a Ground. The Substratum to which it has been referred is insufficient to explain it. For it is only its Possibility, and as the Opposite— which is not Actual, for they are incompatible—is equally Possible, some other explanation must be sought for the fact that the one Possible is Actual, while the other is not. We

cannot, as we have seen, find this explanation within the
Actual in question. We must therefore look for it outside.
The Actual, taken as Contingent, is "no longer in and for itself,
but has its true Reflection-into-self in Another, in other
words, it has a Ground" (*G. L.* ii. 206).

So far Hegel's language is clear. But he adds a perplexing
sentence. "Thus the Contingent has no Ground, because it is
Contingent; and just as much it has a Ground, because it is
Contingent" (*G. L.* ii. 206). This, by itself, would suggest that
it had a Ground and had not a Ground in the same sense,
and that a contradiction arose here which would have to be
transcended. But his previous argument, given in the last
paragraph, makes it clear that he only means that the Contingent has not a Ground within itself, and that it has a
Ground outside itself.

164. In this way we reach Necessity. When the Actual
has a Ground outside itself, it ceases to be Contingent, for that
Ground determines why it exists, rather than its Opposite,
which possessed the same Formal Possibility. And so Actuality
and Possibility coincide. For, now that the Actual has its
Ground, which determines why it exists rather than its
Opposite, its Opposite is no longer Possible (*G. L.* ii. 206, 207).
But this Possibility is no longer the Formal Possibility, which
is always possessed equally by the two Opposites. It is the
Possibility which is limited by the relations of the Actual to
other things. Actuality and Formal Possibility can never
coincide. With this reference to what is external, we pass
over to

B. *Relative Necessity, or Real Actuality, Possibility and Necessity.*

(*G. L.* ii. 207.) Real Actuality is Actuality in relation to
another. This relation to another is also Reflection-into-self.
"The Thing is stable, but has its Reflection-into-self, its determined Essentiality, in something else stable" (*G. L.* ii. 208).
In the same way, the Real Possibility of the Thing is in
another Thing. "The Real Possibility of a fact is therefore
the definitely existing (daseiende) multiplicity of circumstances
which relate themselves to it" (*G. L.* ii. 209).

But this Real Possibility is identical with Necessity. "What is Really Possible can no longer be anything else; under these conditions and circumstances nothing else can follow" (*G. L.* ii. 211). We have gone beyond the Formal Possibility which consists in the absence of internal contradiction, and now find the Possibility of a fact in the absence of any facts which are incompatible with it. But, if nothing is incompatible with its Actuality, it must be Actual[1]. For otherwise it might either be Actual or might not, and so we should have gone back to the position that there can be an Actual with nothing to determine that it, rather than its Opposite, should be Actual. Thus a Real Possibility which does not completely determine Actuality is only imperfect. We may say that the circumstances of a certain enterprise leave it possible either that it should succeed or that it should not succeed. But then the circumstances known to us are only some of the total number. If a complete knowledge of all the circumstances revealed no impossibility of success, success would be certain.

We may sum up Contingency and Relative Necessity by saying that in the first Formal Actuality and Formal Possibility were separate, that the contradiction which this involved led on to Necessity, and that Necessity is now seen to be identical with Real Actuality and Real Possibility. There are not two Necessities, a Formal and a Real, as there are two Possibilities and Actualities. The Necessity which falls within the division of Contingency is the transition to the next division, and is not Formal, but the same Real Necessity which, in the next division, is seen to be identical with Real Actuality and Possibility[2].

But this Real Necessity is only a Relative Necessity. For when we ask why *A* is Necessary, the answer is that it has

---

[1] It is, of course, equally true that if nothing is incompatible with its non-Actuality, it will not be Actual. Actuality has not any prerogative in this respect, such as was sometimes attributed to it in pre-Kantian philosophies.

[2] Hegel certainly speaks (*G. L.* ii. 213, 215) as if the Formal Necessity of Contingency was different from the Real Necessity of Relative Necessity. But I think the only change he means is that, in the latter, Necessity is seen to coincide with Actuality and Possibility, which it did not in the former. And this coincidence comes about through a change in Actuality and Possibility (from Formal to Real), not from any change in Necessity.

its Real Possibility in *B*, *C*, etc. It depends on these, and these are, so far as this relation goes, merely immediate. Thus *A*'s Necessity depends on the mere fact of the existence of *B*, *C*, etc., and is so, in the last resort, Contingent. " The Really Necessary is a limited Actuality, which, on account of this limitation is also, from another point of view, a Contingent" (*G. L.* ii. 212).

165. This difficulty is removed for Hegel by the passage to

C. Absolute Necessity.

(*G. L.* ii. 213.) The nature of this category and the transition to it are extremely obscure. I am inclined to agree with Noël's interpretation (*La Logique de Hegel*, p. 79). The transition seems to consist in the fact that if we took all Existence as a whole it would form a Necessity which was not Contingent, but which had Contingency as an element within itself. It would not be Contingent, for it would have no Ground outside itself. But Contingency would be an element in it, because each part of it would be determined by other parts of it. Each part then would have its Ground outside itself, and, looked at separately, would be Contingent (*G. L.* ii. 213).

Hegel's obscurity here seems to me to be due to the fact that the ideas of this triad are not really, as he supposes them to be, categories distinct from, and leading up to, the categories of Substantiality, Causality, and Reciprocity. The idea of Necessity, as used by Hegel here, is really the same as his category of Causality. The difficulty that the Relatively Necessary is Contingent, because of the immediacy of its external determinant, is really the same difficulty as that which produces the infinite series of Causes of Causes and Effects of Effects. And the only way to escape from it is the way in which Hegel does escape from it, when it recurs a second time under the head of Causation—by means of Reciprocity. And he gets very close to this solution here, when he has recourse to the conception of the system as a whole to transcend the Contingency of the parts. But he does not see that the difficulty is the same in the two places. (If he had seen this, indeed, he would have seen that he was wrong in bringing it in twice.) And consequently he states

his solution here as if it were different from the later one.   It
is this, I think, which accounts for the obscurity.

166.   In this way Hegel reaches

III.   THE ABSOLUTE RELATION.

A.   *The Relation of Substantiality.*

(*G. L.* ii. 219.   *Enc.* 150.)   According to this category the
universe is something which is to be looked at both as a
multiplicity of particulars (the Accidents) and as a unity
(the Substance).   There is thus a certain duplicity, but no
longer the old duplicity which was finally transcended in Inner
and Outer.   Substance and Accidents are not two forms, in
either of which we may regard the reality.   They are two
characteristics of one form, which is the only form which the
reality takes.   We could, according to Hegel, contrast the
reality seen as Whole with the reality seen as Parts, for
although the content was the same in both cases, Whole and
Parts were two separate forms, under either of which it could
be seen.   And the same was true of Force and Exertion.   But
now it is different.   To regard it as Substance is to regard it
also as Accidents, and to regard it as Accidents is to regard it
also as Substance.

Thus the Essence-relation has been transcended.   There
is no longer a Substratum and a Surface, in whose relation
to one another the explanation of reality was to be found.
All that we can say is that Substance—the characteristic of
unity—corresponds to Whole, Force, and the Inner, which
were previously Substratum, and that in the same way
Accidents correspond to the previous Surfaces—Parts, Manifestation, Outer.   But to have a Substratum and a Surface we
want more differentiation than is here permissible.   It may
seem curious that categories in which the Essence-relation is
transcended should fall in the Doctrine of Essence, but we
are now very near the end of that Doctrine.

Is there only one Substance, or are there many Substances,
each having many Attributes?   It seems that, in the sense
in which Hegel uses Substance, there is only One.   The

Absolute Necessity, from which he attempts to derive the
new category, connects the whole universe in one. And of
Inner and Outer (which should have been the immediate
predecessor of Substance, as I shall point out later) we must
say, as of its predecessor Whole and Part, that with such a
conception all existents can be grouped in a single unity.

There is, then, only one Substance. But what are the
Accidents? Accident is generally used as a name for the
qualities of the Substance which has them. Extension and
impenetrability would be said to be Accidents of material
Substance. But this is not Hegel's use. The Accidents of
which he speaks are the things which are parts of the Substance. " They are...existing things with manifold properties,
or wholes which consist of parts, stable parts" (*G. L.* ii. 222).
Although Hegel's special categories of Thing and Properties,
and of Whole and Parts, have been transcended, we must say,
in a more general sense, that the Accidents are parts of the
Substance, and are themselves things with properties.

167. This, then, is what Hegel means by the category.
Is it valid? I believe that it is valid, but that the way in
which he reached it is invalid, and that it should have been
reached directly from Inner and Outer.

In the first place, it *can* be reached from Inner and Outer.
For it is simply the restatement of that category, as a new
Thesis should be of the previous Synthesis. All that we have
said of Substance and Accident is equally true of Inner and
Outer (cp. the last Chapter, Section 151).

Now, if it can be reached from Inner and Outer, Hegel
must be wrong in inserting two triads between them. For
every triad indicates an advance, and there must be something
wrong with the argument when, at the end of the second
triad, we are only where we were before the beginning of the
first one.

And, secondly, the transition by which Hegel does reach
Substance from Absolute Necessity is intrinsically invalid. For,
as I said above, the conception of Necessity is really that of
Causality. Necessity means for Hegel much more than the
fact that reality is certainly determined. If it only meant
that, we should have had Necessity very early among the

categories of Being, and the relation between Surface and Substratum in Essence would have been Necessity throughout. Necessity for him involves two characteristics. In the first place, that which is necessitated must be a Thing—not the mere Somethings of the earlier categories. In the next place, that which determines it must not be its own Substratum—its Ground, Matter, Law, or Force—but some other Thing. It will be remembered that it was the introduction of the idea of Necessity which formed the transition from the Formal Actuality and Possibility, which regarded the thing in its isolation, to the Real Actuality and Possibility, which regarded the thing as connected with others. Now the determination of one thing by another is just what Hegel means by Causality. And, if this is the case, the *Greater Logic* proceeds, in effect, though not in name, from Causality to Substance, and then from Substance to Causality. And this must be wrong. For the same category cannot be both higher and lower in the chain than another category.

Thirdly, Hegel had no right to reach the category of Absolute Necessity at all. For, as I argued above (Sections 157 and 161), the Exposition of the Absolute is not properly deduced from Inner and Outer, nor is Contingency properly deduced from the Modus of the Absolute, so that there are two breaks in the chain.

Thus Hegel had no right to reach the categories of the Absolute and of Actuality (in the narrower sense), and he has no right to go on from them to Substance. On the other hand, by leaving them out, we get a valid transition from Inner and Outer to Substance. It is clear then that they ought to be left out, and, as we shall see, this is just what Hegel does in the *Encyclopaedia*.

168. It is in connexion with Substance that Hegel introduces in the *Encyclopaedia* (Section 151) some remarks on the philosophy of Spinoza, which he dealt with in the *Greater Logic* under the category of the Absolute (*G. L.* ii. 194). The position in the *Greater Logic* was more appropriate. It is true that Spinoza called his sole reality by the name of Substance. But in Hegel's category the whole nature of the Substance is to be found in the Accidents, and they are as real as the

Substance. This is very far from Spinoza's view. Indeed,
according to that tendency in Spinoza's thought to which
Hegel gives most attention, the Accidents, as finite, would
be unreal. Such a view is more appropriately dealt with
under the category of the Absolute, but this category, as I
have said, is omitted in the *Encyclopaedia.*

Hegel says in the *Encyclopaedia* that Spinoza should not
be called an Atheist, but rather an Acosmist. There is great
truth in the view that he was an Acosmist, though it must
be admitted that he did not carry out consistently the principle
that all determination is negation, on which his Acosmism
is based. As to his Atheism, it is beyond doubt that he
denied the existence of a personal or conscious God, but then
Hegel never regarded personality or consciousness as essential
characteristics of God. At times he took God as being the
Absolute Reality, whatever that reality might be. If the
word is used in this sense, nobody but an absolute sceptic could
be an Atheist. At other times he took God to mean the
Absolute Reality conceived as a unity. It is in this sense
that he appears to use it here. In either sense, of course,
it would be true that Spinoza believed in the existence of
God.

169. We now proceed to Causality. The transition lies,
according to Hegel, in the fact that Substance, in its relation
to Accident, is to be conceived as Power. This relation of
Substance to Accident "is only the appearing totality as
Becoming, but it is just as much Reflection; the Accidentality,
which is implicitly Substance, is for that very reason posited as
such; and it is thus determined as a negativity which relates
itself to itself, it is determined as over against itself, as relating
itself to itself and as a simple identity with itself; and is Substance existing for itself and powerful. Thus the relation of
Substantiality passes over into the relation of Causality" (*G. L.*
ii. 223).

In other words, the Substance is conceived as determining
the Accidents. The Accidents are now conceived as something
existing in and for themselves, as a reality separate from the
original Substance, and as themselves Substantial. Thus the
relation of Substance to Accident changes into the relation

between two Substances (the original Substance, and what was originally the Accident), and passing over into

B.   The Relation of Causality

(*G. L.* ii. 223.   *Enc.* 153), we have, as its first form

(a)   Formal Causality.

(*G. L.* ii. 224.) The Accidents, being now, as Hegel tells us, "Substance existing for itself" must be taken as having a separate existence from the original Substance, though they stand in relation to it, and though the content of the two is identical. Thus it is not merely that the conception of Causality has been substituted for that of Substance, but that the two terms in the Substance-relation have been transformed respectively into the two terms in the Causality-relation, the original Substance being the Cause, while the Accidents become the Effect.

It would seem that there is a plurality of Causes, each having a single Effect. For the Accidentality comprised plurality, and if it is taken as Substantial it must be taken as many Substances. And as each Cause is identical in content with its Effect, the plurality of Effect would require a corresponding plurality of Causes.

170. Is the transition valid? I think it is not. For I cannot accept Hegel's argument to prove that what was taken as one Substance must now be taken as two Substances with identical content. So far as I can see the whole transition rests on the phrase quoted above from p. 223, that the relation is Reflection and that therefore "the Accidentality, which is implicitly Substance, is for that very reason posited as such." The Accidents, that is, if I understand it rightly, are so closely related to the Substance, that they themselves are Substance. *B*, let us say, is an Accident of the Substance *A*. Substance and Accident are so closely connected—in Hegel's language, are so reflected into one another—that *B* is implicitly its Substance *A*. From this we proceed to the conclusion that *B* is itself a Substance, over against *A*.

I cannot interpret Hegel's words in any other way than this, and surely this is invalid. It was nothing else but the fact that

Force was implicitly Manifestation, and Manifestation was implicitly Force, which led Hegel to transcend the difference of form previously, and to reach, in Inner and Outer, a category where Surface and Substratum were completely united.   And now he is using just the same argument—that each side is implicitly the other—as a reason for going back to the conception transcended in Inner and Outer, the conception of an identical content in two separate forms.   It is impossible that the same consideration should both disprove and prove this conception.   It seems to me that it did disprove it, that it does not prove it, and that the present transition must therefore be condemned.

It must be noted that in this Formal Causality the Causal relation is not between what would be generally called two different things—things different in content, and on the same stratum of reality.   Causation of this sort does not come in till the next category.   At present the Causation is only between the Substratum, which is Cause, and the Surface, which is Effect, and these have the same content.   For the separation of the two sides has restored the difference between Surface and Substratum.   If we carry on the spatial metaphor which these two terms involve, we may say that Formal Causality is vertical, while ordinary Causality is horizontal.

171.   Hegel now continues.   "In this identity of Cause and Effect the form is transcended, whereby they distinguish themselves as that which is in itself and as that which is posited. The Cause expires in its Effect; thus, equally, the Effect has expired, for it is only the determination of the Cause.   This Causality expired in its Effect is thus an Immediacy, which is indifferent towards the relation of Cause and Effect, and has it outside itself" (*G. L.* ii. 226).

(b)   *Determined Causality.*

(*G. L.* ii. 226.)   "The identity of the Cause with itself in its Effect is the transcending of their might and negativity, and so is a unity which is indifferent to the differences of form, and is the content.—It is therefore only implicitly related to the form, in this case the Causality.   They are therefore posited as separated, and the form as against the content is posited as something which is only immediately actual, as *contingent* Causality.

" Moreover the content as so determined is a content with internal differences (ein verschiedener Inhalt an ihm selbst); and the Cause is determined according to its content, and thereby the Effect also.—The content, since the reflectedness is here also immediate Actuality, is so far *actual* but *finite Substance.*

" This is now the Causal Relation in its reality and finitude. As formal it is the infinite relation of absolute power, whose content is pure manifestation or necessity.   On the other hand, as finite Causality it has a *given* content, and subsides into an external difference to that identity which is one and the same substance in its determinations " (*G. L.* 226, 227).

This is very obscure.   But it seems to me that the same things which were Cause and Effect in Formal Causality are taken as Cause and Effect in the new category.   If *A* is the Cause of *B* by Formal Causality, then, I think, under the new category *A* will still be the Cause of *B*, though the nature of *A* and *B*, and their relation to one another, are conceived rather differently.   The same Identity which connects Cause and Effect in Formal Causality connects them in Determined Causality.   This seems clear, for it is " the Identity," " this Identity," " the Content " all through, without any suggestion of a change in the Identity.   And if it is the same Identity, it must be the same things · which it connects.   The Identity which links together two things of which one was the Substratum of the other, could not connect any other two things. Moreover, if the Causality-relation related things in the new category by other groupings than those of the last category, the transition would have to show some negative character—something which broke down the one system and so made the substitution of the other necessary.   Now there is no such negative element to be found in the transition, which appears to be entirely a direct movement forward, and so leads to the conclusion that if *A* was the Cause of *B* under the first category, it will also be the Cause of *B* under the second.   At any rate, Hegel does not give any indication of why the grouping should change, or how any new one should be formed.

172. But the attempt to regard the things which are joined by Formal Causation as also joined by Determined Causation is impossible. Hegel appears to ignore the fundamental difference which exists between the two. Determined Causation is what is ordinarily known as Causation, with one very important difference. Hegel defines it entirely without relation to Time or Change. Thus while the ordinary conception of Causation is that a change in A produces a change in B, Hegel's Determined Causation only says that the nature of A determines the nature of B. It would be as applicable in a timeless world as in a world of change.

This is no doubt a very important difference. But in spite of the fact that Determined Causation resembles Formal Causation in not involving Time, the points in which Determined Causation resembles the ordinary non-Hegelian conception of Causation are such as to leave a very fundamental difference between Determined and Formal Causation—a difference which, as I have said, Hegel does not recognise.

There are four such points. The first is that, as I said above, Formal Causality does not connect what would usually be called two things—each containing the elements of Surface and Substratum united. It only connects two things one of which is the Surface and the other the Substratum of what would usually be called the same thing. It would not connect, *e.g.*, an axe with a tree, but only the Substance of the axe viewed as one thing, with the Accidents of the axe, now transformed into another thing—the original Substance being Substratum and Cause, and the former Accidents being Surface and Effect. As a consequence of this the content of Cause and Effect in Formal Causality must be identical, since the identity of content between Substance and Accidents is not regarded by Hegel as lost when the Accidents gain a Substantiality of their own.

The second point of difference is that Determined Causality —like ordinary causality—unites the plurality of existence into a system. Things which are different are connected by it[1].

---

[1] Hegel, as we shall see, asserts that in Determined Causality Cause and Effect are identical, but, as we shall also see, he qualifies this by admitting, after all, a certain difference.   And he certainly regards the plurality of existence as related by Determined Causality.

But in Formal Causality there is no such union. Each Effect has its own Cause—identical with it in content, a mere reduplication of it on the level of the Substratum. The different things are not united with one another. Each is split into two, and these two are united by Causality. The other differences —those united by Determined Causality—are not united at all in Formal Causality.

The third point of difference is that in Determined Causality, as Hegel expressly says, a Cause can be (and, indeed, musᵗ be) also an Effect. This is impossible with Formal Causality, since there all Causes are Substrata, and all Effects are Surfaces. Now the same thing cannot be both a Substratum and a Surface.

Fourthly, in ordinary Causation an Effect has a plurality of Causes, and a Cause a plurality of Effects. In Determined Causation Hegel admits, as we shall see, a plurality of remote Causes, though not of immediate Causes. But in Formal Causality there can be no plurality, whether of Causes or Effects, since the Substratum has only one Surface, and the Surface only one Substratum.

173. Hegel makes one attempt to remove these differences in his well-known doctrine of the identity of Cause and Effect, even in Determined Causation. He says, after the transition to Determined Causation has been made, " Through this identity of content this Causality is an analytic proposition. It is the same Fact (Sache) which shows itself at one time as Cause, at another time as Effect" (*G. L.* ii. 227). I shall endeavour to show that Hegel is wrong in asserting this identity, while, even if he had been right, it would by no means have removed the differences between Formal and Determined Causation which he ignores.

There is at any rate a presumption against the truth of this doctrine. It is against the ordinary usage of language. In ordinary empirical propositions about finite things we never find ourselves asserting that A is the cause of A, but always that A is the cause of B. The Cause and Effect are always things which, irrespective of their being Cause and Effect, have different names. The presumption is that there must be some difference between things to which different names are generally given. Let us see how Hegel meets it.

He gives four examples of the asserted identity of Cause and Effect. The first is that rain makes things wet, and that the rain and the wetness are the same water. The second is that the paint is the cause of the colour of a surface, and that it is also the colour of the surface. Again, the cause of a deed is the inner sentiment (Gesinnung) of the agent, and these have the same content and value. Finally, when the cause of the movement of a thing is its contact with another thing, the "quantum of movement" which was the Cause has been transferred to the thing acted on, and is thus the movement which is the Effect (*G. L.* ii. 227, 228).

We must notice, in the first place, that Hegel only gives part of the Cause. For example, the rain-water, by itself, will make nothing wet. Unless the clouds are driven over the house, unless the meteorological conditions allow the rain to fall, the roof will not be wet. Nor could the roof be wet if the house had never been built. The wind, the air, the builders of the house, are all part of the Cause, but they certainly are not identical with the wetness of the roof.

In the second place, rain is not identical with the wetness of a roof, in the sense required here. The rain is detached drops of water falling through the air, the other may be a uniform thin sheet of moisture. They are, from a scientific point of view, different forms of the same matter. But the form is part of the nature of the thing, and, if two things differ in form, they are not identical.

The other examples show similar defects. And so there are two fatal objections to Hegel's position. He only reaches it, firstly, by taking only one Cause of each Effect, although every Effect has many Causes. And, secondly, he only reaches it by assuming that two things are identical if they are formed of the same matter, or if they are of the same value, or have a quantitative equality, ignoring the other aspects in which they differ from one another.

174. Hegel does, indeed, admit (*G. L.* ii. 228) that the Cause has a content which is not in the Effect, but says that this content is a "zufälliges Beiwesen." But, in fact, much of the content of the Cause which is not in the Effect is by no means contingent and unessential, but is an essential part of the Cause, without which it would not produce the Effect. The roof would not be wet except for the action of the wind and the builder. But neither the wind nor the builder is a part of the wetness of the roof.

Again, he admits that the identity is only between the Effect and its immediate Cause, and not between the Effect and its remote Cause (*G. L.* ii. 228). The reason that he gives for this is that the Effect has a plurality of remote Causes. But it is also the case that it has a plurality of immediate Causes. Indeed, the fact that any Effect has a plurality of remote Causes is sufficient to prove that some Effect has a plurality of immediate Causes. If we go back from any Effect along the chain of its Causes, there must be some point in the chain where we pass from a single Cause to the admitted plurality of remote Causes. In that case the last stage (in this backward process) which is a unity will have the members of the first stage which is a plurality as its immediate Causes.

And there is another difficulty. If *A* is the Cause of *B*, and *B* of *C*, then, according to Hegel, *A* is identical with *B*, and *B* with *C*, but *A* need not be identical with *C*. But, unless the point in which *B* is the Effect of *A* is a mere zufälliges Beiwesen with regard to *B*'s causality of *C* (and this cannot always be the case) it would seem that *A* must be identical with *C*. For surely things which are identical with the same thing must be identical with one another.

Lastly Hegel has to admit that, with this interpretation of Causality, it is impossible to apply Causality to the relations of organic and spiritual life (*G. L.* ii. 229)[1]. His examples of improper applications include the assertions that fever could be caused by eating certain foods, and that Caesar's ambition was the cause of the destruction of the republican constitution of Rome. His meaning must therefore be, not merely that the organic and the spiritual cannot enter into causal relations with the inorganic and the material respectively, but that they cannot enter into causal relations at all. But if this category is not applicable to the whole of reality, how can it be derived from

---

[1] This seems quite inconsistent with his previous assertion that the relation between an act and the sentiments of the agent is an example of the identity of Cause and Effect.

earlier categories and lead on to later categories which certainly apply to the whole of reality ? (Of course it is not *completely* adequate to the organic and spiritual worlds, but Hegel's meaning here must be more than this, since no category except the Absolute Idea is completely adequate to any reality.)

Thus we must reject Hegel's theory of the identity of Cause and Effect. It is curious that it should have proved one of the most popular of his doctrines. It is often maintained by writers whose works show little study of the detail of other parts of the dialectic.

175. Even if Hegel had proved the identity of Cause and Effect in the way in which he asserted it, the identity would still be different from the identity in Formal Causality. For, as we saw above, Hegel does admit some difference in the empirical content of Cause and Effect in Determined Causality, though he asserts it to be a "zufälliges Beiwesen." In Formal Causality, on the other hand, it is impossible that there should be any difference between Cause and Effect, except the fact that they are respectively Cause and Effect. In other words, as was said before, Formal Causation is a relation between two aspects of what would commonly be called the same thing. Determined Causality is a relation between what would commonly be called different things.

Hegel has thus failed to remove even the first of the four differences between Formal and Determined Causality, which were enumerated above (Section 172). He does not even attempt to remove the other three—that Determined Causality unites the plurality of the existent, that in it every Cause is also an Effect, and every Effect a Cause, and that in it every Effect has a plurality of Causes—at any rate of remote Causes. None of these features is to be found in Formal Causality.

As Formal and Determined Causality are so different, a valid transition would require a demonstration that, to remove some inadequacy in the conception of Formal Causality, it would be necessary to alter it in each of the four characteristics in which it differs from Determined Causality. And it seems clear to me that he has not succeeded in doing this. Nor does it seem that he realised how much there was to do.

We must therefore reject this transition—one of the most

interesting in the dialectic, since it deals with a problem which has been of such cardinal importance to many philosophies.

176. In the *Encyclopaedia* the treatment of Causality is substantially the same. There is no separate category of Formal Causality, but the transition from Substance to Cause is clearly through the conception of Substance as Cause and Accidents as Effect. (*Enc.* 153, "Substance is Cause, in so far as Substance reflects into self as against its passage into Accidentality, and so stands as the *primary* fact, but again no less suspends this reflection-into-self (its bare possibility), lays itself down as the negative of itself, and thus produces an Effect, an actuality, which, though so far only assumed as a sequence, is through the process that effectuates it at the same time necessary.") This harmonizes with the fact that the *Encyclopaedia*, as well as the *Greater Logic*, maintains the identity of Cause and Effect.

177. Hegel now remarks that, starting from any point, we shall get an infinite series of Causes and Effects. If the original Effect, as being a finite reality, wants a Cause, then the Cause, which is equally a finite reality, wants another Cause, which again will require another, and so on without end. And the same will be true of the Effects.

We have an infinite series, then. But does its infinity involve a contradiction? For, as we have seen before, Hegel does not regard an infinite series as *ipso facto* contradictory. I do not see that there is a contradiction here. At first sight, no doubt, our present series seems to resemble very closely the Infinite Qualitative Series in the *Encyclopaedia*, which was contradictory[1]. But there is an important difference. There the nature of each term was found in its Other, and not in itself. *A*'s nature was only to be found in its other, *B*. But *B* had no nature, except in its other, *C*. Thus *A*'s nature must be looked for in *C*. For the same reason it could not be found there, but in *D*. And so on unendingly. *A*'s nature could be found nowhere, which was contradictory to the fact, already established, that *A* had a nature.

---

[1] The Infinite Qualitative Series in the *Greater Logic* took a different form, and does not resemble the Causal Series so closely. Cp. above, Sections 32 and 35.

Here it is different. A's nature is in itself, not in its Cause, B. That it should be what it is is determined by B, but it falls in A. And thus, as it seems to me, there is no contradiction in an infinite series of Causes. If there is such a series, then A will have an infinite number of relations. It will be related to B, and it will also be related to C, which, as the immediate Cause of B, will be the remote Cause of A. And it will be related in the same way to D, E, and so on infinitely. But there is no contradiction in A's standing in an infinite number of relations.

Again, it follows from the existence of such an infinite series that no mind working in time could ever completely explain anything. For A cannot be explained without reference to the nature of its Cause B, which determines it. But this will not be a complete explanation unless the nature of B is an ultimate fact, neither admitting nor requiring an explanation. If B requires explanation—as will be the case here—by its Cause C, A will not be explained without a knowledge of C, and so on through an infinite series of terms the end of which can never be reached by a mind passing through them successively. But a state of things is not impossible because it could never be completely explained by a mind working in time.

Thus there is no contradiction in this infinite series. And Hegel never says that there is. He calls it a False Infinite (Schlecht-Unendliche) but this is the term which he applies to all infinites of endless succession (as distinguished from the True Infinite of self-determination) whether he regards them as contradictory or not. And his transition to the next category does not depend on any contradiction being found in the infinite series, but developes from the nature of Causation in a point quite independent of the infinite series.

178. To this transition we now proceed. That which is acted on, Hegel tells us, must also itself act ($G.\ L.$ ii. 237). In the first place, the Effect which is worked on anything is also the Effect of that thing ($G.\ L.$ ii. 238). A determines the Effect x in B. But that A should determine that precise Effect is due not only to A's nature but also to B's. The stylus is the cause of the impression made on the wax. But when we consider what a different effect would have been produced by

pressing the stylus on a diamond or on water, we see that the
result produced in the wax is due to its own nature as much as
to the nature of the stylus.

What Hegel says is doubtless true, though he might find
some difficulty in reconciling it with his doctrine of the identity
of Cause and Effect.   For the proof that B is also a Cause of
the Effect determined in it lies in the fact that A determines a
different Effect in B to what it would determine in C.   Now if
A produces different Effects in different things, what becomes
of the identity of Cause and Effect? A cannot be identical
with two things of different natures.

In this way we reach

(c)   Action and Reaction

($G. L.$ ii. 235), where the thing in which the Effect is produced
is recognised as its joint Cause.

179.   From this we proceed to the next category as follows[1].
There is, Hegel tells us, a second sense in which that which is
acted on must also act ($G. L.$ ii. 238).   Not only does B co-
operate in determining the Effect x in itself, but B is also the
Cause of an Effect in A. A's exertion of Causality on B is just
as much a characteristic of A as the result of that exertion,
namely x, is a characteristic of B.   But A cannot determine an
Effect unless there is something to determine it in, nor can it
determine the Effect x unless there is B to determine it in,
for it is only the co-operation of B's nature which makes the
Effect to be x rather than anything else.   Hence B is the Cause
in A of the characteristic "A's co-operation in determining
x."   (That is to say, B is the external Cause of it. A's nature
will of course co-operate.)   Thus we reach

C.   Reciprocity.

($G. L.$ ii. 239. $Enc.$ 155.)   Here "the Activity (Wirken)
which in finite Causality ran out into the process of the false
infinite becomes bent round and an infinite reciprocal Activity
returning into itself" ($G. L.$ ii. 239).

[1] As Hegel places both the transition from Determined Causality to Action
and Reaction, and the transition from Action and Reaction to Reciprocity,
within the section headed Action and Reaction, the distinction between the
two may at first sight be missed, but becomes evident on closer examination.

The question now arises at what points the line of Causality bends round on itself. Hegel's demonstration indicates that two things in immediate causal relation to one another may by themselves form a unity of reciprocal action. At the same time his treatment of this category, and his transition from it by means of the idea of complete Necessity, clearly indicate that the whole of existence is to be taken as forming a single unity of reciprocal activity.

The two positions, however, are quite harmonious. If the principle of Reciprocity is admitted, we can begin with unities as small as we choose but we shall be led on to an all-embracing unity. Suppose we take two things only, A and B, as forming such a unity. If they are the only things in the universe, then the unity is already all-embracing. But, if not, the unity thus formed will have other things outside it. Being thus finite, it will have to be determined from outside. If we call its Cause C, then (A and B) and C will form a larger reciprocal unity, which must again be determined from outside, and so on, till we come to a unity which embraces the whole of existence.

This assumes the truth of the principle that, if several things are taken together as a unity, a Cause for that unity must be found outside it, as if it were a single thing. Hegel unquestionably does assume this, for without it he could not arrive at the final result of this category—that all things are bound in one system of Necessity. But he has not proved it. It would be inapplicable in Formal Causality, and must spring, if it is to be justified, from the special nature of Determined Causality. This nature, we have already seen, Hegel has failed to deduce from Formal Causality.

180. The unity of this reciprocal Activity is called by Hegel, as we saw above, by the name of infinite. This does not mean that the universe of existents is, in the ordinary sense, infinitely large. He speaks here of what he calls the True Infinite—the infinite of self-determination. Such a universe is infinite because it is determined only by its own nature, and not by anything outside it. The absolutely True Infinite will only be reached in the Absolute Idea. But the universe as connected by Reciprocity is relatively a True Infinite as compared with the finitude of a part of the universe or as against the false infinite of endless chains of Causes and Effects.

The system of such a universe as a whole is an ultimate fact, which neither admits nor requires any explanation. And in this consists its infinity, for it is determined by nothing outside it. On the other hand each of the particulars in the system is determined by others, and there is no particular part which does not in this way find an explanation.

But while the infinity which Hegel ascribes to this system is not a "false" infinity of number or magnitude, I do not see that it is impossible for it also to possess a "false" infinity. (On this point Hegel himself says nothing.) If the universe were adequately expressed by the category of Determined Causality, it would necessarily possess such a false infinity, since beyond each thing there would be a fresh thing which was its Cause. With Reciprocity it becomes possible to have a complete system of determination with a finite number of things, and so the number may be finite. But it would be equally possible, I think, to have a complete system of determination with an infinite number of things, and so the number may be infinite.

181. We have now reached the last category of Causality and of Essence. (The transition into the Notion will be considered in the next Chapter.) We have found ourselves able to accept very little of the treatment of the subject in the *Greater Logic*. But the results at which we have arrived are in closer agreement with the *Encyclopaedia*.

Our chief criticisms were two: that the two first subdivisions (the Absolute, and Actuality in the narrower sense) were unjustifiable, and that the treatment of Causality was erroneous. Now the first of these does not apply to the *Encyclopaedia*. Hegel there omits all the categories of the Absolute. Nor does he introduce into the dialectic chain the conceptions which, in the *Greater Logic*, fall within Actuality in the narrower sense. He treats of them, indeed (*Enc.* 143—149), but only in a preliminary discussion before he proceeds to consider the developement of the categories. The result of these omissions is that Substantiality, Causality, and Reciprocity are the three immediate subdivisions of Actuality in the larger sense, instead of, as in the *Greater Logic*, subdivisions of its final subdivision. Instead of being divisions of the fourth order, they are now divisions of the third order.

Thus the *Encyclopaedia* escapes one of the two objections to the *Greater Logic*. The introduction of the excursus on Possibility, Contingency, and Necessity is quite justifiable, so long as they are not treated as categories of the dialectic process. For Necessity and Causality, as I pointed out above, are really the same conception. And the relation of this conception to Possibility and Contingency is well worth consideration, although that consideration is not required, either to reach the conception of Necessity, or to transcend it.

(The *Encyclopaedia*, however, with curious inconsistency, makes the transition to Substantiality from Necessity. This is clearly incompatible with the general line of argument which the *Encyclopaedia* adopts. Since, for it, Possibility, Contingency and Necessity are not a triad in the chain of categories, if Substantiality were deduced from them it would have no connexion with the earlier part of the chain, which would therefore be hopelessly broken at this point. The category immediately before Substantiality, according to the *Encyclopaedia*, is the category of Inner and Outer. It is, therefore, from Inner and Outer that Substantiality must be deduced. And, as I pointed out above, this can easily be done.)

But when we come to our second criticism on the *Greater Logic*, its failure with the category of Cause, we find that the *Encyclopaedia* is in no better position. It has no subdivisions of Cause. But the transition from Substance to Causality is still through the conception of the Substance as the Cause of its Accidents. "Substance is Cause, in so far as Substance reflects into self as against its passage into Accidentality, and so stands as the *primary* fact, but again no less suspends this reflection into self (its bare possibility), lays itself down as the negation of itself, and thus produces an Effect, an Actuality, which, though so far assumed only as a sequence, is through the process that effectuates it at the same time necessary" (*Enc.* 153). With this he holds himself to have arrived at a Causality equivalent to the Determined Causality of the *Greater Logic*. Thus the transition is really the same as in the

Greater Logic. The only result of the omission of Formal Causality as a separate division is to render the argument more obscure.

The *Encyclopaedia* also maintains the identity of Cause and Effect. "So far again as we can speak of a definite content, there is no content in the Effect that is not in the Cause" (*Enc.* 153).

CHAPTER VIII

SUBJECTIVITY

182. The last of the three main divisions of the dialectic is called the Doctrine of the Notion (Begriff). Notion is not, perhaps, a very satisfactory translation of Begriff, but it would be difficult to find a better, and it is the translation usually adopted. The Doctrine of the Notion is divided into three divisions—Subjectivity, Objectivity, and The Idea. (In the *Encyclopaedia* the two first are called the Subjective Notion and the Objective Notion.)

Subjectivity is divided as follows:

I.   The Notion. (Der Begriff.)

    A.   The Universal Notion. (Der allgemeine Begriff.)

    B.   The Particular Notion. (Der besondere Begriff.)

    C.   The Individual. (Das Einzelne.)

II.   The Judgment. (Das Urtheil.)

    A.   The Judgment of Inherence. (Das Urtheil des Daseins.)

      (a)   The Positive Judgment. (Das positive Urtheil.)
      (b)   The Negative Judgment. (Das negative Urtheil.)
      (c)   The Infinite Judgment. (Das unendliche Urtheil.)

    B.   The Judgment of Subsumption. (Das Urtheil der Reflexion.)

      (a)   The Singular Judgment. (Das singulare Urtheil.)
      (b)   The Particular Judgment. (Das partikulare Urtheil.)

(c)   The Universal Judgment.   (Das universelle Urtheil.)

C.   The Judgment of Necessity.   (Das Urtheil der Nothwendigkeit.)

  (a)   The Categorical Judgment.   (Das kategorische Urtheil.)

  (b)   The Hypothetical Judgment.   (Das hypothetische Urtheil.)

  (c)   The Disjunctive Judgment.   (Das disjunktive Urtheil.)

D.   The Judgment of the Notion.   (Das Urtheil des Begriffs.)

  (a)   The Assertoric Judgment.   (Das assertorische Urtheil.)

  (b)   The Problematic Judgment.   (Das problematische Urtheil.)

  (c)   The Apodictic Judgment.   (Das apodiktische Urtheil.)

III.   The Syllogism.   (Der Schluss.)

A.   The Qualitative Syllogism.   (Der Schluss des Daseins.)

  (a)   First Figure.   (Erste Figur.)
  (b)   Second Figure.   (Zweite Figur.)
  (c)   Third Figure.   (Dritte Figur.)
  (d)   Fourth Figure.   (Vierte Figur.)

B.   The Syllogism of Reflection.   (Der Schluss der Reflexion.)

  (a)   The Syllogism of Allness.   (Der Schluss der Allheit.)

  (b)   The Syllogism of Induction.   (Der Schluss der Induktion.)

  (c)   The Syllogism of Analogy.   (Der Schluss der Analogie.)

C.   The Syllogism of Necessity.   (Der Schluss der Nothwendigkeit.)

(a) The Categorical Syllogism. (Der kategorische Schluss.)

(b) The Hypothetical Syllogism. (Der hypothetische Schluss.)

(c) The Disjunctive Syllogism. (Der disjunktive Schluss.)

The only ambiguity in the nomenclature here is that Notion is used both for the primary division of which Subjectivity is a secondary division, and also for the first tertiary division of Subjectivity. Judgment of Inherence and Judgment of Subsumption are not, it will be seen, translations of the titles given by Hegel. But he suggests Urtheil der Inhärenz and Urtheil der Subsumption as alternative names (*G. L.* iii. 94) and, as these seem more expressive than the original titles, I have thought it better to adopt them. In the same way I have called the Schluss des Daseins by the simpler name of Qualitative Syllogism, which is also given by Hegel (*G. L.* iii. 133).

It will be noticed that Judgment and the Qualitative Syllogism have each four divisions instead of three, though the irregularity in the latter case will prove to be more apparent than real.

183. The names of the categories of Subjectivity suggest at first sight that this part of the dialectic deals only with the workings of our minds, and not with all reality. This might account, it would appear, for the name of Subjectivity, and for such names as Judgment and Syllogism among the subdivisions.

But such a use of Subjectivity would not be Hegelian. For Hegel Subjective does not mean mental. It means rather the particular, contingent, and capricious, as opposed to the universal, necessary, and reasonable[1].

---

[1] The only case, so far as I know, in which Hegel uses Subjective in any other way occurs in the *Greater Logic*, when he calls the Doctrines of Being and Essence by the name of Objective Logic, and the Doctrine of the Notion (including Objectivity and the Idea as well as Subjectivity) by the name of Subjective Logic. But he says (*G. L.* i. 51) that this use of Subjective and Objective, though usual, is unsatisfactory.

And when we examine the categories which have the titles of Notion, Judgment, and Syllogism, it is evident that, in spite of their names, they do not apply only to the states of our minds, but to all reality. They follow, by the dialectic process, from the categories of Essence, and the categories of Objectivity and then the categories of the Idea, in like manner, follow from them. They must therefore, if there is to be any validity in the process, apply to the same subject as the categories of Essence and the Idea, which admittedly apply to all reality.

Hegel's own language, too, renders it clear that these categories are meant to apply to all reality. He says, for example, "all things are a categorical judgment" (*Enc.* 177), and again, "everything is a syllogism" (*Enc.* 181).

184. We must look, then, for another explanation of the terminology. We can find it, I think, in the relation of this part of the dialectic to formal logic. Formal logic owes its existence to abstraction. When we take its standpoint we make abstraction of all but certain qualities of reality. Now these qualities, we shall find, are those which are demonstrated to be valid in the categories of Subjectivity.

We find that formal logic assumes that we have the power of ascribing general notions as predicates to subjects, and in this way arriving at complete truth with regard to these subjects. And it also assumes that we are in possession, in some way or another, of various general truths of the type All *A* is *B*, No *A* is *C*, Some *A* is *D*.

On the other hand we find that there are other characteristics of reality of which formal logic takes no account. It makes no distinction between trivial and important propositions. "No man is wholly evil" and "No man has green hair" are, for formal logic, assertions of exactly the same sort. And, in the second place, it only concerns itself with the deduction of one proposition from others. It does not enquire into the validity of the ultimate propositions from which all deduction must start.

Now we shall see that Hegel's Subjectivity begins with the conception of universal notions, and that it soon proceeds to the further conception of valid general propositions—the two assumptions of formal logic. And we shall also see that among the defects which Hegel finds in the course of Subjectivity are, in the first place, the inability to distinguish between the importance of propositions equally true[1], and, in the second place, the failure to take account of ultimate general propositions, while the further failure to take account of ultimate particular propositions, though not mentioned by Hegel, must be taken into account if we are to justify his transition to Objectivity.

This will enable us to explain why the divisions of Subjectivity drew their names from formal logic. The reason is not that these categories apply only to the subject-matter of formal logic, but that the procedure of formal logic involves the validity of these categories in a way in which it does not involve those which come later in the chain. This is, of course, the same principle of nomenclature which we have already found in so many categories, from Repulsion onwards.

We can now understand, also, why the whole division is called Subjectivity. The reason is that it is contingent, and its contingency is the same which we find in formal logic—that the principle of classifying which is adopted is entirely indifferent. For formal logic all universals are of the same importance, and it sees no difference between a classification which arranges pictures by their painters, and one which arranges them by the size of their frames.

185. At the end of Essence we had attained to the idea of completely necessary determination. The category of Reciprocity asserts that everything is so connected with other things that the existence and nature of the one is completely dependent on the existence and nature of the other, and *vice versâ*. And the connexions of this nature, direct or indirect, which belong to each thing, extend to everything else in the universe, so that the universe forms a connected whole.

Hegel tells us that in this complete necessity we find freedom. "Freedom shows itself as the truth of necessity" (*G. L.* iii. 6. *Enc.* 158). In examining this apparent paradox, we must remember that for Hegel freedom never means the power to act without motives, or with an unmotived choice of

---

[1] Cp. his attempt to demonstrate that particular sorts of predicates are appropriate to particular forms of Judgment.

motives.   For him freedom always means absence of external restraint.   That is free which is what its own nature prompts it to be, however inevitable may be its possession of that nature and its action in accordance with it.

If we say, then, that a thing is deficient in freedom, we must mean that, while its inner nature, if unthwarted, would lead it to be *ABC*, it is compelled by external influences to be *ABD* instead.   Now this appeared possible in the categories of Essence.   For there we conceived everything as having an inner nature, which was connected, indeed, with its external relations, but was not identical with them, which could be either in or out of harmony with them, and, in the latter case, would be constrained.   But when we reach Reciprocity we have transcended this view.   The thing has no nature at all, except in so far as it is determined by other things, and in its turn determines them.   What is thus determined is its inner nature.   And thus it reaches freedom.   Since it has no inner nature except the results of this external determination, it is clear that its external determinations can never make it do anything against its inner nature.   This is, indeed, only a negative freedom.   But any more positive freedom requires higher categories.   In necessity we have gained all the freedom which is possible at this stage.

This point is so important that, to prevent ambiguity, it may be well to anticipate some considerations which belong more properly to the Idea.   In self-conscious beings, we can distinguish between free and constrained states, even when we recognise that both states are determined in the same way—as an inner state determined from outside.   A man feels himself free if he can do what he wants, and feels himself constrained if he cannot.   And yet his desire and its gratification are as completely determined in the one case as his desire and its disappointment are in the other.

This, however, does not contradict our previous result.   For an act of volition in a conscious being is not only an occurrence, but an occurrence with a *meaning*—a characteristic which belongs to no occurrences except mental acts.   And while the occurrence of the volition, like any other act, must be in complete harmony with the rest of the universe, its meaning may not be in such a harmony. If a man in the Arctic Circle desires to see a palm-tree, the occurrence of that desire in him will be in perfect harmony with the rest of the universe, for it will be connected with it by reciprocal causation. But the meaning of the act will not be in harmony with the universe. The same nature of the universe which determines his desire for a palm-tree will determine the absence of palm-trees, and so there will, in this sense, be want of harmony between the desire and the universe. Hence there will arise constraint and absence of freedom.

This conflict will require a deeper reconciliation than that which proved effectual in Reciprocity. For here there is something inner which, however it has arisen, deals with the world around it as an independent power. The reconciliation could only take place by a demonstration that the two independent powers do in fact harmonize with one another.

The freedom which is attained by the establishment of complete necessity is only a negative and imperfect freedom, but it is all that can be attained at the point of the dialectic where it is introduced. It is also all that is required, since it removes all the constraint which is, at this point, possible.

186. The first division (*G. L.* iii. 35. *Enc.* 163) is

I. THE NOTION.

A. *The Universal Notion.*

(*G. L.* iii. 36. *Enc.* 163.) The deduction of this category from the last is found at the end of Essence (*G. L.* ii. 242) and is as follows: "The absolute Substance as absolute Form separates itself from itself, and consequently no longer repels itself from itself as Necessity, nor falls as Contingency into Substances indifferent and external to each other, but separates itself. On the one hand it separates itself into the totality, previously the passive Substance, which is original as the reflection into self out of determinateness (Bestimmtheit), as the simple whole which contains its positing in itself, and is posited as therein identical with itself—the Universal. On the other hand it separates itself into the totality, previously the causal Substance, which in its reflection out of its determinateness in itself is negatively determined, and so, as the determinateness which is identical with itself, is likewise the whole, but is posited as the negativity which is identical with itself—the Individual."

I must confess myself unable to follow this. Why is Determinateness more negative in the Cause than in the Effect? The one is as definite as the other, and would therefore, it should seem, have the same element of negativity. And why is the Effect more a simple whole than the Cause? And how could it be so, if the relations of Cause and Effect are reciprocal?

And, again, how does this deduction give us the Universal and the Individual which Hegel proceeds to use? The Universal has to be common to many Individuals, while the Individual has to be determined by many Universals. I cannot see how a passive aspect of Substance can be common to several active aspects, or how one active aspect can be determined by several passive aspects.

187.   But, even if we cannot accept Hegel's own deduction, it is not, I think, difficult to see why Subjectivity, and the Universal Notion in particular, should succeed Reciprocity.

The Universal Notion is, as we shall see, a common quality to be found in two or more things, which are united by their participation in it. Things, again, are united by the reciprocal determinations which have been established by the category of Reciprocity. But these are clearly not the Universal Notions for which we seek. The relation of things which are connected by the same Notion is not a relation of reciprocal causation, but a relation of similarity.

Nevertheless, we know that these things, whose nature is determined by reciprocal causation, are determined by that causation to similarity with one another. For it was shown in the category of Variety that everything is both like and unlike every other thing. From Variety to Reciprocity there are many categories, but in none of them is this particular conclusion transcended. And at the present stage in the dialectic we have the result that the various qualities in the reciprocally determined things must be such that no thing is entirely like or entirely unlike any other thing.

Things, then, are doubly connected—by similarity and by

reciprocal causation. And it is obvious that a thing may be, and generally is, connected by the one tie to things very different from those to which it is connected by the other. A sparrow in England resembles very closely a sparrow in New Zealand, though the influence exerted by one on the other may be as slight as can possibly exist between any two beings on the same planet. On the other hand, the English sparrow's state is largely determined by his relations—positive and negative—to worms and to cats, although their resemblance to him is not great.

Both these connexions have to be worked out further. And this the dialectic proceeds to do. It first takes up the relation of similarity, and works it out through the course of Subjectivity. Then in Objectivity it proceeds to work out the relation of determination—not going back arbitrarily to pick it up, but led on to it again by dialectical necessity, since Subjectivity, when fully worked out, shows itself to have a defect which can only be remedied by the further development of the relation of determination. Finally, the two are united in the Idea as a Synthesis.

188. This, as we have seen, is not the way in which Hegel makes the transition. But it seems to me that in this way it is valid, and I can see no valid alternative. It might be objected that such a transition would destroy the continuity of the dialectic. The dialectic, for Hegel, is unquestionably continuous. Each result must come from the one before it. And here, it might be thought, we have dropped the result gained in Reciprocity, put it aside till we shall have come to Objectivity, and, in order to get started in Subjectivity, gone back to a result which had been gained toward the beginning of the Doctrine of Essence.

This, however, would be a mistake. For if, in one sense, we now start with the conception gained in Variety, that idea has been transformed, or we could not use it here. And it can only be transformed by the application of the conception of complete determination, which came for the first time with the category of Reciprocity. Thus both accusations of want of continuity are answered. We have not gone back to take up a long past result, but are taking it the moment it has been transformed to suit our present purpose.   We have not dropped the result last attained, since it is only through this that the transformation has come about.

Before this point we could not have taken the like and unlike qualities as Notions, because those qualities did not— as the Notions do—express the whole nature of the thing. The thing had these qualities, and they might be said to form part of its nature, but there was also an inner core of Nature, affected by these connexions with the outside, but not completely expressed by them.   This is the characteristic position of Essence.

But when, at the end of Essence, we come to Reciprocity, this is changed.   We saw there that a thing has no inner nature distinct from its outer nature, but that the two are identical.   Thus the whole nature of the thing consists of the qualities in which consist its likeness and unlikeness to everything else.   And thus the transition from Reciprocity is the natural and proper transition to the Universal Notion, since it is Reciprocity which first enables us to regard the like and unlike qualities as Notions.

The transition may then be summed up as follows—the whole nature of everything consists in its qualities, which are determined by the relations of reciprocal causality which exist between it and every thing else.   And, as every thing has some qualities in common with every other thing, the nature of any thing may always be expressed in part by pointing out some common quality which it shares with something else.   These common qualities are Universal Notions.

189.   It is, however, evident that this is only one side of the truth.   If we found that every thing must have some quality in common with every other thing, we also found that no two things could have exactly the same qualities.   And so, if we express in part the nature of A and B by pointing out that they have the common quality X, we are able to assert that it must also be the case that A possesses some quality Y, not shared by B, and that B possesses some quality Z, not shared by A.   These qualities which distinguish the two things, united in their possession of X, are what Hegel calls Particular Notions.

B. *The Particular Notion.*

(*G. L.* iii. 42. *Enc.* 163.) We see from this that a Notion can be used both as Universal and as Particular. The quality Y may be shared by A with other things, and could then be made a Universal, with X as a Particular under it. For example, if we decide to classify a gallery of pictures by their painters, we may bring two pictures together as both painted by Raphael. They may be distinguished from one another by having, one a good frame and the other a bad frame. Here "painted by Raphael" is the Universal, while "having a good frame" and "having a bad frame" are the Particulars. But it would be possible, from caprice or when deciding on repairs of frames, to make the condition of the frames the primary principle of classification. The first Raphael might then be separated from its companion and classed with a Velasquez. Here the Universal would be "having a good frame," and the Particulars would be "painted by Raphael" and "painted by Velasquez."

This brings out the contingency which earns for this part of the dialectic the name of Subjectivity. According to this category, all of the innumerable classifications possible are equally good. Any two things can be brought into the same class, for no two things are destitute of some common quality. Any two things can be separated, for no two things are without some difference in their qualities. There is no distinction made here between a classification based on deep and fundamental similarities, and one based on similarities merely trivial. One similarity is as good as another.

190. At the same time it must be noticed that, while many Notions can be used either as Universals or as Particulars, yet some can be used only as Universals and some, perhaps, only as Particulars. A Universal is a Notion which unites existent things; a Particular is a Notion which divides existent things. Any Notion therefore which is true of all existent things can be used as a Universal, and not as a Particular, since all things are united by their possession of it, and nothing is discriminated, by its possession of it, from anything else. And it is clear that there is at least one Notion which is true of all existent things, namely the Notion of Existence.

Again, while all Notions, being general, are applicable, so far as their own meaning goes, to more things than one, yet it might be the case that some Notion applied only to one existent thing in the universe. Suppose, for example, the universe were such that one being in it, and only one in its whole duration, were yellow. Then the quality of being yellow would be a Particular Notion, but not a Universal. It could be used to discriminate that thing from other existent beings, but not to unite it with any other existent being.

Hegel does not mention—perhaps he did not realise—this three-fold division of Notions which could only be Universal, Notions which could only be Particular, and Notions which could be either. But there is nothing in his language inconsistent with it, nor is the point essential to the dialectic process.

191. For there is no Notion which is neither Universal nor Particular, and so, by a combination of Universal and Particular Notions, we can get all the Notions which are applicable to any thing, and so express its whole nature. And thus we reach

C.   The Individual.

(*G. L.* iii. 60.   *Enc.* 164.) It must be noted that, while the last two categories are the Universal and Particular *Notions*, this is not the Individual *Notion*, but the Individual. In the Thesis the conception was that the nature of each thing was partially expressed by the Notions which joined it to others. In the Antithesis the conception was that the nature of each thing was partially expressed by the Notions which separated it from others. Here in the Synthesis the conception is that by combining both classes of Notions the nature of the thing is completely determined. From this point onward the thing is called an Individual.

192. We now pass to

II.   The Judgment

(*G. L.* iii. 65.   *Enc.* 166), and, in the first place (*G. L.* iii. 75. *Enc.* 172) to

A. *The Judgment of Inherence.*

(a) *The Positive Judgment.*

(*G. L.* iii. 76. *Enc.* 172.) The reality of an Individual, we have seen, was expressible only by a combination of Notions. It must therefore be possible to assert some relation between the Individual and each of these Notions. And this is what is asserted in Judgment. The question which was implicit in the categories of the Notion—how an Individual and a Notion can be connected with each other—becomes explicit in the categories of Judgment.

This problem, to begin with, takes the form that, starting from the Individual, we endeavour to adjust a Notion to it. This is the Judgment of Inherence, as distinguished from the Judgment of Subsumption, in which we start with the Notion and endeavour to connect the Individual with it. The Judgment of Inherence comes first, because, in the preceding categories, the problem was to determine the Individual. And so we start here with the Individual as the *datum*, to which the Notion has to be related. The only relation hitherto considered between an Individual and a Notion has been an affirmative one, and so we start with a Positive Judgment of Inherence.

Hegel expresses this Judgment as "the Individual is the Universal" (*G. L.* iii. 77). If Universal were used here in the same sense as in the categories of the Notion, this would be an inadequate way of expressing the category. For a Notion which can only be Particular is true of an Individual as much as any other Notion. And with respect to one of those Notions which can be either Universal or Particular, there is no reason to call it one rather than the other unless we know whether it is being used to unite or disunite this particular Individual from others. And to determine this, we should have to determine what other Individuals are being considered. Now in the Judgment which we have at present reached, only one Individual is under consideration.

But the fact is that in the course of the Doctrine of the Notion the term Universal is used in very different senses. This is a defect in nomenclature, but one which need not lead to any error on the part of a careful student, as the changes made, and the points at which Hegel makes them, are quite definite. Throughout the categories of the Judgment, Universal means any general idea which is true of an existent Individual.

Hegel takes as an example of this category "the rose is red," and not merely "this is red." This is quite legitimate, if we use the example to remind ourselves that the Individual, which is the subject of the Universal which we are considering, is also the subject of many other Universals—in this case organic, vegetable, and so forth. For we have seen that each Individual must have more than one Universal (in the new sense of Universal introduced in Judgment). But we must not, when enquiring how the Universal can be connected with the Individual, assume that the Individual is already determined by other Universals, since that would beg the question at issue—the nature and possibility of the connexion between a Universal and an Individual.

193. How does this category break down, and compel us to continue the dialectic process? Hegel says (*G. L.* iii. 81. *Enc.* 172) that all statements of the form I is U are necessarily false. If, for example, we say of a rose "this is red" there is a double falsity. Red is not identical with the rose at which we point, for, in the first place, there are many red things in the world besides this rose[1]. And, in the second place, it is not identical with it, because every Individual has more than one quality. The rose will be organic, vegetable, etc., as well as red.

It seems at first sight as if this was a mere quibble. "Of course," it might be answered, "no one supposed that the *is* here was to be taken in the sense of absolute equivalence, as when we say the sum of three and two is five. A change of language will remove the difficulty. Say that the subject *has* the quality of being red, and the criticism ceases to have any force." But Hegel's objection, though I cannot regard it as valid, goes deeper than this.

Hegel's reply would, I conceive, have been as follows. We cannot say that the Individual *has* the Universal. In the

---

[1] If the Universal was one of those predicates which belong only to a single existent Individual, this would not apply. But even then the Universal would not be *identical* with the Individual, though it would denote nothing else.

Doctrine of Essence, indeed, we were able to say that the Thing
had its Properties. But a difficulty has arisen since then.
Before anything can be said to have something else, it must
itself be real. If it is not real, it cannot possess anything.
And so, if we are to say that the Individual has the Universal,
we must previously assign to the Individual some nature other
than that Universal. Now in the case of a Thing and its
Properties, this was possible. For the Thing was conceived as
a Substratum, of which the Properties were the Surface, but
which had a nature in some way distinguished from them.
But this distinction has disappeared in the Notion. Our
Individual is completely expressed by its Universals. It has
nothing else in it. Where, then, can we find a nature for the
Individual which has the Universal ?

Each Individual, of course, has many Universals. But it is
not possible to determine the nature of the Individual which is
asserted to have one Universal, by means of the others which
are true of it. For the difficulty would recur. The Individual
is not identical with these Universals any more than with the
first. We should be compelled to say that it *had* them. And
so the difficulty would arise once more.

194. I do not think, however, that Hegel's argument can
be finally sustained. It is true, no doubt, that the Individual
has no nature except what can be expressed by Universals.
And this would be fatal if it were necessary that a thing, which
was related to its qualities as possessing them, should have a
nature logically prior to those qualities. But I do not see that
this is so. It was doubtless the position in the Doctrine of
Essence, but by this time Hegel regards it as transcended.
The nature of a thing is to be sought in its connexions with
other things—by Universals or by causal relations—and not in
some inner core of reality distinguished from them. This is
certainly Hegel's general position with regard to the difference
between Essence and the Notion, and he has therefore no right
to fall back, in a category of the Notion, on the transcended
conceptions of Essence, in order to demonstrate a contradiction.

Thus I see no contradiction in "the rose is red." We can
state it, to avoid the ambiguity of "is," in the form "the rose
has redness." If we ask what it is which has this redness, no

contradiction arises.   Let us take redness, sweetness, and value
as standing for the whole infinite number of Universals which
are true of any particular rose.   Then, if it is asked, "what is
the nature of this which has redness, sweetness, and value?" the
answer is "its nature is to have redness, sweetness, and value."
This involves no vicious circle.   It does involve the rejection
of the principle that a thing must be logically prior to its
qualities.   But this principle is not true, and is recognised by
Hegel not to be true.   He has therefore no ground, that I can
see, for rejecting this solution.

195.   He does, however, reject it, and passes on.   The
Positive Judgment, he holds, has broken down because the
Individual and the Universal could not be made to coincide.
Now in a Negative Judgment the assertion is precisely that
they do not coincide.   We thus reach

(b)   The Negative Judgment.

(*G. L.* iii. 82.   *Enc.* 172.)   Since the Negative Judgment
is introduced in order to avoid the contradiction which Hegel
finds in the Positive Judgment, it is clear that the Negative
Judgment will have to replace the Positive Judgment altogether.
We must have Negative Judgments, then, which do not involve
any Positive Judgments.

Hegel now points out (*G. L.* iii. 87.   *Enc.* 173) that if we
take a rose which is not red, it will nevertheless have some
colour, and so will fall within the wider class of coloured objects.
And thus we get the Positive Judgment that it is coloured.
Can we ever get a Negative Judgment without such a Positive
Judgment?   Only, he says, if we can deny of the Individual *A*
a Universal *Z*, such that no common Universal would be true
both of *A* and of all those Individuals of whom *Z* would be true.
If we could find a predicate so far removed from *A* as this, the
negative relation between it and *A* would form what Hegel
calls an Infinite Judgment, to which we now pass.

(c)   The Infinite Judgment.

196.   (*G. L.* iii. 89.   *Enc.* 173.)   He now tells us that,
besides this Infinite Judgment, which he also calls the Negative-

Infinite Judgment, there is also a Positive-Infinite Judgment, the Judgment of Identity. This takes either the form " the Individual is the Individual" or else the form " the Universal is the Universal" (*G. L.* iii. 90).

It is quite true, of course, that if all Universals are denied of Individuals, we shall still be able to assert these barren tautologies, and they will be the only positive assertions which we shall be able to make. But Hegel's treatment of these identities as if they were a subdivision of the Infinite Judgment is misleading. The true Infinite Judgment—the Negative-Infinite—denies the Universal of the Individual, and is in its proper place in the chain of attempts to determine the relation of the Individual to the Universal which runs right through the Judgments of Inherence and Subsumption. The affirmations that the Individual is the Individual, and the Universal is the Universal, have no place in this chain. They are true here, as they are true at every point after Individual and Universal have been once introduced. But they do not form a category at this point. The attempt to explain the nature of existent reality by the affirmation that anything is itself belongs to the category of Identity at the beginning of Essence.

Hegel appears to have intended to express the same view in the *Encyclopaedia* on this point as he had already expressed in the *Greater Logic* (*Enc.* 173). But he makes the whole argument unintelligible by making the Positive-Infinite Judgment (there called simply Identical) *precede* the Negative-Infinite Judgment (there called simply Infinite). By doing this he throws the transition from Negative Judgment into obscurity which can only be cleared up by comparison with the *Greater Logic.* This obscurity is increased by the extreme condensation which prevails in the whole treatment of Subjectivity in the *Encyclopaedia.*

197. Hegel's transition from Infinite Judgment is as follows. He takes as examples of Infinite Judgments, " the rose is not an elephant," " the understanding is not a table," and he says that, although correct or true (richtig oder wahr) they are nonsensical and trivial (widersinnig und abgeschmackt) (*G. L.* iii. 90. *Enc.* 173). And it certainly is true that such Judgments are seldom, if ever, worth the trouble of asserting

A Negative Judgment is interesting in proportion as the Individual of whom the Universal is denied, resembles those Individuals of whom it could be affirmed. Thus "the elephant is not carnivorous" is a more interesting and important proposition than "the oak is not carnivorous," while this, again, is better worth asserting than the equally correct proposition "the binomial theorem is not carnivorous."

But this would not be sufficient for Hegel's purpose. For to pass from Infinite Judgment to the Judgment of Subsumption it would be necessary to show that there is some contradiction in Infinite Judgment. And this is not done by showing that the propositions which, from the point of view of Infinite Judgment, would describe the universe, are trivial and unimportant. It would be necessary to show that they would be, taken by themselves, contradictory, whereas Hegel admits them to be correct and true.

The fact is that Hegel does not do justice to his own position. The examples he gives are not contradictory, but then they are not Infinite Judgments. "The understanding is not a table" is not an Infinite Judgment. For an understanding has certain Universals in common with tables. Tables and understandings, for example, are both substances and both existent. A real Infinite Judgment is impossible. In an Infinite Judgment the Subject, of which the Predicate is denied, must have no Universal in common with the Individuals of whom the Predicate could be affirmed. This is clearly impossible, if all Individuals have any Universal common to all of them. And all Individuals have, at any rate, the common Universal of Individuality. There cannot, therefore, be any Judgment which is really Infinite.

It seems to me that Hegel was mistaken in making Infinite Judgment a separate category, and in making it the Synthesis in the triad of Judgment of Inherence. For an Infinite Judgment is only a Negative Judgment which can be true without any Positive Judgment being true. If "A is not Z" is not Infinite, then A has some Universal Y in common with the Individuals which are Z, and this would be the basis of a Positive Judgment. Now the transition from Positive to Negative Judgments involved that no Positive Judgments are true, and thus in reaching the category of Negative Judgment we had already reached the position of Infinite Judgment which should not, therefore, be a separate category.

Moreover, Infinite Judgment does not form a proper Synthesis for the triad of Judgment of Inherence. As a Synthesis it ought to transcend the opposition between Positive and Negative Judgments, while in fact it merely developes it[1].

198. It would be easy, however, to recast the divisions, so as to avoid this defect, without departing from the main line of Hegel's argument. The category of Negative Judgment breaks down because it requires that only Negative Judgments should be true of Individuals, which is impossible, since at any rate the Positive Judgment, " this is an Individual," is true of every Individual. Then the argument by which Hegel passes to Judgment of Subsumption from Infinite Judgment would take us from Negative Judgment to a Synthesis which contains the principle of Subsumption, and which, by the usual " collapse into immediacy" will take us to the Singular Judgment, the first subdivision of Subsumption.

That argument is as follows (*G. L.* iii. 93). In the Judgment of Inherence "its movement showed itself in the predicate" while the subject was what was regarded as fundamental. But in the Judgment of Subsumption the fundamental element is the predicate "by which the subject is to be measured, and in correspondence to which the subject is to be determined."

Both Positive and Negative Judgments of Inherence—this appears to be the line of Hegel's thought—have broken down. The difficulty has arisen from the inevitable incompatibility of the subject and the predicate in the Judgment of Inherence. How can this be changed? So far we have started with the subject and endeavoured to fit the predicate to it. And we have failed. There remains the alternative of starting with the predicate, and endeavouring to fit the subject to it. Instead, that is, of asking what Universal is true of a given Individual, we shall ask of what Individuals a given Universal is true. The last triad was called Judgment of Inherence because the question was what Universals belonged to, or inhered in, an

---

[1] This point is partially obscured by Hegel's treatment of Identical Judgment, which suggests that it is a subdivision of Infinite Judgment.

Individual.   Here the question is what Individuals are brought under a Universal, and our new triad is called

B.   *The Judgment of Subsumption.*

(*G. L.* iii. 91.   *Enc.* 174.)   This introduces, for the first time, the possibility of a distinction of Quantity in Judgment.   When we started with the Individual, all Judgments applied to one Individual only.   But the answer to our present question may be either that the Universal applies to one Individual, or to several.   And these several can either be some of those who possess a second Universal, or all of those who possess it.   Our Judgment may be "this is Z," or "some Y are Z," or "all Y are Z."   It can be either Singular, Particular, or Universal.

199.   Hegel gives another characteristic of this triad, which apparently forms the ground for its other title of Judgment of Reflection.   "If examples are to be given of the predicates of Judgments of Reflection, they must be of a different kind than those of the Judgments of Determinate Being[1].   In the Judgment of Reflection is given for the first time a really determined content, that is, a content at all....In the Judgment of Determinate Being the content is only something immediate, abstract, undetermined.   Thus the following can serve as examples of Judgments of Reflection : man is mortal, things are perishable, this thing is useful or hurtful.   Hardness and elasticity of bodies, happiness, etc., are characteristic predicates of this sort.   They express an essentiality, which however is a determination by means of Relations, or a unifying (zusammenfassende) Universality" (*G. L.* iii. 92.   *Enc.* 174).

The point apparently is that a predicate must now assert some relation of the subject with another subject.   But all the examples are not happily chosen.   Useful and elastic, indeed, assert a relation, but perishable and happy do not seem to assert a relation any more than red does, which is taken by Hegel as an example of a Judgment of Determined Being.

I do not think Hegel is justified in ascribing this second characteristic to the new triad.   He has now made it differ from the former in two respects, (*a*) the predicates must express

---

[1] It will be remembered that Judgments of Inherence are also called Judgments of Determinate Being.

relations, (*b*) the predicate, and not the subject, is the *datum* from which we start. If the new category is to have both these characteristics, he is bound to show that they are some-how connected, so that we are forced, if we modify our previous conception in one respect, to modify it also in the other. So far as I can see, he does not make any attempt to do this. And it seems difficult to conceive how it could be done. What is there in the fact that a predicate expresses a relation, that should involve the fact that the predicate, rather than the subject, should be taken as the *datum*? Or what is there in the fact that the predicate, rather than the subject, should be taken as the *datum*, which should involve the fact that the predicate taken should be one which expresses a relation?

If the changes, then, are separate and unconnected, which of them is really the characteristic idea of the new triad? It seems clear that it is Subsumption, and not Relational Predicates which must be taken as the meaning of the new stage, if the argument is to be considered valid. For we saw above that the change to Subsumption was a real attempt to remove the difficulty which Hegel found in Judgments of Inherence—the impossibility of finding a predicate which should coincide with the subject. Now a change to Relational Predicates does nothing to remove this difficulty. If there really were, as Hegel believed, a contradiction in "this rose is red," owing to the want of coincidence between the subject and the predicate, there would be just the same contradiction in "this rose is useful."

Again, it is clearly essential to the new triad that the distinction of Quantity should be introduced. The subdivisions of the triad turn entirely on Quantity, and without it we should not reach the Universal Judgment, which is vital for the rest of the argument of the dialectic. Now, as we have seen, the change to Subsumption does involve the introduction of Quantity into Judgments. But the change to Relational Predicates would not. If we continued to take the subject as the *datum* for starting, there would be no more reason to make distinctions of Quantity in predicating utility than in predi-cating redness.

For these reasons I think that we must regard Hegel as

having illegitimately added the change to Relational Predicates, when he ought to have confined himself to the change to
Subsumption.

(a)   The Singular Judgment.

200. (*G. L.* iii. 94. *Enc.* 175.) All Judgments of Inherence
are, as we have said, Singular in form.   The Judgment of Subsumption, which is derived from the Judgment of Inherence,
will consequently start as a Singular Judgment.   Its outer
form, therefore, will be exactly the same as in a Positive
Judgment of Inherence—for example, "this is red " or "this is
useful."   But the difference is that, in the former triad, the
singularity of the Judgment was an essential part of its nature
as a Judgment of Inherence.   Here, on the other hand, it is
merely the form with which we start, which can be modified if
it is found not to be suitable.

201.   This Hegel considers he has already shown, in his
criticism of the Positive Judgment.   We must pass on to

(b)   The Particular Judgment.

(*G. L.* iii. 94. *Enc.* 175.) The example Hegel gives of this
is "some men are happy."   It will be noticed that the change
is more than a mere increase in the number of Individuals.
Our Singular Judgment had only one Universal—the Universal
in the predicate.   For, as we saw above (Section 192), although,
even in Judgments of Inherence, we may speak of " this rose "
and not simply " this," it is only to remind us that the Individual
is, in point of fact, a concrete Individual with many qualities.
We did not make our assertion of redness in any way dependent
on the Individual being a rose.   It would have been as good
an example of the category if w had only said "this is red."
Here, however, it is the nature of our Judgment to have a
Universal in the subject as well as in the predicate.   The
subject is defined in relation to this Universal.   It is "some
men."

It is necessary that the Particular Judgment should take
this form, if it is to remove the difficulty which Hegel finds in
the Singular Judgment.   For if we merely took a plurality of
separate Individuals, instead of a single Individual, we should

leave the difficulty untouched. It would occur about each Individual separately, and the only change would be that it would be repeated many times over. It is not transcended till we have grouped the Individuals under another Universal, and so made the Judgment the expression of the relation between two Universals.

The statement "some X is Y" is, however, ambiguous. It may mean "some, but not all, X is Y," or it may leave it doubtful whether there is any X which is not Y. Hegel takes it here in the former sense. " In the judgment ' some men are happy' is implied the immediate consequence 'some men are not happy'" ($G.$ $L.$ iii. 95). In this, however, he seems to me to be wrong. He has no right to put any more into this new category than is required to avoid the inadequacy of the previous category. Now all that is required for that purpose is that the Individuals in the subject should be united by all being X. It would not be at all helped by the existence of other X's which were not Y.

If we take the Particular Judgment in the second sense— as leaving it doubtful if any X is not Y—then, apart from the necessity of transcending the inadequacy of Singular Judgments, we can see that, if Individuals have Universals at all, Particular Judgments must be true. For the relation of any number of Individuals, A, B, C, etc., to the Universal Z, which they all possess, can be expressed in a Particular Judgment, " some Y is Z," if any other Universal Y can be found which also belongs to A, B, and C. And, whatever A, B, C, etc., are, this is always the case. If there are at least two Universals which are common to all Individuals, any two Individuals which have one common Universal must also have another common Universal. And the Universals of existence and individuality—not to mention any others—are common to all Individuals. So, when we have predicated a Universal of two or more Individuals, however dissimilar in other respects those Individuals may be, we know that some other Universal may always be found, which they have in common, and can express the fact in the form of a Particular Judgment.

Of course, the higher we have to go for the Universal in the subject, the less information we get. "Some judges are

corrupt" gives us more information than "some functionaries
are corrupt," and the latter again gives us more information
than "some men are corrupt." But though the importance of
the proposition which we can obtain will vary, some proposition
of this form will always be true.

202. But while Particular Judgments are true, the category
of Particular Judgments developes a contradiction. By taking
it as a category we undertake to express the nature of the
existent by it. And this cannot be done. For if a Particular
Judgment is true, then something else must be true which is
not expressed in the Particular Judgment. The Particular
Judgment says of a certain class that some of its members have
a certain Universal. This leaves it possible that some have not
got it[1]. Thus of every member of the class we assert that it
may or may not have it. But this is not the whole truth.
For the truth about certain members of the class is that they
do have it. And the truth about certain members of the class
may be that they do *not* have it. Thus assertions of actual
possession or non-possession must be true about each member,
while all that the Particular Judgment gives us about each
member is an assertion of possible possession.

Now we cannot take them one by one, and, pointing to each
in turn, say that *A* has it, *B* has it not, and so on. For then
we should have got back to predicating Universals directly of
Individuals, and this has already been decided to be in-
admissible. Since the Individuals of the subject, then, are not
to be taken individually, they must be united by a Universal—
there is no other way. And it will not be sufficient to unite
them by a Universal which covers other Individuals besides
them, since this will give only a Particular Judgment. There
is only one course left. We must group our Individuals by
means of a Subject-Universal which just covers them, so that
we can say that wherever the Subject-Universal is found the
Predicate-Universal will be found too. In other words, we
must be able to make general propositions, and say "all *X* are
Z." It is not necessary, indeed, that all *Z* should also be *X*.

---

[1] If we take the Particular Judgment as Hegel does himself (*G. L.* iii. 95,
loc. cit.) this is not only possible, but necessary. The rest of the argument
would be unchanged.

The position may be that all Z are either X or W, and that all X, and likewise all W, are Z. But every individual which is Z must have some other Universal, which Universal is never found in any case without Z.

(c) The Universal Judgment.

203. (*G. L.* iii. 96. *Enc.* 175.) The advance which is made in this category is evident and striking. Here, for the first time, we become entitled to assert general propositions, other than the general propositions which make up the Logic itself. That is to say, for the first time science becomes possible. However certain it might be that nothing happened without a cause, and that everything was in relations of reciprocal causality with everything else, this would not be sufficient for science. Unless the results of that determination could be expressed in general propositions, so that we could say that some Universals are always or never found in conjunction with others, it would be impossible to classify, to predict, or to explain.

This is the point at which scepticism of a certain type stops. It will admit that there really are Universals shared by more than one Individual, but it denies that there really are any general laws connecting one Universal with another. It does not merely assert that many general laws which we at present accept may possibly be erroneous, which no one could, in the present imperfect state of our knowledge, reasonably deny. It asserts that there are no true general laws at all, known or unknown, and that all inferences are erroneous which conclude the presence or absence of one Universal in an Individual from the presence or absence of another Universal.

Hegel's answer would be that there must be true general propositions, as this is the only way in which the contradiction which appears in the Particular Judgment can be removed. Let us recapitulate. The Individuals of which a certain Universal is predicated must be either isolated or connected. If they are connected, it can only be by a second Universal introduced into the subject. And this Subject-Universal may either include other Individuals, of which the Predicate-

Universal is not true, or it may include only those of which the Predicate-Universal is true.   We have thus three cases. The first gives the Singular Judgment.   The second gives the Particular Judgment.   We have seen that both of these, when taken as categories, involve contradictions, and must therefore be transcended.   There remains only the third alternative, and this gives us Universal Judgments.

In thus transcending the categories of Singular and Particular Judgments we do not assert that no Singular or Particular Judgments are true.   It may be quite true to say "this is red," or "some roses are red."   What we have gained in this triad is the knowledge that "this" (whatever it may be) could not be red unless it possessed some other Universal, which is never found except where redness is found also. And the same will be true of each individual rose which is, in fact, red.

The whole force of the argument for this category rests, of course, on Hegel's view that there is a contradiction in the category of Positive Judgment.   Without that we could never have proceeded to Negative Judgment, or passed over to Subsumption.   I have endeavoured to show that Hegel was not justified in rejecting Positive Judgment for the reasons given by him.   In that case we must pronounce the transition to Universal Judgment unsound, without raising the question whether, if the contradiction in Positive Judgment could have been justified, Hegel could finally have transcended it by the course which he has taken.

It is possible that the gap which this leaves in the dialectic process could be supplied.   For example, it might be the case that a consideration of what is involved in the complete reciprocal determination established at the end of Essence might lead us by a shorter path to the validity of the category of Universal Judgment.   But an attempt to consider this question would take us too far from Hegel to permit its introduction here.

We now leave the direct consideration of the Individual for the present, since our Judgment has become a relation between Universals.   This will develope a certain one-sidedness which will be counterbalanced in Objectivity.

C. *The Judgment of Necessity.*

204. (*G. L.* iii. 101. *Enc.* 177.) It is to be noticed that the Necessity is not in the connexion of Universals, but in the determination of Individuals under them. The truth about the universe is now taken as expressed in Judgments of the type "all X are Z." This Judgment is not held as necessary, for there is nothing given as yet to necessitate it. But what is now necessary is the determination of the Individual. Of any Individual which is X it can be said, not only that it is Z, but that, since it is X, it must be Z. And here we get the conception of Necessity.

(a) *The Categorical Judgment.*

205. (*G. L.* iii. 101. *Enc.* 177.) This, as is to be expected, is a restatement of the Universal Judgment. When, in the Universal Judgment, we found that all X were Z, that could not mean only that, in point of fact, each Individual which was X was also Z. For then the Universal Judgment would only be the abbreviated expression of a series of Singular Judgments, and could not, therefore, transcend the defects of Singular Judgments. The Universal Judgment must mean that the presence of the one Universal *involves* the presence of the other. And the only difference which we find when we pass to the Categorical Judgment is that the assertion of the connexion between the Universals is rather more explicit. This is marked by discarding the form of Subsumption which was still left in the Universal Judgment. Instead of saying "all lions are mammals," we now say "the lion is a mammal."

Hegel tells us here, as he did before with Judgments of Subsumption, that this form is only appropriate to certain Universals. "The rose is a plant" is a legitimate Categorical Judgment, but not "the rose is red" (*G. L.* iii. 102). Presumably the Universals appropriate to Judgments of Reflection, such as transitory or useful, would also be inappropriate here. He does not in any way define the class of Universals appropriate to Judgments of Necessity. The examples he gives are "the rose is a plant," "this ring is gold," and (in the *Encyclopaedia*) "gold is a metal."

It seems to me that this view, like the corresponding view in Judgments of Subsumption, is unjustifiable. If Hegel regards the change as first introduced in the passage from Universal to Categorical Judgments, which his words seem to suggest, this is inconsistent with the fact that he does not treat this passage as involving any advance in the dialectic, but merely as a restatement. If, on the other hand, he regards it as first introduced in the transition from Particular to Universal Judgments, he does not give any reason why this change should accompany the change from Particularity to Universality. He does show why we cannot be satisfied with a category of Particularity and why we must proceed to Universality, but he gives no indication of any necessity for changing, at the same time, the class of predicates employed.

And, again, when we come to the Syllogism of Determinate Being, we find that any restriction on the character of Universals has disappeared, though it is difficult to imagine—and we find nothing in Hegel to help us—how such a restriction, when once made, could again be removed. On all these grounds I think that the limitation to a special class of Universals must be rejected.

206. Hegel now proceeds to

(b) The Hypothetical Judgment.

(*G. L.* iii. 103. *Enc.* 177.) If by this category had been meant, as would naturally have been supposed, a view of existence which could be expressed in the form "if anything is X, then it is Z," there would have been no difficulty. It is clear that if the lion is a mammal, then, if anything is a lion, it is a mammal. The Categorical Judgment involves the Hypothetical. The only possible criticism would be that the Hypothetical Judgment is a mere restatement of the Categorical, and that this relation, though appropriate between a Synthesis and a new Thesis, is out of place between a Thesis and an Antithesis in the same triad.

But this is not the Hypothetical Judgment which Hegel has in view. His example, both in the *Greater Logic* and in the *Encyclopaedia*, is, "if A is, B is." He expands this in the

Greater Logic, "the Being of A is not its own Being, but the Being of another, of B."

Here, again, Hegel seems to me quite unjustified in his procedure. The whole of Subjectivity is devoted to determining the nature of Individuals by means of Universals. This is what was being done in Categorical Judgment. It is what is done again, in the next category, in Disjunctive Judgment. Is it possible that between these there should be inserted a category which determines, not the nature, but the existence, of an Individual, and which determines it, not by Universals, but by another Individual? It would at any rate require a very clear deduction of the necessity of such a category before we could accept it. Now all that Hegel says is "the Categorical Judgment corresponds for the first time to its objective universality by this necessity of its immediate being, and in this way passes over to the Hypothetical Judgment" (*G. L.* iii. 103). This might serve to explain the transition from "the X is Y" to "if anything is X, it is Y," where X and Y are both Universals. It entirely fails to justify the transition from "the X is Y" to "if A is, B is," where A and B are Individuals. Nor would the return from Individuals to Universals at the transition into the Disjunctive Judgment be any more intelligible (cp. *G. L.* iii. 105). The category must then, in my opinion, be rejected.

(c) *The Disjunctive Judgment.*

207. (*G. L.* iii. 105. *Enc.* 177.) Although Hegel's transition from Categorical to Disjunctive Judgments thus breaks down, we can see that a transition from Categorical to Disjunctive Judgments is necessary.

We know that there are cases in which it is true that all X are Z, while it is false that all Z are X. The proof of this is as follows. Any two Individuals, as we have seen, will have some Universals in common, and each of them will have some Universals which the other has not. Let us take Z as standing for a Universal common to some two Individuals, and Q and R as two Universals each of which belongs to one of them only. The first Individual will be ZQ, and the second ZR. Now as any predication of Universals of any Individual can only be made by means of a Universal Judgment, there must be some

X such that all X will be ZQ.   Then all X will be Z, but all Z will not be X.   For all X are Q, and all Z are not Q, since there is the class ZR, of which our second Individual was an example.

We know, therefore, that in some of our Universal (or Categorical) Judgments the predicate will be wider than the subject.   All X will be Z, but there are some Z which are not X. Now these Individuals, which are not X, cannot be Z as simply isolated Individuals.   This, according to Hegel, was proved when we transcended Positive Judgments.   Each of these Individuals must have some Universal, with which Z is connected by means of another Categorical Judgment.   How many of them there may be we do not know, but we do know that every Individual which has Z, must have one of them.   Thus we arrive at the conclusion that all Z is either X, or W, or V, where W and V represent an unknown number of Universals.

Of course this does not exclude the possibility that in some cases the connexion of the Universals is reciprocal, so that not only all X is Z, but all Z is X.   This cannot, for the reasons just given, be true in all cases, but it can in some.   Thus we may say that the category before us asserts that for every Universal Z there may be found a group of Universals, X, W, V, such that whatever is X, W, or V is Z, and that whatever is Z is either X, W, or V, and asserts further that in some cases the group X, W, V, may contain only a single Universal, but that it is impossible that this should be so in all cases.

The necessity of passing from Categorical Judgment to Disjunctive Judgment applies, of course, to the nature of existence and not to our knowledge about it.   If Categorical Judgments are true of existence, then Disjunctive Judgments are true of existence.   But if our knowledge enables us to make a Categorical Judgment on any subject, it by no means follows that it will enable us to make the corresponding Disjunctive. I may know that the lion is a mammal, without knowing the complete list of species, to one of which every mammal must belong.   In the same way a Positive Judgment can be known without knowing the corresponding Universal.   I may know that this Individual is red, without being able to determine what Universal it possesses, the possession of which involves redness, though, if Hegel is right, such a Universal must exist.

208. The two sides of the Judgment are now, according to Hegel, "identical" (*G. L.* iii. 110). By this he means that they have the same denotation. Every *Z* is either *X* or *W* or *V*, while all *X*, all *W*, and all *V* are *Z*. Thus the denotation of *Z* is the same as the denotations of *X*, *W*, and *V* added together. "This Unity," he continues, "the Copula of this Judgment, in which the extremes have come together through their identity, is thereby the Notion itself, and, moreover, the Notion as posited; the mere Judgment of Necessity has thus raised itself to the Judgment of the Notion."

D. *The Judgment of the Notion.*

209. (*G. L.* iii. 110. *Enc.* 178.) This transition appears to relate exclusively to the relation of the Subject with the Predicate. But here, as with Judgments of Subsumption and Judgments of Necessity, Hegel introduces, along with this distinction, the further distinction that only a special sort of Predicates are appropriate for Judgments of this form. The examples he gives are good, bad, true, beautiful and correct. All these, as he remarks, have reference to some ideal (ein Sollen). But he establishes no connexion between these Predicates on the one hand, and, on the other, the closer relation between Subject and Predicate which formed the transition to Judgments of the Notion. Nor is there any connexion between the use of such Predicates, and the three subdivisions of Judgments of the Notion, of which the first is

(a) *The Assertoric Judgment.*

(*G. L.* iii. 112. *Enc.* 178.) The example given of this is "this deed is good." This does not appear to differ from a Categorical Judgment, except in the sort of Predicate used. But the Assertoric Judgment does differ from the Categorical Judgment in another characteristic, though this characteristic does not seem to have any relation to the closer connexion of Subject and Predicate which was given in the passage quoted above as the characteristic of Judgments of the Notion.

The new difference concerns, not what is asserted, but the

justification which he who asserts it possesses for his assertion. "Its proof is a subjective assurance" (*G. L.* iii. 113).

210. And this gives the transition to the next category, for, as Hegel goes on to remark, "over against the assurance of the Assertoric Judgment there stands with equal right the assurance of its opposite." If the only ground for believing this deed to be good is that the assertion is made, then we are plunged in doubt. For it is equally possible to make the assertion that this deed is not good, and one assertion is as good as another. This doubt takes us to (*G. L.* iii. 114. *Enc.* 178)

(b)   *The Problematic Judgment.*

211. Hegel does not give any reason why we must pass from this category to the next. He merely gives the transition without justifying it. Instead of simply saying "the deed is good," we must say "the deed of such and such a nature is good." Here the nature of the deed is, in effect, given as a reason why we should accept the Judgment that it is good rather than the Judgment that it is not good. This is

(c)   *The Apodictic Judgment.*

(*G. L.* iii. 116. *Enc.* 178.) The characteristic of the Subject, thus given as the reason why the Subject should have the Predicate, is said by Hegel to be the Copula of the Judgment become "completed or full of content (erfüllte oder inhaltsvolle); the unity of the Notion again restored out of the Judgment, in the extremes of which it was lost." From this Hegel makes his transition to Syllogism.

212. Is this triad of the Judgment of the Notion valid? I believe that it is not, and that the transition ought to go direct from Disjunctive Judgment to Syllogism. In support of this I would urge four considerations.

In the first place, grave suspicion is thrown upon the triad by the fact that, if it is accepted, it gives Judgment as a whole four subdivisions instead of the three which are essential to Hegel's method. The excuse which he gives for this is that of the "three chief kinds of Judgment parallel to the stages of Being, Essence, and Notion," the second "as required by the character of Essence, which is the stage of differentiation, must be doubled" (*Enc.* 171). This however cannot be accepted as a justification for Judgment having four subdivisions, when other stages have only three. For, throughout the whole dialectic, the second subdivision of the three in each stage always corresponds to Essence, and, if this involved dividing it into two, four subdivisions would be the invariable rule, and not the exception.

The second difficulty is still more serious. The Assertoric, Problematic, and Apodictic Judgments are distinguished from one another, and from those which precede them, not by any distinction in the propositions asserted, but by distinctions as to the characteristics of mental states of those who assert the propositions. An Assertoric Judgment is one believed firmly, but without a reason. A Problematic Judgment is one which is regarded as possibly, but not certainly, true. An Apodictic Judgment is one which is believed firmly, with a reason for believing it.

Hegel, indeed, denies (*G. L.* iii. 111) that these categories are thus subjective. But he does not explain what other meaning they can have, and when he comes to treat them in detail, as we have already seen, his treatment is inexplicable except on the hypothesis that they have this meaning.

For the Assertoric Judgment clearly differs from those which go before it in something else besides the sort of Predicates applicable. This is evident both from the transition to it, and from its name. And if this new feature is not " our subjective assurance" of it, why does Hegel, on p. 113, give that account of it? And what else could that new feature be? And how, if it were not a question of beliefs rather than propositions, could two be opposed to one another with equal right, as Hegel in the transition to Problematic Judgments asserts that they are?

So, too, with the Problematic Judgment. This arises because two incompatible Assertoric Judgments about the same Subject are held with equal right. Now this cannot possibly produce any new Judgment about the Subject, but may very well produce a doubt and uncertainty about each of them. It seems impossible to deduce anything else here, and this makes the distinction relate entirely to the way in which we believe the truth. And the name clearly indicates the same fact. Problematic means doubtful, and no proposition is doubtful except in relation to the knowledge of some particular knower. I may be doubtful whether *A* is *B*, but *A* cannot be doubtfully *B*. It is *B* or it is not.

The same is, I think, the case with the Apodictic Judgment. The examples Hegel gives are not decisive. The nature of the deed might be given either as the reason why it was good, or as the reason why I believed it to be good. But it seems clear to me that Hegel regarded the Apodictic Judgment as differing from the Assertoric and Problematic in the same manner in which the Assertoric and Problematic differ from one another. In that case the Apodictic Judgment is also a category which applies to beliefs only, and not to all realities, and the reason given in it is not the reason of the fact believed, but the reason of the belief.

If Hegel has introduced either two or three categories of this sort here, his treatment is clearly invalid. The whole argument of the dialectic rests on the supposition that all the categories are applicable to the same subject-matter—namely all existent reality. Again, the Disjunctive Judgment clearly applied to all existence, and not merely to beliefs. How could we deduce from it a new category which applies merely to beliefs ? It seems impossible to conceive how such a deduction could be justified, and certainly Hegel does not attempt to justify it. And, in the same way, how could he be justified in passing back, from categories which deal merely with beliefs, to categories which deal with all existence? And, by the time he reaches Syllogism he has certainly done this.

213. In the third place, the transition to the Judgment of the Notion seems to me erroneous. It is no doubt the case, as was said above, that Judgments made according to Hegel's category of Disjunctive Judgment have the same denotation for their Subjects and their Predicates. But I cannot see how this would enable us to pass to the Judgment of the Notion, where the denotations are not identical, though the connotations are said to be more closely connected. Nor can I see why Assertoric, Problematic, and Apodictic Judgments should be

the subdivisions of Judgment of the Notion, defined as Hegel
has defined it.

In the fourth place the Judgment of the Notion can be
removed without destroying the continuity of the dialectic.
For it is not difficult to see that Syllogism necessarily follows
from Disjunctive Judgment. Syllogism starts, as we shall see,
with the position that it is necessary to give some reason why
the two Universals in a general proposition are connected with
one another. Now this necessity will be seen so soon as we find
that two Universals are connected in such a way—that is, in
the Categorical Judgment. In the Disjunctive Judgment the
question becomes more pressing, since the alternative nature
of the connexion renders it more obvious that we must face the
problem. Z is in some cases X, in some cases W, and in some
cases V. Why, in each case, is it the one and not the other?
Thus Syllogism could follow directly from Disjunctive Judgment.
For these four reasons I think that the Judgment of the Notion
must be rejected.

214. We now pass to

III. THE SYLLOGISM.

(*G. L.* iii. 118. *Enc.* 181.) The essential characteristic
here is the mediation of the connexion between two Universals.
The connexion, in the first place, is made by what was, in
Apodictic Judgment, the reason (cp. above, Section 211).
This is based on another Universal. The reason that the deed
was good was that its nature had a certain characteristic, and
such a characteristic is expressed by a Universal. Thus mediation is by a third Universal, which gives us

A. *The Qualitative Syllogism.*

(*G. L.* iii. 121. *Enc.* 183.) This is again divided by Hegel,
the subdivisions being named after the Figures of formal logic.
We shall have to consider later whether this is valid, but there
is at any rate no doubt that, if we are to have these divisions,
we must begin with the First Figure. For the linking of
Universals gives Universal Propositions, some of which are
Affirmative. And Universal Affirmative Propositions can only
be proved by the First Figure.

(a)   First Figure.

(*G. L.* iii. 122.   *Enc.* 183.)   Hegel says that this category can be expressed as I P U.   The Subject of the conclusion, that is, is an Individual, the Predicate of the conclusion is a Universal, and the Middle Term is a Particular.

This seems unjustifiable.   The distinction between Particular and Universal Notions at the beginning of Subjectivity (cp. above, Section 190) does not apply to the Middle and Major terms of a Syllogism of the First Figure, and if Hegel means anything else here by Universal and Particular, he does not tell us what it is.

Nor has he, I think, any right to bring in the Individual here.   In the Categorical Judgment the result reached was a connexion of two Universals.   In several places between that and the present stage Hegel speaks as if the Subject of the Judgment might or must be an Individual, but he never expressly acknowledges this transition, or attempts to justify it.   We have no right here to deal with any connexion except that between Universals.

Nor does the formal logic, of whose Figures he has availed himself to provide names for his categories, offer any excuse for the introduction of the Individual.   For the Individual is not recognised by formal logic, which treats "Caesar is mortal" as a proposition of exactly the same type as "all Bishops are mortal."

215.   How is the inadequacy of the First Figure proved? Hegel makes two objections to its validity.   The first is as follows.   The Subject has many characteristics which may be used as Middle Terms, and each Middle Term, again, can connect it with many Major Terms.   Thus it is "contingent and capricious" (zufällig und willkürlich) with what Major Term the Subject will be connected, and also what Predicate will be given it in the conclusion (*G. L.* iii. 127. *Enc.* 184).

This is quite true.   All Cambridge Doctors of Divinity are Anglican clergymen, and are graduates of the University. From the first of these, as a Middle Term, we can conclude either that they have been ordained, or that they are incapable of sitting in Parliament. From the second we can conclude, either that the Graces for their degrees passed the Senate, or that they were presented for their degrees by a member of the University. All four conclusions are true, but it is quite contingent and capricious which we shall take. There is nothing in the idea of the Subject "all Cambridge Doctors of Divinity" to decide which we shall prefer to the others.

But how does this produce a contradiction? The Subject is united, by two Middle Terms, to four Predicates. But why should this not be the case? If, indeed, we had to choose one in preference to others, a difficulty would arise, for no ground of preference is given. But there is no necessity to choose. For all these Judgments can be true of the Subject together.

The defect which Hegel thinks that he has found here is like the defect which he says constitutes the inadequacy of the category of Variety (cp. above, Section 116). But while it was a defect there, it is not one here. There the whole point of the category was to range things by their Likeness or Unlikeness to one another. And no such arrangement was possible, if everything was connected with everything else both by Likeness and Unlikeness.

Here it is different. No doubt it is the case that Individuals, or classes of Individuals, are Like or Unlike one another, by reason of the Universals which can be predicated of them. But the point here is not arrangement simply as Like or Unlike, but arrangement as sharing or not sharing certain Universals. Thus arrangement is possible though each Individual or class should be Like or Unlike every other, because it would be in virtue of different Universals.

There is thus no necessity to take one grouping rather than another, because the different groupings are now compatible, which was not the case in the category of Variety. And thus the fact that the preference of one grouping to another would be "contingent and capricious" while it is a valid objection to the category of Variety, is not a valid objection here.

Hegel asserts (*G. L.* iii. 127) that this contingency involves that contradictory Predicates must be held true of the same Subject. He bases this on the statement that "Difference, which is in the first place indifferent Variety, is just as

essentially Opposition (Entgegensetzung)." But he makes
no attempt to prove that the two different Predicates must
necessarily be incompatible Predicates, which is what his
sentence must mean if it is to bear out his assertion.   And
his examples (*G. L.* iii. 128) do not help him. The first which
he gives—the rest are substantially similar—is " If from the
Middle Term that a stick was painted blue, it is concluded that
it therefore *is* blue, this is concluded correctly ; but the stick,
in spite of this conclusion, can be green, if it has also been
covered over with yellow paint, from which last circumstance,
taken by itself, would result that it was yellow."

It is true that a stick cannot at once be blue and green.
But the first conclusion—that it is blue—could only be reached
from the Minor Premise which Hegel gives, "this stick has
been painted blue," by the help of the Major Premise "whatever has ever been painted blue is now blue." And this Major
Premise is notoriously false, so that one of the contradictory
conclusions has not been proved. In each of the other examples
he gives the same fallacy is present. The contradictory conclusions do not follow legitimately from the diverse premises,
but only follow by the aid of other premises which are false.

216. But Hegel also gives another objection to this category,
and this, I think, must be accepted as valid. We reached the
category by taking the position that two Universals which are
connected with one another must have their connexion mediated
by a third.   But the third Universal, being connected with the
first and the second, will, on the same principle, require a fourth
and a fifth Universal to mediate these connexions. The four
connexions so established will require four fresh Universals,
and so on infinitely (*G. L.* iii. 130.   *Enc.* 185).

The Infinite Series thus established will involve a contradiction, for the earlier members are logically dependent on the
later, as no Universal can mediate till it is connected with the
Universals it mediates, and, to be connected, it must itself be
mediated by Universals given in later members. Thus Hegel
rejects the category, on this second ground also, as invalid.

217.   Hegel considers that these defects require the alteration of the Middle Term. The Individual is now become the
Middle Term, and the Syllogism will no longer be represented

by I P U, but by P I U. And in this he finds a transition to what he calls

(b) Second Figure.

(*G. L.* iii. 132. *Enc.* 186.) By this, however, he means, as he explains in the *Greater Logic* (iii. 135), what is generally called the Third Figure. (In the *Encyclopaedia* he also uses the name in this unusual sense, without any warning that he has departed from the common custom.)

The defect here, according to Hegel (*G. L.* iii. 134), is that the new form "ought to correspond to the Species, that is, the Universal Schema, I P U. But to this it does not correspond... the Middle Term is on both occasions Subject, in which therefore the other two terms inhere." The fault is thus in the position of the Middle Term—the same characteristic which, as we see in formal logic, prevents a Syllogism in this Figure from having any but a Particular conclusion.

218. Hegel then tells us that "the Individuality connects the Particular and the Universal in so far as it transcends the determination of the Particular;...the extremes are not connected through their determined relation which they had as Middle Term; it is therefore not their determined unity, and the positive unity, which it still has, is only abstract Universality" (*G. L.* iii. 136). The Middle Term is thus U, and the new form of the Syllogism is I U P. This, according to Hegel, gives us

(c) Third Figure.

(*G. L.* iii. 137. *Enc.* 187.) This is what is usually called the Second Figure. This leads only to negative conclusions. Hegel mentions this (*G. L.* iii. 138), but does not regard it as the ground of the inadequacy of the category. The inadequacy lies in the fact that the Universal, which is the Middle Term, has no inherent connexion with either of the extremes, and would have to be connected with them by a fresh process, independent of the original Syllogism. All this, he says, is just as contingent as in the preceding forms of the Syllogism.

(d) Fourth Figure.

219. (*G. L.* iii. 139. *Enc.* 188.) This is not the Fourth Figure of formal logic, which he rejects as useless (*G. L.* iii. 138.

Enc. 187). What he substitutes for it is what he calls the Mathematical Syllogism, of which, he tells us, the formula is U U U. Its principle, he also tells us, is "if two things are equal to a third, they are equal to one another." The three equal things are apparently taken as the three terms.

The relation between the three things in question, however, is by no means the relation between the terms of a Syllogism. The third thing, whose equality to each of the others is the basis of the argument, may be said to mediate between them, but not in the same way as the Middle Term of a Syllogism does. And if we were to take this Fourth Figure seriously, there would be the additional difficulty that it would disregard the triadic movement of the dialectic.

Hegel, however, does not take it seriously. The Fourth Figure is not a legitimate and necessary stage in the dialectic process. It is only the result which would be reached if we took the wrong track. This seems clear from the following passage. "The merely negative result is the disappearance of qualitative determinations of form in mere quantitative and mathematical Syllogisms. But what we really get (was wahrhaft vorhanden ist) is the positive result, that the mediation does not take place through an individual qualitative determination of form, but through the concrete identity" of the extremes. "The defect and the formalism of the three Figures of the Syllogism consists just in this that such an individual determination had to serve as their Middle Term. The mediation has thus determined itself as the indifference of immediate or abstract determinations of form, and as positive Reflection of the one into the other. The immediate Qualitative Syllogism is thus transferred into the Syllogism of Reflection" (*G. L.* iii. 141). Thus the real movement of the dialectic is from the Third Figure to the Syllogism of Reflection. Under these circumstances it seems curious that Hegel should have given the Fourth Figure as a separate heading, as if it were a real category.

220. I have given the transitions from each Figure to the next without criticising the validity of each transition taken by itself, because I believe that the argument is invalid as a whole. The Second and Third Figures appear to me to be unjustified.

What Hegel calls the First Figure should, in my opinion, be the whole of an undivided category of Qualitative Syllogism, and from this the transition should be made directly to Syllogism of Reflection.

Hegel gave, as we saw above, two objections to the validity of the First Figure. The first was the contingency of the Middle Term relatively to the Subject, and of the Predicate relatively to the Middle Term. The second was the infinite series of mediations which would be required. The first objection, as I endeavoured to show, was unfounded. If this is really the case, then any valid transition to the Second Figure must be determined by the second objection.

Now this is not what happens. The Second and Third Figures do not even profess to remove this defect, or to alter it in any way. The infinite series of mediations would arise in them just as inevitably, and exactly in the same way, as in the First Figure. The transition, therefore, is invalid.

And not only do the Second and Third Figures fail to remove the defects of the First, but they reintroduce defects which had been long ago transcended. For the (Hegelian) Second Figure can only prove Particular conclusions, and the (Hegelian) Third Figure can only prove Negative conclusions, and we saw, when we treated of Judgments of Inherence and Subsumption, that no category could be possible according to which only Negative, or only Particular, propositions were true. These categories therefore, so far from being more adequate than the First Figure, are less adequate.

Hegel seems more or less to realise this when he condemns the Second Figure on the ground that it does not, as it should do, "correspond to the Species, that is, the universal Schema, I P U" (*G. L.* iii. 134; cp. above, Section 217). For I P U is, according to Hegel, the Schema of the First Figure. But if the Second Figure is wrong because it is not the First, how can it take its place in the dialectic series as the successor of the First?

I have not thought it necessary to consider whether Hegel was right in appropriating the Schema P I U to his Second Figure, and I U P to his Third Figure. The enquiry is superfluous if, as I have tried to show, the Second and Third

Figures have no rightful place in the dialectic at all. And again any enquiry as to the particular appropriation is superfluous, if, as I have also tried to show (cp. above, Section 214) Hegel was wrong in introducing the conceptions of Individual and Particular *terms* into any of the Figures of Qualitative Syllogism.

221. The omission of the Second and Third Figures will not leave any gap in the dialectic process. For we can pass quite legitimately from the First Figure to the Syllogism of Reflection. If every connexion of Universals must be mediated by a Universal, we are involved in a contradictory infinite series. But this might be averted if Universals were mediated by something else, for perhaps the connexions of this something else with a Universal might not again require mediation. What else could mediate the connexion of Universals, except Universals? There is nothing left but Individuals[1]. We have seen above (Section 202) that it is impossible that the Universal Judgment should be *equivalent to* a series of Judgments about mere Individuals. We have now to consider whether the Universal Judgment can be *based on* such a series of Judgments. This would take us direct to Hegel's Syllogism of Reflection from his First Figure.

222. On all these grounds, therefore, I think the Second and Third Figures should be rejected. We now arrive, whether by the argument just given, or by Hegel's argument quoted above, at

B.   The Syllogism of Reflection.

(a)   The Syllogism of Allness.

(*G. L.* iii. 149. *Enc.* 190.) In this category the fact that all Z are X is held to be dependent on the facts that this, that, and the other things which are Z are also in point of fact X. "This, that, and the other" here include *all* the things which are Z. Since each of them individually is X, it is certain that all Z are X. If the House of Lords has a gallery for strangers, and the House of Commons has a gallery for strangers, then all houses of the British Parliament have galleries for strangers.

---

[1] It will be remembered that both the Universal Notion and the Particular Notion of the beginning of Subjectivity have, since the beginning of Judgment, been classed together as Universals (cp. above, Section 192).

This category corresponds to the logical process called Perfect Induction, and not to any form of Syllogism. Hegel, however, speaks of a Syllogism of Allness. His example is " all men are mortal, Caius is a man, therefore Caius is mortal." This differs, according to him, from the ordinary Syllogism of the First Figure, because the Major Premise is reached by a complete enumeration of Individuals—though, of course, in the example he has taken, this could not be the case.

It seems to me, however, that Hegel is wrong here. No doubt we can use the result of the Perfect Induction as the Premise of a Syllogism. But what corresponds to the Syllogism of previous categories is not the Syllogism which Hegel gives here, but the proposition he takes as Major Premise. In Qualitative Syllogism two Universals were mediated by a third Universal, and this mediation made the Syllogism. Here two Universals are mediated by an enumeration of Individuals, and it is the proposition thus reached which corresponds to the Syllogism in Qualitative Syllogism. The change is that while in Qualitative Syllogism we reach the conclusion " all men are mortal" by some such argument as " all men are animals, and all animals are mortal," here we should reach it by an enumeration of Individuals. What was done before by Syllogism is not now done by Syllogism but by enumeration, and thus the name of Syllogism here is incorrect.

223. Hegel's objection to this Syllogism (*G. L.* iii. 151. *Enc.* 190) is that the conclusion presupposes the Major Premise. We could not know, in this way, that all men were mortal, unless, among others, we knew that Caius was mortal. Thus we cannot prove the mortality of Caius from the mortality of all men. This is, no doubt, correct, but, as was said above, the category is exemplified in the assertion that all men are mortal, not in the assertion that Caius is mortal, and the objection is therefore irrelevant.

Hegel now proceeds to

(b) *The Syllogism of Induction.*

(*G. L.* iii. 152. *Enc.* 190.) Here we have a category which corresponds to ordinary Induction. The connexion between the two Universals is mediated by the fact that they do occur

together in *some* of the Individuals included in the denotation
of the Subject.   We conclude that all men are mortal, because
it is so as a matter of fact in those cases which we have
examined.

The transition to this category is not brought out very
clearly by Hegel, but we can see that it will remove the defect
which he found in the last.   When we have established by
induction that all men are mortal, we may conclude that Caius
is mortal without necessarily arguing in a circle.   For Caius
may not have been one of the men on whose mortality we
founded the general statement.   He may, for example, be still
alive.

The defect which Hegel finds in this category is that our
enumeration of the Individuals can never be complete.   (*G. L.*
iii. 154.   *Enc.* 190.)   It is not at first evident why we should
wish to have it complete, since then we should get back to the
previous category, which has already been abandoned as inadequate.   But as he ends his criticism with the words " the
conclusion of Induction remains problematic " he appears to
have in his mind the fact that no general conclusion arrived at
by Induction can be more than probable, and that therefore we
can never, by means of such a conclusion, arrive at absolute
certainty as to any Individual.   The only Individuals as to
whom we can be certain are those whose natures formed the
basis of our Induction.   And these are not the whole number.

224.   The defect of Induction compels us, according to
Hegel, to pass to

(c)   *The Syllogism of Analogy.*

(*G. L.* iii. 155.   *Enc.* 190.)   The example which he gives of
this is " the earth has inhabitants, the moon is an earth, therefore the moon has inhabitants."   If we remove the ambiguity
in the use of earth, it might be put as follows : " the planet on
which we live is an earth, and is inhabited ; the moon is an
earth, therefore it is inhabited."   This is an Induction, based
on a single instance.   It does not seem, however, that the fact
that there is only a single instance, is essential to the category.
Hegel says (*G. L.* iii. 157) that earth is taken here " as something concrete, which in its truth is just as much a universal

nature or species, as it is an individual"; and he continues that the category breaks down because we cannot tell whether the first Individual has the second quality because it has the first quality, or for some other reason. We cannot, *e.g.*, be sure whether it is because it is an earth, or for some other reason, that this planet is inhabited. If it were for some other reason, we could not be sure that the moon shared the quality of being inhabited.

It seems, therefore, that Analogy is Induction made explicit. When, in Induction, we conclude that, since A, B, C, etc. are all both X and Y, therefore all things which are X are Y, we also implicitly conclude that there is some intrinsic connexion, direct or indirect, between X and Y. If there is no such intrinsic connexion, our conclusion would be illegitimate. And this connexion between the qualities X and Y is made explicit in Analogy. It is the impossibility of being certain of that connexion, as has just been pointed out, which wrecks Analogy. And it is this impossibility, also, which prevented us from ever reaching an absolutely certain Induction.

225. From this category Hegel passes to the Syllogism of Necessity as follows: "The Syllogism of Reflection, taken as a whole, comes under the Schema P I U : in it the Individual as such still forms the essential determination of the Middle Term; but in so far as its immediacy has transcended itself, and the Middle Term is determined as Universality in and for itself, in so far the Syllogism has come under the formal Schema I U P, and the Syllogism of Reflection has passed over into the Syllogism of Necessity" (*G. L.* iii. 159).

This transition seems to me unconvincing. It is true that there is a certain appropriateness in calling the Middle Term of the explicit Induction of Analogy by the name of Universal. And the nature of the Middle Term of the new category is also such as to give some appropriateness to the description of it as Universal. But in the two cases Universal is used in different senses. It means much more in the Categorical Syllogism, which is the first form of Syllogism of Necessity, than it did in the Syllogism of Analogy.

It is natural that it should do this. For the Categorical Syllogism is not, as we should expect from its position, a mere restatement of the Syllogism of Analogy after a collapse into Immediacy. The Syllogism of Analogy has, according to Hegel, broken down, and the transition to the Syllogism of Necessity removes a contradiction. The new category must be an advance, then, and not a mere restatement, and it is an advance, for it contains, as we shall see, an entirely new conception.

If this is the case, Hegel's account of the transition must be wrong, for he speaks as if the Universality of the Middle Term in Analogy had already brought us to the Syllogism of Necessity, and as if, therefore, there was no real advance.

226. The criticism which I venture to suggest on the triad of Syllogism of Reflection is that, here as in the Qualitative Syllogism, the subdivisions are unjustified. The conception which Hegel treats, under the Syllogism of Allness should have been the sole content of an undivided Syllogism of Reflection. No doubt Induction and Analogy, as processes of acquiring knowledge, are quite different from so-called Perfect Induction. But categories are descriptions of reality and not processes of acquiring knowledge, and I cannot see that any separate description of reality corresponds to these processes.

The category which we reached in the Syllogism of Allness asserted that the validity of Universal Judgments depends on the fact that every Individual, which possesses the Subject-Universal, possesses, as a matter of fact, the Predicate-Universal also. We have seen that this category corresponds to the logical process of Perfect Induction. But how shall we find a second category to correspond to the logical process of Induction in the ordinary sense of the word?

The difference between the processes of acquiring knowledge is that in Perfect Induction the conclusion is based on an examination of all the Individuals who possess the Subject-Universal, while in ordinary Induction we examine only some of them. Hegel's category of Induction would thus have to mean that the validity of Universal Judgments depends on the fact that *some* of the Individuals, which possess the Subject-Universal, do, as a matter of fact, possess the Predicate-Universal also.

What could be meant by this dependence on *some* of the

Individuals ? In the case of the Judgment all X are Y, it is clear that it cannot mean that the rest of X (those which are not included in the " some ") are not-Y, since the conclusion is that they are all Y. It could only mean that, while every X was Y, yet some of them were Y in their own right, and exercised some power which caused the other X's to be Y, and so made the general proposition true.

This conception would not be in any way an advance on the Syllogism of Allness, nor would it remove any of the difficulties to which that category was exposed. On the contrary, it would add to them by introducing a new complexity—the difference between the " some " X's and the other X's—which had not been deduced from the previous category, and could not be justified.

The logical process of Induction can give a natural and reasonable meaning to the " some "—namely that though, if the law is true, every X is Y, yet there are only some cases in which this has been ascertained when the Induction is made. But the distinction between known and unknown cases is irrelevant to the metaphysical category.

Thus we must reject the category of Induction. And, if Analogy is only explicit Induction, Analogy must go too. This leaves Allness, as the sole form of the Syllogism of Reflection.

Here, as with the Qualitative Syllogism, the error seems to have arisen from Hegel's attempt to push a parallel too far. There is one category which has a real resemblance to the Syllogism of deductive logic, and another which has a real resemblance to induction as a whole. But the attempt to find categories corresponding to the different figures and the different varieties of induction has led to errors.

And here, as with Qualitative Syllogism, the dialectic process goes all the better for the simplification. The undivided Syllogism of Reflection is the Antithesis of which Qualitative Syllogism was the Thesis. The transition from the one to the other was shown above (Section 221).

And this new Antithesis, we can see, will break down. For we saw, in dealing with Judgments of Inherence and Subsumption, that a Judgment about an Individual could only be

valid when it was dependent upon a Universal Judgment.
Since all Individual Judgments must be based upon Universal
Judgments, it is obviously impossible that all Universal
Judgments should be based upon Individual Judgments.

It thus becomes evident that it is impossible that all
Universal Judgments should be mediated. Whether we
attempt to mediate them by Universals or by Individuals we
have found that insuperable difficulties presented themselves.
Only one alternative remains—to assert that some, at any rate,
among Universal Judgments, do not require mediation. And
this takes us on to Hegel's next category

C. The Syllogism of Necessity.

(a) The Categorical Syllogism.

227. (*G. L.* iii. 161. *Enc.* 191.) The first feature of the
Categorical Syllogism is that the Middle Term is the essential
nature of the Subject of the conclusion, and, in the same way,
the Predicate of the conclusion is the essential nature of the
Middle Term. And thus the contingency disappears, which
arose from the fact that the Subject might be taken as connected
with any one of several Middle Terms, and each Middle Term
as connected with any one of several Predicates (*G. L.* iii. 162).
This contingency, it will be remembered, was treated by Hegel
as a defect of the First Figure. He regards it as finally
removed here, making the assumption that a Term can only
have one " essential nature," so that there is here no alternative
Middle Term for a Subject, and no alternative Predicate for
a Middle Term.

"Since," he continues, " the connections of the extremes
with the Middle Terms have not that external immediacy
which they have in the Qualitative Syllogism, the demand for
a proof does not come in here in the same way as in the
Qualitative Syllogism, where it led to an Infinite Series"
(*G. L.* iii. 162). In this way the second defect of the First
Figure is removed. It is clear, therefore, that Hegel regards
the essential connections of the Categorical Syllogism as being
ultimate connections. They may be used to mediate, but they
do not themselves require mediation.

Here, then, for the first time, Hegel regards the defects of the First Figure as transcended.   And this confirms my view that the subdivisions of Qualitative Syllogism and Syllogism of Reflection are mistaken.   For the special defect of each category should be cured when we reach the next Synthesis. And, by the simplification I propose, Syllogism of Necessity is the next Synthesis after these defects have manifested themselves.

The connexions in the new category are, according to Hegel, "essential," so as to remove the first defect of the First Figure, and ultimate, so as to remove its second defect.   If I was right in my previous contention that the first defect—the contingency—has not been shown to involve the inadequacy of the First Figure, and that the only real necessity for a transition lay in the second defect, we shall have to take a somewhat different view, since the "essentiality" of the connexions will not have been deduced.   We shall only be able to say that the connexions are ultimate—that certain propositions of the form "all X is Y" are true, without any mediation of the connexion being either possible or necessary.

Whatever other characteristic the connexions may have, they are certainly ultimate.   And, therefore, I think Hegel is wrong in calling this category by the name of Syllogism, for reasons analogous to those which made me regard the name of Syllogism as improper when applied to Allness, Induction, and Analogy (cp. above, Section 222).   The categories of Qualitative Syllogism were called by the name of Syllogism because, from the point of view of those categories, every proposition had to be mediated by two others, which were the premises, while it was the conclusion.   Now we have reached a point where we see that all propositions need not be mediated in this way, but that some do not require mediation.   Thus the characteristic which made the name appropriate is gone.   That characteristic was the fact that the truth of every proposition depended on the truth of two others from which it followed logically.

The Syllogism which Hegel gets here is one in which a derivative and mediated conclusion follows from two ultimate premises.   And it is, of course, true that many propositions have a derivative truth of this kind, dependent on the truth of two ultimate propositions. But the essential characteristic of this category—the characteristic which enables it to remove the defects of the First Figure—is not that the ultimate Judgments can mediate, but that they do not themselves require mediation. In other words, the essential characteristic is not that they can be the premises of Syllogisms, but that they need not be the conclusions of Syllogisms. And this logical priority of the ultimate Judgments to Syllogisms, makes the name of Syllogism inappropriate here. A better name for the category, I suggest, would have been Ultimate Laws.

(b) The Hypothetical Syllogism.

228. (*G. L.*°iii. 164. *Enc.* 191.) Hegel's example of this is "if *A* is, *B* is; but *A* is, therefore *B* is." It seems to me that Hegel has erred here in the same way as in the Hypothetical Judgment (cp. above, Section 206). From the ultimate Categorical Judgment "all *A* is *B*," it certainly follows that the ultimate Hypothetical Judgment, "if anything is *A*, it is *B*," is also true, and that this can be made, if we wish to do so, a premise in a Syllogism.

But, as we have just seen, Hegel's Hypothetical Syllogism is not this, but something quite different. And how are we to pass from "all *A* are *B*," where the same Individuals are *A* and *B*, and "are" is only a copula, to "if *A* is, *B* is," where *A* and *B* are different Individuals, and "is" seems to be an assertion of existence? Hegel does not tell us how this can be done—he does not seem indeed to realise the greatness of the difference—and I fail to see how such a transition is to be demonstrated. Nor do I see how we could make the further transition from it to "*A* is either *B*, *C*, or *D*" of the Disjunctive Syllogism, since that takes us back again to the same type of proposition as we found in Categorical Syllogism.

229. The transition to the Disjunctive Syllogism from the Categorical Syllogism is, I think, valid, although it appears to violate the triadic movement by moving directly without an Antithesis. (The valid Hypothetical "if anything is *A*, it is *B*" will scarcely serve as an Antithesis, since it is only a restatement of the Categorical.)

The transition is as follows. We have seen that the nature of Individuals must be based on Universal Judgments. And we also saw (Section 207) that from the fact that every Individual is Like and Unlike every other Individual it follows that some of these Universal Judgments must be such that it is true that all X is Z, when it is false that all Z is X.

If this is the case, it will follow that there are not only true Judgments of this type, but true ultimate Judgments. For we have now reached the conclusion that the whole content of all Judgments must be found in ultimate Judgments. The derivative Judgments only combine what is found in their ultimate premises, and give no new truth. The nature of Individuals is therefore based on ultimate Universal Judgments. And as that nature requires for its expression Judgments that all X is Z, while all Z is not X, there must be true ultimate Judgments of this type.

Those Individuals which are Z without being X must be connected with Z by one or more other Universals, whose connexion with Z is ultimate. And thus we reach the conclusion that the nature of the universe is expressed by Universal Judgments of the type that all Z is X, W, or V, where all X, all W, and all V are Z, and where V and W represent a number of Universals which may vary indefinitely from zero upwards, though we know that in some cases it is greater than zero[1]. Thus we reach

(c)   The Disjunctive Syllogism

(*G. L.* iii. 167.   *Enc.* 191.), for this, as given by Hegel, is a Syllogism of which the Major Premise is one of these Judgments.

230. The position at which we have arrived is that the nature of the universe is expressed by ultimate Universal Judgments which are such that by their means is expressed both the Likeness and the Unlikeness which every Individual bears to every other Individual.

Hegel would regard all these ultimate Judgments as forming a single hierarchy, without cross-classifications. For he says

---

[1] It can be zero in some cases, because these are cases where it is true both that all X are Z, and that all Z are X (cp. Section 207).

that, in the Syllogism of Necessity, every Subject has only one possible Middle Term, and every Middle Term only one possible Predicate. Thus everything has only one higher class to which it can immediately be referred, and cross-classifications would be impossible.

Whether this single system of classification could possibly explain the whole complex nature of existence is a difficult problem which Hegel does not discuss. In the absence of any treatment of the subject by him, it is sufficient to say here that the conclusion that each Subject could only have one possible Middle Term, and each Middle Term only one possible Predicate, arose from the asserted necessity of removing the " contingency " in the First Figure. If, as I have tried to show, that contingency is not a defect, and need not be removed, the conclusion will not be justified. In that case, the connexion of Universals, expressed by the ultimate Judgments can be more complex, and can admit of cross-classifications.

231. In the ultimate Disjunctive Judgments found in Disjunctive Syllogisms we have the conception of the Self-Differentiating Notion. (So far as I know, the phrase is not Hegel's own. At any rate he does not use it frequently. But it is often used by commentators, and it expresses a conception which has great importance for Hegel.) This conception is simpler than the name would suggest. It means nothing but a Notion, which is always accompanied by one of a certain number of subordinate Notions, the connexion between the first Notion and its subordinates being intrinsic—not due to any outside circumstance, but to the nature of the terms—and also being ultimate and not derivative. (In the case of the Notions contemplated by the present category the subordinate Notions are of less extent than the self-differentiating Notion, and they are peculiar to it, so that no cross-classification is possible.)

Let us, for example, assume that it is true that all finite spirits must be either angels, men, or brutes. Then if the connexion between the terms is not external, but intrinsic, and not derivative but ultimate, the Notion of a finite spirit would be one which was said to differentiate itself into angels, men, and brutes.

The conception of a self-differentiating Notion has often

been misunderstood. It has been supposed that by such a Notion Hegel meant one from whose nature the nature of the subordinate Notions could be deduced by pure thought. We should only have to take the conception of the class, and examine it with sufficient care, and it would proceed to develope the conceptions of its sub-classes. The mythical German who conducted his zoological studies by endeavouring to evolve the idea of a camel from his inner consciousness was acting very much in this manner.

Such a theory is obviously incorrect, nor do I believe that there is the slightest evidence to support the view that Hegel held it. The only case in which Hegel professes to evolve anything by pure thought is in the dialectic. He there evolves only categories, which are themselves forms of pure thought. But most of the Notions which Hegel held to be self-differentiating contain an empirical element. And there is nothing to suggest that Hegel believed that a new empirical idea could ever be produced by pure thought.

Nor, even in the dialectic, does Hegel give us a Notion differentiating itself by pure thought. The lower (in the sense of the less adequate) passes into the higher, but the higher (in the sense of the more extensive) never splits itself up into the lower. (This very important distinction has, I think, sometimes escaped the notice both of disciples and of critics of Hegel, and this has sometimes led to considerable confusion.)

The self-differentiation of a Notion, then, does not imply any inherent dialectic. It only means that it is an ultimate and intrinsic characteristic of that Notion, that it is always united with one of several others. What those others are must be discovered by us through observation and experiment, and, when they are found, the conjunction must be accepted by us as an ultimate fact.

Some of the mistakes about the self-differentiating Notion may be due to the name, which is rather misleading. The active participle suggests a logical, if not a temporal process, and so leads us to suppose that the unity is the agent which produces the plurality, and is therefore prior to it. This might to some extent be remedied if we were also to use the correlative phrase of a self-unifying multiplicity, which would be as true a description of the same fact.

With the Disjunctive Syllogism we reach the end of Subjectivity. The treatment of Subjectivity in the *Encyclopaedia* does not differ from that in the *Greater Logic*, though its extreme condensation renders it more obscure.

CHAPTER IX

OBJECTIVITY

232. The divisions of Objectivity are as follows:

I. Mechanism. (Der Mechanismus.)

    A. The Mechanical Object. (Das mechanische Objekt.)

    B. The Mechanical Process. (Der mechanische Process.)

        (a) The Formal Mechanical Process. (Der formale mechanische Process.)

        (b) The Real Mechanical Process. (Der reale mechanische Process.)

        (c) The Product of the Mechanical Process. (Das Produkt des mechanischen Processes.)

    C. The Absolute Mechanism. (Der absolute Mechanismus.)

        (a) The Centre. (Das Centrum.)

        (b) The Law. (Das Gesetz.)

        (c) Transition from Mechanism. (Uebergang des Mechanismus.)

II. Chemism. (Der Chemismus.)

    A. The Chemical Object. (Das chemische Objekt.)

    B. The Chemical Process. (Der chemische Process.)

    C. Transition from Chemistry. (Uebergang des Chemismus.)

III. Teleology. (Die Teleologie.)

    A. The Subjective End. (Der subjective Zweck.)

    B. The Means. (Das Mittel.)

    C. The Realised End. (Der ausgeführte Zweck.)

233. We saw reason in the last chapter to reject the view that Subjectivity meant the inner as opposed to the outer. It meant that which is contingent or capricious, as opposed to that which is universal and inevitable. It is thus natural that the next division should be called Objectivity. The contingent and capricious character of the classification, which had been present through the subdivisions of Notion and Judgment was recognised, at the beginning of Syllogism, in the First Figure, as a defect which proved the inadequacy of the category, and was finally transcended in the Syllogism of Necessity, the classification in which, according to Hegel, was no longer contingent and capricious, but universal and necessary. It is natural, therefore, that the next division, which preserves this result, should be called Objectivity.

234. Hegel's account of the transition to Objectivity is as follows. " The Syllogism is mediation, the complete Notion in its position (Gesetztsein). Its movement is the transcending of this mediation, in which nothing is in and for itself, but each is only as it is mediated by another. The result is therefore an Immediacy, which has arisen through transcending the mediation, a Being, that is just as much identical with the mediation and with the Notion, which has restored itself out of and by means of (aus und in) its Otherbeing. This Being is therefore a fact, which is in and for itself—Objectivity " (*G. L.* iii. 170. Cp. also *Enc.* 193).

I cannot regard this as satisfactory. The line of the argument appears to be that at the end of Subjectivity the mediation is merged, that this produces immediacy, and that this forms the transition to Objectivity. But how has this mediation been merged? Surely it has not been completely merged. It is true that in the Disjunctive Syllogism it is an immediate fact that Z is either X, or W, or V, and that the connexions of X, W, and V with Z require no mediation. But, in any particular Individual, Z will be connected either with X, or with W, or with V, and not with all three. Mediation will therefore be necessary to determine with which of them it *is* connected, and a transition based on the absence of mediation is incorrect.

Moreover, when we consider the detail of Objectivity, we

find that mediation is not dispensed with, but that there is mediation, though of a different sort from that in Subjectivity—the new sort of mediation being directed to the issue just mentioned, the connexion of Z with X, *e.g.*, rather than with W or V.

235. I venture to suggest a line of argument which I believe to be valid in itself, and also to lead, as Hegel's own does not, to the mediation which he describes in the categories of Mechanism.

In the last chapter (Section 187) I sketched this transition in anticipation. In considering the transition from the last categories of Essence to Subjectivity, I pointed out that "things are doubly connected—by similarity and by reciprocal causation. And it is obvious that a thing may be, and generally is, connected by the one tie to things very different from those to which it is connected by the other." And I submitted that the dialectic "first takes up the relation of similarity, and works it out through the course of Subjectivity. Then in Objectivity it proceeds to work out the relation of determination—not going back arbitrarily to pick it up, but led on to it again by dialectical necessity, since Subjectivity, when fully worked out, shows itself to have a defect which can only be remedied by the fuller development of the relation of determination."

We have now reached the end of Subjectivity, and we have found that it does, in fact, possess such a defect. Our position at the end of Subjectivity was that the nature of the universe could be explained by judgments of the type "every Z is either X or W." But such knowledge is necessarily incomplete. For of any given Individual which is Z, we know it is either X or W, but we do not know which it is. And yet it is certain that it is one of them, and that it is not the other. How is this to be determined? Subjectivity cannot do it[1]. We require a

---

[1] Hegel makes the ultimate Disjunctive Judgment the Major Premise of a Syllogism, the conclusion of which determines the Individual. "Every Z is either X or W, this Z is not W, therefore it is X." In this case however, he has introduced a Minor Premise which is not a Universal Judgment, and has thus gone beyond Subjectivity which has transcended, and never re-introduced, Judgments other than Universal.

further determination of objects which their inner nature, as we are able at this stage of the dialectic to understand it, cannot give us. What can remain? It can only be determination from outside. And thus we are naturally led back at the end of Subjectivity to the conception of the reciprocal connexion of Individuals by determination—that very conception which we had temporarily ignored while dealing with Subjectivity. Thus the argument takes the course that might be anticipated from the nature of the dialectic. When we left one element of Reciprocity behind, and, in the Thesis of the Doctrine of the Notion, devoted ourselves to developing the other side only, we could predict that the incompleteness thus created would require us to develop the other element of Reciprocity in the Antithesis. And this is exactly what has happened. We are now on the point of beginning the Antithesis—namely Objectivity—and the course of the argument has led us back to the ignored element in Reciprocity.

I. MECHANISM.

236. (*G. L.* iii. 180. *Enc.* 195.) In the first place, Hegel says, the Individuals, now called Objects, are taken as merely externally connected by this reciprocal determination. And this is Mechanism, whose character, he tells us, is that " whatever relation takes place between the connected things, that relation is alien (fremde) to them, does not belong to their nature, and, although it unites them with the appearance of a One, remains nothing more than a collocation, mixture, or heap (Zusammensetzung, Vermischung, Haufen) " (*G. L.* iii. 180).

A. *The Mechanical Object.*

(*G. L.* iii. 181. *Enc.* 195.) The definition of this, as often happens in the dialectic, is identical with that of the larger division, of which it is the first subdivision. The other two subdivisions modify and correct the characteristic idea of Mechanism. But here it is given in its full extent. Each Object enters into external relations of reciprocal determination with all others outside it, but these external relations are not affected by, and do not affect, the internal nature of the Objects related. In the *Encyclopaedia* the category of the Mechanical

Object is known as Formal Mechanism, and this expresses the nature of the conception better than the title in the *Greater Logic*.

When we are dealing with any subject-matter accessible to our experience, so extreme a view as this can only be accepted as a methodological expedient. It may sometimes be convenient, for some temporary and limited purpose, to consider things *as if* their external relations had no influence on their inner nature, or their inner nature on their external relations. But experience teaches us, too plainly to be disregarded, that every external relation which holds of any of the things which we perceive does affect the inner nature of that thing, and that, on the other hand, the external relations which hold of things are largely determined by their inner nature.

Atoms, however, cannot be directly perceived, and in their case, therefore, empirical knowledge is powerless to check the errors of theory. And the theory of Atoms has sometimes got very near to the position of Formal Mechanism. It would not, indeed, assert that the inner nature of the atoms was entirely a matter of indifference to their outer relations. They could not, for example, repel one another, except by some property of impenetrability. But it has been asserted that a change in their outer relations makes no change in their inner nature, and that their inner nature has no influence in deciding which, of various possible relations, should be the one into which they should actually enter.

Hegel says that this is the standpoint of Determinism (*G. L.* iii. 183). The expression does not, at first sight, seem very appropriate, since one of the chief characteristics of the category is that the inner nature of the Object is not determined by its outer relations. But it is the determination of the outer relations themselves to which Hegel refers here, and the significance of the name is negative. It denotes the fact that, so far as these reciprocal determinations are concerned, there is no *self-determination* on the part of the Object. If we ask why it is determined in this way rather than that, we can only attribute it to determination by another Object. In no case can the Object be self-determined in these reciprocal determinations, for its inner nature has nothing to do with them.

237. This category, Hegel tells us, breaks down because of the contradiction which arises between the indifference of the Objects to one another, and their connexion with one another (*G. L.* iii. 184). He takes the reciprocal determination of two Objects as introducing an identical element in each of them. This is to be expected, for, as we saw in Chapter VII., he regards Cause and Effect as identical, and the reciprocal determination which we have here is, of course, reciprocal causation. But this error—if, as I have previously maintained, it is an error—does not affect the validity of his position that there is a contradiction between the indifference of the Objects and their connexion by reciprocal determination.

In the earlier stages of Essence there would have been no contradiction in such a case. For there the Surface and the Substratum were conceived as having natures more or less independent of each other, though more or less connected. To determine the Surface would not necessarily involve the determination of the Substratum. Thus, if the inner nature of the thing were taken as Substratum, and its relations of reciprocal determination with other things were taken as Surface, the two might be as independent as this category requires.

But in the course of the Doctrine of Essence we learned that the inner nature of a thing cannot be *merely* inner, but that it, and the whole of it, must be manifested by the external nature of the thing. And, conversely, no outer nature can be entirely outer. There can no more be anything in the Surface which has not its root in the Substratum, than there can be anything in the Substratum which does not manifest itself in the Surface.

And thus the category of the Mechanical Object contains a contradiction. It demands that the inner nature of the Object shall be indifferent to its external relations of reciprocal determination. But these external relations belong somehow, and in some respects, to the Object, or there would be no meaning in calling them the external relations of that Object. They are not its inner nature. They must, therefore, be its outer side, or part of its outer side. Thus the category of the Mechanical Object demands an outer side which does not affect the inner side. And this is just what was proved in the Doctrine of Essence to be impossible.

If then the outer relations and inner nature of the Object are not absolutely independent, how do they stand to one another? The *primâ facie* assumption, since they at any rate profess to be different, is that they are two separate realities acting on one another. The arguments given above, indeed, suggest that the connexion is closer than this, but Hegel prefers to approach the truth gradually, by stating and transcending this view of the interaction of separate realities. This forms the second subdivision of Mechanism, and he entitles it

B. *The Mechanical Process.*

(*G. L.* iii. 184. *Enc.* 196.) In the *Encyclopaedia* this category is called "Differenter Mechanismus," which Wallace translates Mechanism with Affinity. The significance of this name appears to be that one Object is no longer as suitable as another to enter into any particular relations. Since the inner nature has some influence on the outer relations, only those Objects can enter into any particular relations whose inner nature possesses particular qualities.

238. Hegel divides this category into three subdivisions. This seems to me mistaken, for the first subdivision, so far as I can see, only repeats the conception of the Mechanical Object, while the third is only the transition to Absolute Mechanism. Thus the second subdivision gives the only conception peculiar to the triad, and might have been taken as the undivided category of Mechanical Process. (This course is taken by Hegel in the *Encyclopaedia*.) The first subdivision is called (*G. L.* iii. 186)

(a) *The Formal Mechanical Process.*

239. Of this Hegel says (*G. L.* iii. 190) that the determination which the Object receives through it is merely external. It is this which makes me think it identical with the last category, the essential characteristic of which was the externality of the determinations. If this is so, the same arguments which carried us into Mechanical Process will carry us into its second subdivision,

(b) *The Real Mechanical Process*

(*G. L.* iii. 190), where it is admitted that the reciprocal determinations do affect the inner nature of the Object.

To this category, Hegel says (*G. L.* iii. 192), belongs the idea of Fate—a blind Fate, conceived as crushing and ignoring the Objects which are in its power. This conception of the sacrifice of the Object to the order of things outside it could not have arisen in the category of the Mechanical Object, since there the interior of any Object was quite untouched by external circumstances, and could not be sacrificed to them. And in the next category, that of Absolute Mechanism, the opposition of inner and outer is replaced by the perception of their unity, and with it there vanishes the idea of Fate as an alien and crushing power—to return again, on a higher level, in the category of Life, but to be again transcended in the category of Cognition. But, between the Mechanical Object and Absolute Mechanism, our present category is precisely the proper sphere of Fate. For outside and inside are connected just so much that the former may act on the latter, just so little that there is no harmony between them. Fate has the individual Objects in its power, "subjectos tanquam suos, viles tanquam alienos."

If we carry this line of thought one step backwards we may say that if we looked at man under the category of the Mechanical Object, we should get a morality not unlike that of the Stoics. For morality is in the long run concerned only with the inner states of people, which are the only things which possess ultimate value[1]. If everyone was happy, virtuous, and otherwise good, all external relations would be quite indifferent to morality, which only cares for external matters in so far as they affect the goodness (in the widest sense) of conscious beings. And if the inner nature of man, as of all other Objects, were independent of his external relations, then, whatever his circumstances, it would be in the power of each man to be completely good. Such a view would, of course, tend to produce absolute indifference to the affairs of the external world.

But from such a view as this we are necessarily driven, if

---

[1] The view that nothing but the states of conscious beings possesses value as an end is not universal, but is maintained by almost all philosophers. The arguments in the text would have no validity for those who denied this view.

we do not refuse to look facts in the face, to the Fatalism
which we have seen to be characteristic of the category of the
Mechanical Process. It is all very well to say that a man has
the power to be free, virtuous and happy under any circumstances. But the circumstances may include a badly trapped
sewer which sends him out of the world, or a blow on the head
which sends him into an asylum, or an education which leaves
him with a complete ignorance of virtue, or a lively distaste
for it. It is useless to try to escape from our circumstances.
Such an "escape from Fate is itself the most unhappy of
all Fates" as Hegel says elsewhere. For the attempt to
escape generally deprives us of much of our power over our
circumstances, while it by no means deprives them of their
power over us.

240. Hegel does not state explicitly the arguments which
lead from this category to the next, but we can easily supply
them, for they were really anticipated when we passed from the
Mechanical Object to the Mechanical Process. There is no
opposition between the inner and outer nature of an Object,
because there is no difference between them. They are only
the same thing seen from different points of view. The internal
nature of each Object consists of qualities. And all these
qualities are only in that Object because they are externally
determined to be so. The general laws which we dealt with in
Subjectivity can never by themselves assign any quality to any
Object. They can only say that if one quality is there, another
will, or will not, be there. They are only hypothetical. The
actual existence of any quality in any Object is due to the
relations of reciprocal determination with other Objects which
form its outer nature.

Thus the internal qualities are only the expression of the
outer relations. But the outer relations are just as much only
an expression of the inner qualities. If A and B are related
by reciprocal determination, then A's qualities will be an
expression of its relation to B, and B's qualities of its relation
to A. But again the relation of A to B which determines B's
qualities will be an expression of A's qualities. For if A's
qualities had been different, it would have determined B
differently. And likewise the relation of B to A which

determines A's qualities will be an expression of B's qualities[1].

And so, to come back to Fatalism, we see that it is really impossible for the inner nature of an Object to be crushed. If the inner nature of an Object is said to be XYZ, then either it has it, or it has it not. If it has it, it has it, and then the inner nature is not crushed, but exists in its fulness. But if it has it not, then XYZ is not the Object's inner nature at all, and the Object is not in the least crushed or thwarted because it is not XYZ. Why *should* it be XYZ, if in point of fact it is not?

Of course this would not be a solution of the problem of Fate for self-conscious beings, but this is because the nature of a self-conscious being cannot be adequately brought under our present category. In the case of any being with a power of conscious self-determination, the inner nature will include volitions of some sort, and if outside circumstances prevent those volitions from being realised, then we can intelligibly speak of the inner nature being thwarted. For the inner nature in such a case is not *merely* a fact, but it is a fact part of which is a demand, and a demand can be real and yet unsatisfied.

Thus Hegel says "Only self-consciousness has a true (eigentlich) fate; for self-consciousness is free, in the individuality of its I it is in and for itself, and can place itself over against its objective universality, and treat itself as alien against it" (*G. L.* iii. 193). This true fate is not transcended till we reach a higher category.

We thus reach (*G. L.* iii. 193)

(c)   *The Product of the Mechanical Process,*

which Hegel treats as identical with the first subdivision of Absolute Mechanism, to which we now proceed.

C.   *The Absolute Mechanism.*

241. (*G. L.* iii. 194. *Enc.* 197.) This is divided in the *Greater Logic* into three subdivisions, the first of which is

---

[1] I venture to think that, if Hegel had worked this out further, it would have provided a more satisfactory transition to Teleology than is afforded by Chemism. But it would take us too far from Hegel's text to attempt to develope this view.

(a) The Centre.

(*G. L.* iii. 194.) According to this category, every Object is
the centre of a system composed of all the other Objects which
influence it. As everything in the universe stands in reciprocal connexion with everything else, it follows that each of
these systems embraces the whole of existence, and that they
are distinguished from each other by the fact that each has
a different Centre.

Since Hegel has connected the Mechanical Object with
Determinism, and the Mechanical Process with Fatalism, we
may say that in Absolute Mechanism we return again to the
conception of Freedom, which we reached at the end of
Essence. For Freedom, according to that conception, only
consists in acting according to one's nature, and we now see
that there is no power in the universe which could possibly
make any Object do anything not in accordance with its nature.
Freedom, in the higher sense in which it is applicable to
conscious beings, is not reached till the "true fate" has been
transcended, which Hegel speaks of above (*G. L.* iii. 193).

We have, then, the Central Object, the determining Objects,
and the relations between them. The surrounding Objects are
called by Hegel the Relative-Central Objects, while the relations themselves are, somewhat curiously, called the Formal
Objects.

Each of these, Hegel points out, may be called the Universal.
He apparently means by the Universal that term which is taken
as uniting the other two. And any one of the three may occupy
that position. The Central Object may be taken as uniting
the other two, since those determining Objects could only have
those relations with just that Central Object. (If there were
a different Central Object they would determine it differently,
and so be in different relations to it.) But again we may
consider the determining Objects as the Universal. For that
Central Object could only have those relations with just those
determining Objects. And again the relations may be taken as
Universal. For that Central Object could only be connected
with those determining Objects by just those relations (*G. L.*
iii. 196. *Enc.* 198).

242. It should be noticed that the example of the category given by Hegel in both Logics (*G. L.* iii. 197. *Enc.* 198) is misleading. He makes either the State or the Government take the place of the Central Object, while the citizens are the determining Objects. Now the State and the Government differ from the citizens, not only as one citizen does from another, but in a more fundamental way. And thus the example would suggest that there are some Objects which are by their nature fitted to be the Central Objects of systems, while others are fitted only for the humbler position of determining Objects. But this, as we have seen, would be a mistake. For every possible Object is equally subjected to the category of Mechanical Process, and we saw in the course of the deduction that every Object to which the category of Mechanical Process was applicable, became the centre of a system of Absolute Mechanism.

Indeed, we may say that the example, in the form which it takes in the *Encyclopaedia*, is not only misleading, but incorrect. For there he speaks of the State as the Central Object. Now the State is not an Object distinct from the citizens, which can act and react on them, as each of them does on the rest. It is, as no one realised more fully than Hegel, a unity of which the individual citizens are the parts. It is, no doubt, for Hegel a very close unity, and not a mere aggregate, but still it is a unity which only exists in the citizens, and not side by side with them. And thus the citizens cannot be determining Objects with the State as their Central Object.

The example as given in the *Greater Logic* cannot be called positively incorrect. For Hegel there speaks only of the Regierung, and not, as in the *Encyclopaedia*, of the State also. Now Hegel probably took Regierung to mean a separate class— the king, civil servants, etc.—and, if so, it would form a separate Object by the side of the citizens, which could enter into relations of Mechanism with them. But the example would still be misleading, as suggesting an intrinsic difference between those Objects which were fitted to be Central Objects, and those which were not.

243. We now enter on the course of argument which leads to Chemism by the gradual obliteration of the independence of the Object. This is not fully attained in the *Greater Logic* till the category of Chemical Process, between which and our present category three others intervene. In the *Encyclopaedia*, however, where Absolute Mechanism and Chemism are undivided categories, the whole movement is performed in a single stage. It will, I think, be better to state and criticise the argument in this simpler form, before tracing the more elaborate course of the *Greater Logic*.

The statement of the *Encyclopaedia* is as follows (199). "The immediacy of existence, which the objects have in Absolute Mechanism, is implicitly negatived by the 'fact that their independence is derived from, and due to, their connexions with each other, and therefore to their own want of stability. Thus the object must be explicitly stated as in its existence having an Affinity (or a bias) towards its other—as not-indifferent."

I conceive that Hegel's meaning is this. The whole nature of each Object depends on the relation between it and other Objects. But each of these relations does not, of course, belong exclusively to the one Object, but is shared by it with another. The nature of a particular piece of wax consists, for example, partly in the fact that it has been melted by a particular fire. But this melting is just as much part of the nature of the fire. The fact is shared between the wax and the fire, and cannot be said to belong to one of them more than to the other. It belongs to both of them jointly.

Thus the only subject of which the relation can be predicated will be the system which is formed by these two Objects—Objects which are now said to be in Affinity with (different *gegen*) one another. This, then, will be the true unity determined by this relation. But two Objects cannot form a closed system, since all Objects in the universe are in reciprocal connexion. Our system of two Objects will have relations with others, and will be merged with them, in the same way in which the original Objects were merged in it, since the relations, which alone give individuality, are found to be common property, and so merge their terms, instead of keeping them distinct. The system in which all the Objects, and all their relations, are contained, becomes the only true Object, of which all the relations contained in the system are adjectives. The individual Objects disappear, and we reach the category of Chemism.

I think that this is what Hegel means, and at any rate it is quite clear that, when he has reached Chemism, he regards the different Objects as having collapsed into one Object. But I cannot see that this is justified. The conclusion from the essentiality of the relations to the unreality of the terms could only be valid if things lost their reality and stability in so far as they were connected with others. But the reverse of this is true. We have seen, with gradually increasing clearness as the dialectic advanced, that it is to their relations with what is outside them that all things owe their independence and stability.

244. We now proceed to the argument of the *Greater Logic*, whose elaboration does not introduce any really new factors, though it rather confuses the issue. At the end of his treatment of the category of the Centre, Hegel says " the system, which is the merely external determination of the Objects, has now passed over into an immanent and objective determination ; this is the Law " (*G. L.* iii. 198).

(b)   The Law.

(*G. L.* iii. 198.) Of this he says on the same page " This reality, which corresponds to the Notion, is an ideal reality, different from the former reality which only strove ; the Difference, which was previously a plurality of Objects, is taken up into its essentiality, and into the pure universality."

This, however, does not take us more than one step on the way to Chemism, for the Objects are still possessed of a separate existence. " The soul is still sunk in the body " (*G. L.* iii. 199). The Law, apparently, is recognised as more important than the Objects which it connects, but it has not removed their stability.

245. Now, however, Hegel proceeds to prove their instability by an argument similar to that employed in the *Encyclopaedia*. " The Object has its essential stability only in its ideal centrality, and in the law of the centrality ; it has therefore no power to resist the judgment of the Notion, and to maintain itself in abstract undetermined stability and exclusion" (*G. L.* iii. 200. The phrase "judgment of the Notion" has clearly no reference to the particular division of Subjectivity which bore that name). We thus reach (*G. L.* iii. 199)

(c) Transition from Mechanism.

246. Here we have the Object in its Chemical form, no longer stable, but unstable by reason of its Affinity towards the related Object. Thus we pass to

II. CHEMISM.

(*G. L.* iii. 200. *Enc.* 200.) Chemism is not further divided in the *Encyclopaedia*, but in the *Greater Logic* it has three subdivisions, of which the first is

A. The Chemical Object

(*G. L.* iii. 200), which appears to be exactly the same as Transition from Mechanism[1]. We have again Objects, still different from one another, but unstable by means of their Affinity.

247. Now, however, he proceeds to argue, as in the *Encyclopaedia*, that "the Chemical Object is not comprehensible by itself, and that the Being of one is the Being of the other" (*G. L.* iii. 202). With this merging of the Objects into one, he reaches

B. The Chemical Process.

(*G. L.* iii. 202.) Here the full conception of Chemism is attained, and we have come to the same point which was reached in the *Encyclopaedia* by the simpler argument given above.

The Object produced by merging the other Objects into one is called the Neutral Object. This name, and the expression that the Object has "sunk back to immediacy" (*Enc.* 202) suggest that the Neutral Object is undifferentiated. And we

---

[1] This is not in accordance with the general method of the dialectic. Transition from Mechanism is a subdivision of the fifth degree, while the Chemical Object is a subdivision of the fourth degree. Thus they do not stand to one another as Synthesis and new Thesis, and it is only categories which do this which, according to the general method of the dialectic, are identical in content.

can see that this would naturally be the case. For, in proportion as the related Objects lost their several reality, the relation between them would lose its reality. The relation of melting only exists between a fire and a piece of wax, if they are taken as different, though connected, Objects. If there were no fire and no wax there would be no relation of melting. Thus besides the separate Objects and their qualities, the relations also have gone, and nothing remains which could differentiate the Neutral Object.

248. The category now reached gives us, says Hegel, an oscillation between the Neutral Object on the one hand, and, on the other hand, two Extremes, distinct, but connected and in a state of tension. It is, I think, clear that Hegel is asserting a category of alternation and not an alternation of categories. It is not, according to him, that we alternately regard existence as a Neutral Object and as a tension of Extremes, but that we hold throughout our treatment of the Chemical Process a position which asserts that the existent itself continually passes from one of these forms to the other.

The passage to Chemical Process—this appears to be Hegel's meaning—gives us the Neutral Object. But the Neutral Object is undifferentiated, "it has sunk back to immediacy." It has therefore no true unity. So it splits up into the Extremes, which are the old separate Objects. But the Extremes, being "biassed and strained"—that is, in connexion with each other, fall back into the Neutral Object, and the process goes on *ad infinitum*. This endless oscillation is apparently Hegel's ground for rejecting the category as inadequate. (The account of this in the *Encyclopaedia* is clearer than that in the *Greater Logic*, but the meaning of both is the same.)

249. To the validity of this argument there appears to me to be two objections.

In the first place, if such a Neutral Object were reached, it would not split up into Extremes, as Hegel makes it do, but would vanish altogether. Such a Neutral Object could have nothing outside it, for it is to be co-extensive with a mechanical system, and we have seen that every mechanical system is co-extensive with the universe. And again the Neutral Object, being undifferentiated, could have nothing inside it. It would have no determination left, external or internal. In other words, it would have returned to Pure Being, which, as we learned at the beginning of the Logic, is equivalent to nothing. We should be back again where we started, and the dialectic process could never pass this point, but would always return back on itself in a circle which could never be transcended.

But even supposing that the Neutral Object did split up into its Extremes, and that the perpetual oscillation between it and them could be established, where is the contradiction in this that could take us on to the next category? The continual oscillation is, of course, what Hegel calls a False Infinite. But a False Infinite, as we have seen, though always regarded by Hegel as something valueless and unsatisfactory, is not regarded by him as necessarily involving a contradiction. It is only certain False Infinites which he regards as doing so. He gives no reason why this one should be counted among them, nor do I see what reason could be given. But, without some demonstration that this particular False Infinite is contradictory, we have no valid transition to the next category.

I submit, therefore, that the conception of Chemism is unsatisfactory, alike as regards the transition to it, the conception itself, and the transition from it, and that it must be rejected. And, as I said above (Section 240, note), I believe a more attentive consideration of the category of Absolute Mechanism might very possibly yield a new category, which would in its turn offer a valid transition to Teleology.

250. Hegel's transition to the next category is made by arguing that this oscillation shows the inadequacy of the forms —Neutral Object on the one hand, and Extremes on the other— which succeed one another in the Chemical Process, and that this inadequacy leaves the Notion which was (imperfectly) shown in each of them, standing free from them (*G. L.* iii. 208. *Enc.* 203). I quote the account in the *Encyclopaedia*, which seems to me more clearly expressed than the corresponding passage in the *Greater Logic*, though I do not think there is any difference in meaning. Speaking of the processes from Neutral Object to Extremes, and from Extremes to Neutral Object, he says that each " goes its own way without hindrance from the other.   But that want of inner connexion shows that they are finite, by their passage into products in which they are merged and lost.   Conversely the process exhibits the non-entity of the pre-supposed immediacy of the not-indifferent Objects.—By this negation of immediacy and of externalism in which the Notion as such was sunk, it is liberated and invested with independent being in the face of that externalism and immediacy."

This is Hegel's argument, and its meaning does not seem to me doubtful.   Its validity is not so clear.   It is not evident why the fact that each form gives place to another form, in unending oscillation, should enable us to assert that the Notion, which is the uniting principle of both, should be able to do without either.   It is still less evident why we should be entitled to assert, as Hegel proceeds to do, that the Notion thus freed embodies itself in the form of the category of Teleology.

In this way Hegel passes to (*G. L.* iii. 206)

C.   *Transition from Chemism.*

251.   The question arises, with regard to the Notion of which Hegel has just spoken (which we may conveniently distinguish as the Chemical Notion), whether there are more than one of such Notions in the universe, or whether there is only one.   The answer will be of considerable importance, not only with reference to the present category, but throughout the divisions of Teleology and Life.   Hegel's language gives us no reason for one answer rather than another, but it seems to follow logically from his treatment of Chemism that there can be only one Chemical Notion.   For it seems clear that there can be only one Chemical system.   It is true that there were many systems of Absolute Mechanism, and that the transition to Chemism professed to show that each system of Absolute Mechanism must now be regarded as a Chemical system.   But apparently they would have all to be regarded as the same Chemical system.

It must be remembered that each system of Absolute Mechanism contained all the Objects in the universe.   The systems were only differentiated from one another by the fact

that each system had a different Object for its Centre.   Now
this possibility of differentiation disappears in the Chemical
system.   A Chemical system is made up of a Neutral Object
and Extremes.   Two Chemical systems could not be differentiated from each other by means of different Neutral
Objects, for the Neutral Object is the result of merging all the
Objects of the universe together, and therefore there could
only be one in the universe.   Moreover, if the Neutral Object
is undifferentiated, there could be nothing to distinguish one
Neutral Object from another.   And Hegel appears to regard
the Neutral Object as capable of splitting into Extremes in one
manner only, so that the Chemical systems could not be
differentiated from one another by the possession of different
Extremes.   Thus we seem forced to the conclusion that there
is only one Chemical system, and, therefore, only one Chemical
Notion.

252.   The category of Transition from Chemism, as a
Synthesis, is naturally identical with the Thesis of the new
triad.   We pass at once, therefore, to this new triad, which is

III.   Teleology.

(*G. L.* iii. 209.   *Enc.* 204.)   The Chemical Notion has now,
Hegel tells us, become the End.   The End is the element of
unity in the categories of Teleology, and the correlative element
of plurality is the Means.

Hegel departs considerably from the common usage in the
meaning which he gives to the terms Teleology, End, and
Means.   What is generally meant by Teleology is what Hegel
calls "finite and outward design," in which some independently
existing object is used by some self-conscious being as a means
for carrying out some plan which he has conceived.   In "outward design" the Means and the End can exist independently;
for the End can exist in the mind of the designer, even if there
are no available Means to carry it out, while the objects which
are used as Means do not derive their entire existence from
that use, but may have existed before the End was formed,
and might still have existed, if the End had never been
formed.

Hegel tells us that his use of these terms resembles Kant's, of whose conception of Teleology the best example is to be found in organic life (*G. L.* iii. 213. *Enc.* 204). By the help of this, and of the indications given by Hegel in the discussion of the subdivisions of the category, we can, I think, see what Hegel means by a Teleological system. It is, on the one hand a system the intrinsic nature of whose parts is dependent on their place in the system. Not only their external relations, but their whole nature, can only be explained, or even described, by reference to the system, and, through the system, to the other members of it. On the other hand the unity, the End, can only be stated as the unity which does connect just those parts. It cannot have a separate description, as is the case with the Ends of "finite design."

We can see that a living body offers the best possible example of this, though not quite an adequate one[1]. For the parts of an organism at any rate approximate to that degree of close connexion in which none of them have any nature at all which is not expressed in and dependent on their place in the system. And, on the other hand, if we ask what is the nature of the unity which holds together the parts of any organism, we can only say that it is the unity which does express itself in just those parts connected in that way. It is, it must be noted, this organic unity which is the End of the organism, in Hegel's and Kant's use of the word. The purpose of its creator or its parent, in creating or begetting it, or the purposes which the spiritual being connected with it uses it to fulfil, are only Ends of finite design.

253. A similar unity to this may be found in a picture, in so far as it possesses aesthetic merit. For then the explanation and justification of each detail in the picture will be found in its place in the scheme of the picture as a whole, and, through that, in its relation to the other details. On the other hand, if we ask what the scheme of the picture is, what is the unity which makes it aesthetically meritorious, we can only say that it is the unity which is expressed in just those parts, arranged in just that manner. It admits of no separate statement.

---

[1] The failure of organisms to afford an adequate example of Teleological unity will be discussed in the next chapter (Section 266).

Here, again, we must distinguish this inner unity of the picture, which is its End in the Hegelian sense, from the purpose of the artist to represent a particular scene in his picture, and from the more fundamental purpose which led him to paint the picture—desire for fame, for money, or the like. These are only Ends of finite design, and they admit of statement in other terms than simply that they are the End of this picture.

In ordinary language the term Means may signify either the material in which an End is embodied and realised or the instruments by which that material is adapted. If I propose as an End to make a statue, both the marble and the chisel would be called Means to my End. But when Means is used as the correlative to End in the Hegelian sense, there is no question of instruments, and the Means are simply the plurality in which the unity of the End is embodied. That this is the case appears also from the two arguments by which Hegel demonstrates the inadequacy of the category of Means (see below, Sections 259, 260).

254. We can now see that Teleology is a Synthesis of the positions of Mechanism and Chemism. In Mechanism the unity of a system of Objects is one of themselves—the Central Object. The unity is not yet a distinct moment in the system, correlative to the plurality of Objects. In Chemism, on the other hand, the unity of the system is regarded as more funda-mental than the plurality, for the result of the category is that the Chemical Notion is inadequately expressed by its mani-festations. In Teleology the two sides are balanced. The unity is a moment in the system distinct from the moment of the plurality of the parts of the system, and as fundamental as that plurality. On the other hand the unity is no more fundamental than the plurality, for it has no separate nature, but is just the unity which does unite that particular plurality in that particular way.

The End may be called a Universal, and rightly, since it unites the system, and is common to every part of it. But it must be noticed that it is quite a different sort of Universal from that which we had in Subjectivity. There the Universal was a common quality. Here it is an organising principle.

The highest point of Subjectivity was the Ultimate Disjunctive Judgment which formed the Major Premise of the Disjunctive Syllogism. Let us take as an example, "all finite spirits must be angels, men, or brutes." Then the fact that a certain existent Individual was a finite spirit and a man would not in any way determine whether any other finite spirits existed, or to which of the three possible varieties they belonged. But if there exists a living human stomach, then, in so far as a living being is an adequate example of Hegelian Teleology, its existence will determine the existence of other living human organs which are not stomachs. For the living stomach could only exist as a manifestation of the organic unity of a human body, and such a unity must also manifest itself in other organs which are not stomachs.

We have here, even more distinctly than at the end of Subjectivity, the idea of a self-differentiating unity, by which is to be understood, as I said above (Section 231), not a unity, from whose nature the nature of its differentiations can be deduced by pure thought, but a unity which, not through some external accident, but from inner necessity, is only to be found in a particular multiplicity. This multiplicity, however, is as ultimate and fundamental as the unity. It does not proceed from the unity, and is only dependent on it in the same way that the unity, in its turn, depends on the multiplicity— namely that the existence of each involves the existence of the other.

We saw, in treating of this conception in the last chapter, that, although the existence of the unity involves that of the differentiations, and conversely, yet it does not follow that, if we know the nature of the unity, we should be able to deduce from it what were the differentiations of that unity. To recur to our previous example—a complete knowledge of what is meant by a finite spirit will not necessarily enable us to deduce that all finite spirits must be men, angels, or brutes. In dealing with the self-differentiating Notion of Teleology we may go further. We can be quite certain that we shall never be able to deduce the nature of the differentiations from our knowledge of the nature of the unity. For, as we have seen, the End in Teleology does not admit of being stated except as the unity which holds together just those differentiations in just that manner. And thus we cannot know the nature of the unity except in so far as we know the nature of the differentiations.

255. Hegel's use of the terms End and Means in this category seems to me very unfortunate. For, in ordinary language, the principal point in the significance of these terms is that the Means, as Means, exist only for the sake of the End, while the End exists for its own sake. The End has ultimate value, the Means only derivative value. Now it is an essential characteristic of Hegel's category, that the plurality, which he calls the Means, is just as fundamental and important as the unity, which he calls the End. But the contrary is almost irresistibly suggested by the associations called up by the words, and even Hegel himself seems sometimes to forget in what a different sense from the common one he is professing to use them.

Again, we must remember that, with the Hegelian use of the words, there can be no such thing as an unrealised End, or an inadequate Means. An End only exists at all in so far as it is the unity which unites the Means—*i.e.* which is realised by them, and, conversely, the Means only exist in so far as they are unified by, and express, the End, and can therefore offer no resistance to its realisation.

And with this use of the words the conception of a realised End loses altogether that implication of value which it has when the words are used in their ordinary significance. In the latter case, to begin with, the assertion that an End is realised is not a tautology. An End adopted is not necessarily realised, and the realisation brings in a fresh element. And that fresh element is the harmony between the purpose of a conscious being on the one hand, and the surrounding reality on the other. This certainly involves pleasure, and, if pleasure be taken as a good, it also involves good. And thus, with "finite and outward" Ends, their realisation takes us into the world of values, since, at the lowest, the realisation implies that some conscious being has got what he wanted.

But with Ends, in the Hegelian sense of the word, it is quite different. In the first place, to say that an End is realised, is now, as was explained above, a mere tautology.

And, in the second place, an End, in this sense, is only the inner unity of existence. It has no necessary relation to the purpose of any conscious being, and no implication of value.

256.   The End, we have seen, is a unity as compared to the plurality of the Means. But the question still remains whether there is only one Teleological system and one End for the whole universe, or whether there are a plurality of Ends. Hegel does not make this clear.

Logically, it would seem, there ought only to be one End. For there is no doubt that it is the Chemical Notion which becomes the End, and we have seen above (Section 251) that there can be only one Chemical Notion.

And there seem very grave difficulties in the way of the assertion of a plurality of Ends. Have the separate Ends separate Means or not ? If they have, then the universe—the whole of existence—is broken up into different systems unconnected with one another. For the principle of connexion, according to this category, lies wholly in the End, and two Ends could not be connected.

Such a view of the universe, at this point of the dialectic process, would be completely unjustifiable. It is scarcely possible that Hegel could have supposed it justifiable. At any rate, if he had made so great and striking a change at this point he would certainly have mentioned it explicitly, and as he gives no indication whatever of it, the hypothesis of a plurality of Ends, each with its distinct Means, must be rejected.

But it is equally impossible that a plurality of Ends should all have the same Means. For the things which are the Means will be related to one another in various ways, and these various relations will unite them all into a single system. Now, as we saw above, the unity which unites just those things in just that way, will be an End to those Means. And they can have none other than this. It is the unity of the system in which they are, and they are not in more than one system, for the system means all the relations which exist between them[1].

---

[1] In Absolute Mechanism the same Objects formed many systems. But then each system took the whole from the point of view of one Object as Centre, and there were many of these points of view. Here, where the unity of the system is not found in one of its parts, but is a distinct element, this source of plurality has failed.

Thus a plurality of Ends could neither have separate Means nor the same Means, and thus the plurality of Ends is untenable. No doubt minor systems might be discovered within the all-embracing system, and the unity of each of these might be taken as an End, but these systems would have relative Ends. The systems would be parts of the all-embracing system, and their Ends only Means to the one ultimate End.

On the other side, it must be admitted that the End is transformed into the Organism, and that Hegel unquestionably maintains a plurality of Organisms. But, in view of the arguments given above, it seems that we must say that there is only one End to the whole universe, and that the transition to the plurality of Organisms was unjustifiable.

A. The Subjective End.

257. (*G. L.* iii. 217. *Enc.* 207.) The full unity between Means and End is not attained till we reach the last division of Teleology. At first they are only regarded as of equal importance and as closely united. Each is still a separate entity with a separate nature of its own, though it could not exist except in conjunction with the other. This view dominates the two first subdivisions of Teleology. Whether Hegel could have avoided these, and could legitimately have proceeded direct from Chemism to the final form of Teleology is a question which it seems impossible to answer, on account of the difficulty of seeing precisely how he does pass from Chemism to Teleology as a whole.

The first subdivision of Teleology is called by Hegel the Subjective End. It regards the Means as possessing no definite quality of their own except that they are a plurality. One Object is as good as another in any position in the system of manifestations of the End. If the Object *A* fills the place *X* in the manifestation of the End, that does not imply any special fitness in *A* to manifest *X*. *B*, or any other Object, would have done quite as well. All that the Objects are wanted for is to provide a plurality.

258. The contradiction involved in this category is not hard to discover. For, while it asserts the Means to have separate natures, apart from that End which they carry out, it defines the Means so as to reduce this separate nature, and consequently the Means themselves, to nothing.

The interconnexions of the various Means with one another form the End, which the Means carry out. The End is the unity of the Means, and it is clearly to the End that these interconnexions, which unite the Means to one another, must be referred. Now the present category asserts that one Means would always do as well as another in carrying out the End, and, consequently, that the intrinsic nature of the Means has no relation to the End. It follows that the intrinsic nature of the different Means has no relation to the connexions between them. These connexions, however, form the whole of the external nature of the Objects which are considered as Means, and we saw, when we were dealing with Absolute Mechanism, that the inner nature is completely expressed in its outer nature. To maintain that anything has a core of its own apart from and unaffected by its relations to outer things would be to go back to the earlier categories of Essence, whose insufficiency has been demonstrated much earlier in the dialectic. Therefore this intrinsic nature which the Means are asserted to possess can neither be their outer nature nor their inner nature—and what else is left for it to be? Clearly nothing. And thus the Means, having no nature, would be non-existent.

To suppose, then, that the Means have no intrinsic adaptation to the End, is to destroy the possibility of their having a nature at all, and so the possibility of their existing at all. If, therefore, they are still to retain any externality whatever to the End, that externality must be harmonious to the End. The nature of each Means must consist in its fitness to carry out the End—its fitness to fill one particular place in the system of which the End is the unity. It thus ceases to be indifferent which Means are employed in manifesting the End in a particular way—that is, at a particular place in the system. Only those Means can do so which are fitted for the task by their own nature. We thus approach more closely in one respect to the ordinary significance of the word Means, which includes some special capability in the Object to carry out the End. It is thus appropriate that the next category should be called

B.   The Means.

(*G. L.* iii. 221.   *Enc.* 208.)   Here, as elsewhere, we must remember the special meaning of End and Means as Hegel uses them.   Though the Means have a certain externality to the End, and a certain distinction from it, yet it is not held that they could exist apart from it.   The position throughout Teleology is that the Means could not exist if they did not embody the End, nor the End if it were not embodied by the Means.   And so it may be misleading to speak here of the Means as *fitted* to embody the End.   The relation of the Means to the End is not a mere potentiality, as when, in the non-Hegelian sense of the terms, we say that a spade is a Means for digging.   For Hegel the Means only exist as embodying the End, and when we speak of them as being fitted for it, we only mean that their intrinsic nature co-operates in the manifestation, and is no longer considered as indifferent to it.

259.   This category, in its turn, is found to be inadequate. Of this Hegel gives two demonstrations, the first of which is to be found in the *Greater Logic* only, while the second occurs both there and in the *Encyclopaedia*.   They may be said to be based on the same general principle, but raise perfectly distinct points, and must be considered separately.

In the first (*G. L.* iii. 229) he says that if we accepted the position of this category we should be forced to insert, between the End and the Means, a second Means, and then, between the End and this second Means, a third Means, and so on *ad infinitum*, and that this involves a contradiction.   Let us expand this argument.

If the End and the Means are to be taken as distinguishable entities, then it is clear that each of them must conform to all the conditions which are necessary to the existence of any entity.   Now we have seen in the course of the dialectic that no entity of any sort can be a blank or undifferentiated unity. Therefore the End cannot be such a unity, but must be differentiated.   This, indeed, has already been admitted, and the work of the Means is to differentiate it.   But—and here the root of the inadequacy appears—if the End has an existence distinguishable from the Means, it must have a differentiation

distinguishable from the Means. Now the element of differentiation in a differentiated unity cannot be evolved from or
produced by the element of unity. It must be correlative with
it, and equally ultimate.

Within the End, therefore, and apart from the Means, there
must be such an element of differentiation. But the definition
of a Means, as we have seen, is just the plurality which
differentiates a unity in this way, and this element of differentiation will therefore be a second Means, between the End
and the first Means. And, now that it is a Means, it will,
according to the present category, be a separate entity from the
End. By the same reasoning as before, the End will require
some differentiation independent of this new Means, and this
differentiation will become a third Means, between the End and
the second Means. And this process will go on *ad infinitum*.

Such an infinite process as this clearly involves a contradiction. By the hypothesis the End and the first Means are
united. But we now find that their union must be mediated.
It depends on the union between the End and the second
Means. But this union again requires mediation, and so on.
All mediated connexions must depend on some immediate
connexion. But in this chain every connexion requires
mediation, and there is no immediate connexion. Then there
can be no mediated connexion either, and so no connexion at
all. But, by the hypothesis, there is a connexion. And thus
we reach a contradiction.

260. Hegel's second argument (*G. L.* iii. 230. *Enc.* 211)
is that the Realised End will, according to the present category,
be nothing but a Means, that it will consequently require
another Realised End beyond it, which in turn will be nothing
but a Means, and so on *ad infinitum*. This also requires some
expansion.

When End and Means are taken in their common and un-
Hegelian sense, there is a clear distinction between the Means
and the Realised End. A block of marble and a chisel may be
taken as Means to the End of making a statue, but no one
could mistake either the block or the chisel for the statue which
is their Realised End. But it is different when the terms have
their Hegelian sense. For then the Means is not merely an

Object which might be made to realise the End. It is an Object which does realise it, and which realises it necessarily, and by its intrinsic nature. The Means therefore is an Object whose nature is such that it realises the End. (If we are speaking of a single Object, it is better, except for the sake of brevity, to say "which participates in realising the End," since of course an End can only be realised in a plurality of Means.)

Now what is the Realised End? Is it anything more than this? It can be nothing more. The only form a Realised End can take is that of an Object whose nature is such that it manifests the End. And therefore, for Hegelian Teleology, there is no difference between the Means and the Realised End.

This conclusion we shall find later on to be the truth. But it is inconsistent with the position of the present category, and the attempt to combine the two produces a contradiction. For the Realised End is the union of the End and Means, and, if these are taken as in any way distinguishable, it cannot be the same as either of them. Hence when we find that our Realised End is identical with the Means, we cannot regard it as really the Realised End. If it is one extreme of the relation it cannot be the union of both. We take it then, according to Hegel, simply as the Means, and look for another Realised End beyond it. (It may be added, though Hegel does not mention it, that it would have been equally correct to take it simply as the Realised End, and then to look for another Means to mediate between it and the End. The infinite series thus started would lead to a contradiction, in the manner indicated in Section 259.) But the new Realised End would also necessarily be identical with the Means, for the same reasons as before, and our search would have to be continued *ad infinitum*. Such an infinite series would involve a contradiction, for there would be no term in which the End was realised, and therefore it would not be realised at all, while, by the hypothesis, it is realised.

261. The category which involves such contradictions must be transcended. And the way to transcend it is clear. The whole of the difficulty arose from the fact that End and Means were taken as separate entities. It was this that forced us to insert, between Means and End, an infinite series of new Means.

And it was this which gave us the choice, either to insert another infinite series of Means between Means and Realised End, or else to prolong the series of Means infinitely forward, in the vain attempt to reach a Realised End which was different from a Means.   We can get rid of the contradictions only by dropping our supposition that End and Means are in any way separate entities.   We know from the first category of Teleology that they can only exist if they are connected.   But now we are driven to the conclusion that they are two aspects of the same entity.   Existence is a differentiated unity.   The End is the aspect of unity, the Means the aspect of differentiation. The relation of the aspect of unity to the aspect of differentiation, and the relation of the various differentiations to one another were considered above (Sections 252—254).   With this we pass to the final subdivision, to which Hegel gives the name of

C.   The Realised End.

(*G. L.* iii. **224.**   *Enc.* **209.**)   The appropriateness of this name lies in the fact that the Realised End is the unity of the End and Means, and that we have come to the conclusion that End and Means are not two realities connected with each other, but two aspects distinguishable within a single reality.   And thus this category takes its name from the unity of the two sides—that is to say, from the Realised End.   (The unity of the two sides with one another, must, of course, be carefully distinguished from the unity of the differentiations, which is one of those two sides.)

Thus we learn that the universe is as much One as it is Many.   It is a reality in which the aspect of unity—the End—which makes it One, is as fundamental, and no more fundamental, than the aspect of plurality—the Means—which makes it Many.   This equipoise of unity and plurality may not be reached here for the first time in the dialectic, but our return to it when both unity and differentiation have been so fully developed, has a greater significance than its previous occurrence could have.   And thus we reach the end of Objectivity.

The treatment of Objectivity in the *Encyclopaedia* only varies in the fact that Mechanical Process, Absolute Mechanism, and Chemism are not, as in the *Greater Logic*, further divided. The first two, at any rate, of these changes, seem to be improvements.

CHAPTER X

THE IDEA

262. The last section of the dialectic is divided as follows :

I. Life. (Das Leben.)

    A. The Living Individual. (Das lebendige Individuum.)

    B. The Life-Process. (Das Lebens-Process.)

    C. The Kind. (Die Gattung.)

II. The Idea of Cognition. (Die Idee des Erkennen.)

    A. The Idea of the True. (Die Idee des Wahren.)

       (*a*) Analytic Cognition. (Das analytische Erkennen.)

       (*b*) Synthetic Cognition. (Das synthetische Erkennen.)

    B. The Idea of the Good. (Die Idee des Guten.)

III. The Absolute Idea. (Die absolute Idee.)

It should be noticed that within II. there are only two divisions, the Synthesis being absent, and that the same is the case with the subdivisions of II. A. Cognition (Erkennen) has its meaning so extended that, as will be seen later, it covers Volition as well as Knowledge.

263. In the last division of Objectivity, Realised End, we had reached the result that the whole of existence forms a system of differentiated parts, the unity of the system being as fundamental as the differentiation of the parts, and the differentiation of the parts, again, being as fundamental as the unity of the system. In this system the intrinsic nature of each part is dependent on its place in the system. It can only be explained, or even described, by reference to the system, and,

through the system, to the other members of it.   On the other
hand, the unity can only be described as the unity which does
connect these parts.   It has no nature which can be stated
apart from them, just as they have no nature which can be
stated apart from the unity.

This conception, which formed the Synthesis of the last triad
of Objectivity, is naturally reproduced in the Thesis of the first
triad of the Idea.   And this is the conception which we find in
the category of the Living Individual.

The general conception of the Idea is, according to Hegel,
the unity of the Subjective Notion and Objectivity.   (*G. L.* iii.
240.   He also calls it the unity of the Notion and Objectivity.
G. L. iii. 238.   *Enc.* 213.   This phrase is less appropriate than
the other, since Objectivity is also part of the Notion.)   In
Subjectivity the Individuals were connected by their similarities
and dissimilarities, which were realised as forming their inner
and intrinsic nature.   In Objectivity there was added to this
connexion the further connexion of each Individual with other
Individuals by means of causal relations[1].   But this was conceived at first as a species of connexion which was external to
the Individuals connected, and did not form part of their
natures.   This externality was gradually eliminated, but did
not completely disappear until the final category of Realised
End.   Then the determination of each Individual by others
was found to consist in their relation to one another in a Teleological System, while the inner nature of each is found to be an
expression of its place in the Teleological System.   Thus in
Idea the connexion of Individuals is, as in Objectivity, inclusive
of the mutual determination of each Individual by every other
Individual, while, at the same time, the whole connexion of
Individuals is, as in Subjectivity, part of their inner nature.

Hegel, however, says that "in a more general sense" the
Idea is also "the unity of Notion and Reality (Realität)"
(*G. L.* iii. 240).   This seems incorrect.   By Reality Hegel
appears to mean the plurality in which the Notion is expressed.
Now if he speaks of the conception of such a plurality in which

---

[1] This connexion by causal relation was, of course, first reached in Reciprocity, but its development was not taken up again until Objectivity had
been reached.

the Notion is expressed, that conception is not reached for the first time in the Idea, since both in Subjectivity and Objectivity the Idea was recognised as having such a plurality. If, on the other hand, he speaks of a detailed knowledge of that plurality, or of the actual existent plurality itself, these are not reached in the Idea. The whole dialectic deals only ·with à *priori* conceptions, and we cannot acquire by it any knowledge of the different characteristics of particular Individuals, which—for us at any rate—can only be known empirically. Still less can the actual Individuals themselves be part of the dialectic.

I. LIFE.

264. (*G. L.* iii. 244. *Enc.* 216.) We must, of course, bear in mind here, as with other categories named from concrete phenomena, the relation between those phenomena and the category. The category of Life does not apply only to what are commonly called living beings, but is equally true of all reality. Nor does Hegel profess to deduce by the dialectic process all the empirical characteristics of biological life. The choice of the name is due to the fact that this is the category of pure thought which is most usually and naturally employed in dealing with the phenomena of life.

Hegel is, I think, clearly right in saying that it is this category which is thus employed in dealing with the phenomena of life. In so far as any matter is held to form a living organism, it is held that the nature of each part of that whole is only capable of explication or description by reference to the organism as a whole, while that organism can only be described as the unity which is the unity of just those parts[1]. (This is the case when the organism is looked at by itself, and for itself. If the organism is regarded as connected with a conscious Spirit, and as used by that Spirit as a means to its own ends, more can be said about the organism. But then we are considering something beyond biological life.)

---

[1] We may compare Kant's account of an organised being. (*Critique of Judgment*, Section 65.) "In the first place it is requisite that its parts (as regards their presence and their form) are only possible through their reference to the whole....It is requisite secondly that its parts should so combine in the unity of a whole that they are reciprocally cause and effect of each other's form."

It is for this reason that he calls this category Life, and that he calls the element of unity by the name of Seele, and the element of plurality by the name of Body. It is not easy to find an English equivalent for Seele, in the sense in which it is used by Hegel, and I have therefore retained the German word. Soul would be misleading, since the modern use of that word is to designate what is otherwise called Spirit. But Seele means for Hegel nothing but the unity of which the body is the plurality—the element of unity in biological life.

In the case of Life Hegel makes it even more explicit than he does when dealing with other categories with concrete names, that he *intends* to keep strictly to pure thought, and to avoid all empirical intermixture. For he expressly warns us against supposing the Life spoken of in the dialectic to be identical with the life of concrete experience, whether the latter be taken by itself, or as a manifestation of Spirit (*G. L.* iii. 245—246). But he fails to carry out his intentions. The category of Life, as treated by him, possesses two important features which are found in the phenomena studied in biology, but which cannot, as it seems to me, be legitimately deduced by the dialectic process, and which ought not, therefore, to have been ascribed to the category.

265. In the first place, the question arises whether the universe consists of one example of the category of Life, or of many such examples. Each of these examples may be called an Organism. Are there many such Organisms, or only one?

It seems to me that the right answer to this would have been that there is only one. The whole universe, as I have maintained in the last chapter, forms one Teleological System, and, as it is the Teleological System which, in the new Thesis, is re-stated as the Organism, there should be only one Organism. And in the next category, Cognition, the individual cognizing Selves appear to correspond to the parts of the Organism, while the cognized Whole—which embraces the whole universe— corresponds to the Organism. This, also, indicates that the universe ought to be conceived as one Organism.

But Hegel takes a different view. According to him the universe, as seen under this category, consists of a plurality of Organisms, each of which has a plurality of parts. The Organisms are in relation to one another, and so may be said to form a unity of some sort, but this larger unity—which does embrace the whole universe—is not an Organic unity.

He seems to have been led into this error by the analogy offered by biology, which deals with a multitude of living beings, each of which is an organic unity, while they do not together form an organic unity.   And this error vitiates, I think, his whole treatment of the categories of Life.

266.   The second case in which, as it seems to me, Hegel has been misled by biological analogies is in treating the living Body[1] as an *inadequate* manifestation of the Seele.   On this, as we shall see, he endeavours to base the transition to the next category.   Now there is nothing in the dialectic to warrant this view.   In the Teleological System the nature of the unity was just that it was the unity which did connect those parts. If Hegel had not demonstrated the validity of this conception, he would have had no right to affirm the category of Teleology, nor, consequently, the category of Life.   But if he had demonstrated its validity, how could he be justified in saying that the parts are not an adequate manifestation of the unity?

But the analogy of biology would suggest that the manifestation could be inadequate.   For, although biological life is the best example known to us of this category, it is not a perfect example.   The parts of a biological organism have some existence independently of the organism of which they form part, since the same matter which now forms part of a living body, existed before that body was formed, and will exist when it has decomposed.   Its condition while in the body is in some respects different from its condition outside the body, but it retains certain characteristics unchanged.

Hegel quotes with approval (*Enc.* 216) Aristotle's remark that a hand separated from the body is only a hand in name, not in fact.   But if this is given as a characteristic which is confined to the parts of living beings, the statement cannot be justified.   A hand is changed more or less by being cut off— but so is a piece of granite changed, when it is cut out of the quarry.   The granite remains more or less the same after the

---

[1] Here, and wherever I write Body with a capital initial, I mean the element of plurality in Hegel's category of Life.   When I mean the body as known to biology I write the word without a capital.

separation, and so does the hand. Even when the hand eventually decays, the atoms, or other units, into which it is resolved, are in many respects the same as they were before the hand was cut off. Thus the difference here between the organic and the inorganic is only a matter of degree.

And, on the other hand, the organism in biology is independent, to a certain degree, of its parts. For during the life of an organism, much matter is added to it, and much, which previously belonged to it, is excluded from it, while the organism is regarded as being the same through all these changes.

Since the biological organism and its parts are thus more or less independent of one another, the possibility of an inadequate manifestation of the organism by its parts would arise. But this relative independence is not a characteristic of the category of Life, as given in the dialectic, and Hegel is not justified in asserting the possibility, under that category, of an imperfect manifestation.

The approval which Hegel gives to Aristotle's statement about the hand, seems to indicate that he did not fully realise the imperfect nature of biological unity, to which, as I submit, the possibility of an inadequate manifestation is due. But the fact that biological manifestations were sometimes inadequate—and that so the organism died—was clearly before him. And it was this, I think, which led him to suppose the possibility of inadequate manifestation in his category of Life.

Hegel says that Life is the Idea in the form of immediacy (*G. L.* iii. 249. *Enc.* 216). It appears from what he says later with reference to the process by which this category is transcended, that he connects the immediacy of Life with the possibility of an inadequate manifestation. A particular arrangement of parts, which in point of fact exists, may or may not manifest the Seele adequately. If it does manifest it adequately this is a mere fact, which can be recognised as true, but cannot be demonstrated as necessary.

A. *The Living Individual*[1].

267. (*G. L.* iii. 249. *Enc.* 218.) Three characteristics of the Living Individual are given by Hegel—Sensibility,

---

[1] Individual here stands for Das Individuum, and not, as elsewhere in this book, for Das Einzelne.

Irritability, and Reproduction.   These correspond, he says, to
the Universal, the Particular, and the Individual (Das Einzelne).
They are not divided off, either in the text or in the table of
contents, as separate subdivisions of the category of Life, but
it would seem that Hegel does regard them as such, since the
third seems to be taken as a Synthesis of the other two, and to
form the transition to the next category of the Life-Process.
The transition from the Thesis to the Antithesis, however, is
not very clear.   It would seem that both are reached directly
from the general idea of Life, rather than the second from the
first.   All three assume that there is something outside each
Organism.   This naturally follows from Hegel's view that there
is a plurality of Organisms, for then each of them will have
other Organisms outside it.

In the first place, then, an Organism which is related to
other things outside it, will be affected by them, and will
receive impressions from them.   By reason of the unity of the
Organism, these impressions will not only affect that part of
the Organism which first receives them, but will also affect the
Organism as a whole and in its unity.   This affection of the
whole by what happens in any part is what Hegel calls Sensibility (*G. L.* iii. 253.   *Enc.* 218).   (Here, as afterwards with
Irritability and Reproduction, the name, like the name of Life,
is only applied to the logical conception because that conception
is *exemplified* in what is commonly called Sensibility.   It does
not imply that all existence has the empirical characteristic of
Sensibility.)

In the second place, the Organism will in its turn affect
whatever is outside it.   It will do this by means of the part of
its Body which is in immediate relation with the particular
outside thing in question.   But this part of the Body will be
determined to its particular nature by the Seele, the unity of
the Organism.   And this action of the whole Organism, through
its part, on what is outside it, is called Irritability (*G. L.* iii. 254.
Enc. 218).

The third stage is the maintenance of the Organism as a
whole, through, and by means of, its relation to what is external
to it.   In the *Greater Logic* he says that this, on its theoretical
side, may be called Feeling (Gefühl) and on its "real" side

may be called Reproduction (Reproduktion) (*G. L.* iii. 254).
In the *Encyclopaedia* only the name Reproduction is used
(*Enc.* 218).

When Reproduction is found in a series of names which are
taken from biological science, we should naturally suppose it to
mean that the characteristic after which this category was
named was the power possessed by living beings of producing
other beings of their own species.   But this is not the case.
Hegel's language, in both *Logics,* is clearly incompatible with
this, and moreover the propagation of the species is found later
on as an example of a more advanced stage of the category
of Life.

The Organism, then, preserves itself in its own identity
through its relation to what is outside it.   Throughout this
triad of the Living Individual, it is assumed that each
Organism must enter into relation with what is outside it, and
that it is by means of these relations that it will maintain
and express its own nature.   This necessarily follows, if it is
admitted that there is a plurality of Organisms, and that,
consequently, every Organism must have something outside it.
For the different parts of the universe cannot be unconnected,
nor can their connexion be anything merely external to them.
It must be a connexion in which the nature of those different
parts must be expressed.   This results from previous stages of
the dialectic.   The only illegitimate assumption is the primary
assumption that there is a plurality of Organisms.

268.   With this conception of the relation of the Organism
to the outside world we reach

B.   The Life-Process

(*G. L.* iii. 255.   *Enc.* 219), which consists in just such a self-
maintenance of the Organism by means of its external relations.
The empirical characteristic of living beings which Hegel com-
pares to this category is the process of assimilation, by which
the animal or vegetable not only maintains itself by its relation
to what is external to its body, but, in that process of maintenance, actually converts it into a part of its body (*G. L.*
iii. 258.   *Enc.* 219).

In this connexion Hegel says that the living being "stands

face to face with an inorganic nature" (*Enc.* 219). This, taken literally, could not apply to the relations of the Organism under this category. All the universe is not, according to Hegel, one Organism, but it consists of nothing but Organisms, and thus no Organism could be in relation to anything inorganic, since nothing inorganic exists.

This, however, does not affect the accuracy of the category. For all that the category requires is that the Organism should stand in relation to something with which it is not in organic relation. And this condition, as we have seen, is satisfied if the Organism stands in relation to other Organisms.

In speaking of this category in the *Greater Logic* Hegel says that "the self-determination of the living being has the form of objective externality, and since the living being is at the same time identical with itself, it is the absolute contradiction (Widerspruch)" (*G. L.* iii. 256). I do not see why he should have said this. Of course this category, like all categories from Becoming onwards, contains, synthesised in its unity, moments which if unsynthesised would contradict each other. But they do not contradict each other when synthesised, so that the name of Contradiction is not appropriate. And, if it were appropriate to a category which synthesised moments which contradict one another, it would be equally applicable to all categories except Being and Nothing.

In connexion with this contradiction, and the division (Entzweiung) which it involves, Hegel introduces Pain. It may be doubted whether it is worth while to carry so far the parallelism between the empirical characteristics known in biology and the characteristics of the logical category. If it were, it would seem as if Pain should rather be introduced in connexion with the inadequacy of the manifestation—a point not yet reached.

269.   The transition to the next category appears to be by the idea of Universality. In the Life-Process the Particularity of the Organism is transcended, and it is elevated to Universality, by reason of its connexion of itself with that which is external to it, while it maintains its own nature in that connexion. "Through the external Life-Process it has thus posited itself as real, universal Life, as Kind" (*G. L.* iii. 259).

C. The Kind.

(*G. L.* iii. 259. *Enc.* 220.) Hegel's view is, apparently, that the idea of the Kind is now the Seele, or principle of unity, of each Organism. And it is the inadequacy of any particular Body to manifest the general idea of the Kind, on which he relies to demonstrate the inadequacy of all Organic manifestation.

270. This view seems to me to be quite unjustified. It is true that the Universal element in the Organism becomes more explicit when we realise that it not only manifests itself in its own Body, but maintains itself in and by means of its relation to what is outside its Organism. And it is true that a Kind, or species, is Universal as compared to the Individuals which belong to it. But the transition from one to the other is quite illegitimate, for they are two quite different Universals. The Universal which constitutes a Kind is a Universal such as was discussed under Subjectivity—a common quality, or group of qualities, which can be shared by various Individuals. It was because this sort of Universal proved inadequate as a description of existence that the dialectic passed in Objectivity to the Universals of Systems. The Universal throughout Objectivity, and now in Life, has been the Universal which is the unity of a System, a Universal which belongs to and unites certain differentiations, so that each of them has its definite place in the System, and, by means of this systematic connexion, the existence of one differentiation determines the existence of another. This is clearly quite a different notion from such·a Universal as "lion." The latter denotes a group of qualities which may be, as in point of fact it is, shared by many beings, but which does not unite them in any sort of system, since the existence of one lion does not determine the existence of any others—at least, does not determine it by virtue of their common Universal. If all lions but one were annihilated, the survivor would not be any less a lion, while, on the other hand, if all the organs of a living body but one were annihilated, the one which remained would no longer be part of an organic unity.

Hegel has therefore no right to substitute one conception of Universal for the other at this point as if they were equivalent

—especially as in doing so he substitutes a conception which he had demonstrated to be defective for the higher conception which had transcended the defect.

271. Since, according to Hegel's view, the Seele of the Organism is its Kind-Universal, the Organism, as being only a particular Individual, is unable to manifest this Seele adequately. The inadequacy is displayed in two ways. Firstly, the Individual propagates its Kind, by producing other Individuals which belong to the Kind (*G. L.* iii. 261. *Enc.* 220). Secondly, the Individual dies (*G. L.* iii. 262. *Enc.* 221).

I cannot see that Hegel has justified his view that the Body of the Organism will be inadequate to manifest its Seele. He has transformed the System-Universal, with which Organism started, to a Class-Universal, which is not the Seele of the Organism. And there seems no reason whatever to say that a particular Organism cannot manifest such a Class-Universal of a Kind. The Class-Universal of the Kind of lions, for example, consists of certain general qualities—the qualities of being vertebrate, mammal, carnivorous, etc. There is no reason why a particular Organism should not possess all these qualities, and, if it does, it is an adequate manifestation of the Class-Universal[1].

The statement that the inadequacy is shown in Propagation also seems to me mistaken, because I cannot see what characteristic of the category of Organism, as reached in the dialectic, could possibly correspond to Propagation. The other biological facts whose names have been used—Life, Seele, Body, Sensibility, Irritability, Assimilation, are, as we have seen, examples of certain characteristics of the category. But there has been no demonstration in the dialectic that one of the Organisms of a particular Kind would be produced by another Organism of

---

[1] It is possible that Hegel may have vaguely conceived the Idea of the Kind as including an Ideal of the way in which the Class-Universal *should* be possessed, so that a lion who was not a lion in the best sort of way was not an adequate manifestation of the Idea of a lion. But he has not explicitly stated, still less justified, the introduction of this fresh element into the Idea of a Kind. And all that would follow would be the *possibility* that no lions were, in this sense, adequate manifestations of the Idea of the Kind. It would not follow that no lion *could* be an adequate manifestation, which is what Hegel asserts.

the same Kind, nor anything which even suggests that this would be the case. And nothing but a production of one Organism by another could appropriately be named after the biological fact of propagation.

The biological fact of death could doubtless be taken as an example of the change which would take place if an Organism, as defined by the category, broke up so that the parts of its Body ceased to be connected with one another by the Seele, and so ceased to form an organic Body. .Such a dissolution would be incompatible with the conception of Organism, as Hegel first deduced it, for according to that the parts would have no nature apart from their connexion in the Organism, and could not, therefore, exist when it was dissolved. But Hegel, as we have seen, takes the Organism to be an imperfect manifestation of its Seele, and so the parts, which do exist in the Organism, might possibly exist otherwise.

But while the inadequacy of the manifestation would thus *allow of* the dissolution of the Organism, Hegel's attempt to treat that dissolution as an *expression* of the inadequacy of the Organism must be condemned as invalid. For the inadequacy of the Organism to express its Seele is, according to Hegel, necessary and invariable. If the inadequacy is inconsistent with the existence of the Organism, the Organism can never come into existence at all, and therefore can never dissolve. If the inadequacy is not inconsistent with the existence of the Organism, then the dissolution of the Organism cannot be accounted for by the inadequacy[1].

272. Death and propagation, while they proclaim the inadequacy of the manifestation, also, according to Hegel, furnish the escape from the inadequacy. "The process of Kind, in which the individual Individuals (die einzelnen Individuen) lose in one another their indifferent immediate existence, and die in this negative unity, has also for the other aspect of its product the Realised Kind, which has posited itself as identical

---

[1] There remains the possibility that the inadequacy, though not inconsistent with the existence of the Organism, would cause such friction among its parts as to wear it out after a time. But such a quantitative relation could never, I think, be proved à priori, as it must be if it is to form part of the dialectic. And certainly Hegel makes no attempt to prove it.

with the Notion.   In the Kind-process the separated individualities of the individual lives pass away; the negative
identity, in which the Kind returns to itself, while it is on one
side the production of individuality, is on the other side the
transcending of individuality, and thus is the Kind which
comes together with itself, the Universality of the Idea which
is becoming for itself" (*G. L.* iii. 262. Cp. *Enc.* 221, 222).

Thus Hegel finds the solution of the inadequacy in the
conception of the Kind as a whole, which remains while its
members die.   He reaches this conception by means of the
conception of Propagation, which, as I have endeavoured to
show above, is unjustified.   But this need not invalidate the
present step, since we should have a right to conceive of the
Kind as a whole, even if its members were not connected by
any tie analogous to propagation in biology.   And, again, while
Hegel was not justified in taking Death—the dissolution of the
Organism—as the expression of the inadequacy of the manifestation of the Seele, it is still possible that Organisms may
dissolve.

But, when we have reached the conception of the Realised
Kind, is the idea of the Kind manifested with less inadequacy
than it was before ?   It seems to me that this is not the case.
The idea of the Kind, as we have seen, is simply that group of
Universals which are possessed by every member, actual or
possible, of the Kind.   These are manifested in the separate
members of the Kind, or nowhere.   It is, for example, the
individual lions who are carnivorous, not the species as a unity,
for the species as a unity cannot eat flesh.   Now Hegel has
arrived, rightly or wrongly, at the conclusion that the individual
Organisms cannot, in any case, adequately manifest the idea of
the Kind, which is their Seele.   And, if that is correct, they
cannot manifest it adequately when we take them all together,
and call them the Realised Kind.   The grouping them together
will make no difference to the inadequacy in the case of each
Organism, since the inadequacy, according to Hegel, is a
necessary characteristic of an Organism.   And, if the manifestation is not adequate in the case of particular Organisms,
it cannot be adequate at all, for it only occurs in the particular
Organisms.

273. It may be replied, possibly, that Hegel has, legitimately or illegitimately, changed his conception of the idea of a Kind, and that that idea is not, for him, a Class-Universal, but a System-Universal, which can be realised in all the members of the Kind taken together, though it cannot be realised in any one of them separately.

There seem to me, however, three objections to this view. In the first place, if Hegel had meant this, he would have held that all the members of each Kind formed together one single Organism, for an Organism, for him, means a system of parts which manifests, as a whole, a unity which none of the parts could manifest separately. Now there is nothing in Hegel's language to suggest that the Kind is now to be regarded as itself an Organism. He never assigns to it either Sensibility, Irritability, or Reproduction, all of which he considers as essential for an Organism.

In the second place, if he had taken this view, he would have departed very materially from the analogy of biology, where a species, or other kind, does not mean an organic whole, the existence of one member of which involves the existence of all the rest, but a class composed of all the beings who have certain common qualities. We have seen that, up to this point, Hegel has been keeping very close to the biological analogy of the category—much closer than he was justified in doing. Is it probable that, at this point, while still using biological names profusely, he should have so far departed from the biological analogy, without a word of warning or justification?

In the third place, if the Kind really were meant now to be a System-Universal, which would only be manifested through all the members of the Kind taken together, then, if Death were brought in at all, it could only be on the view that Death did not really remove the individual from the Kind, and so did not destroy the totality required for the manifestation. But this is certainly not Hegel's view. It is clear from the passage last quoted that the adequacy of the manifestation in the Realised Kind is not dependent on the irrelevancy of Death to the question of manifestation. On the contrary, it is only because "the separated individualities of the individual lives pass away" that the manifestation can become adequate.

Those lives, therefore, cannot be members of an Organism in which the adequate manifestation occurs, and as they are members of the Kind, the Kind is not an Organism.

274.   Thus we must, I think, take the Kind-Universal to be, as is certainly suggested by its name, a Class-Universal and not a System-Universal.   And in that case, as I pointed out above, the Realised Kind cannot give a more adequate manifestation than the separate members.   Nor does the introduction of Death help the matter, though Hegel seems to think that it does so.   The inadequate manifestations successively pass away, in the successive dissolutions of Organisms, but they leave nothing better behind them.   So long as there are any Organisms left, they are only inadequate manifestations of the idea of the Kind.   If, on the other hand, they all passed away, there would not be a Realised Kind at all.

We must, therefore, I consider, reject as invalid the solution which Hegel offers us in the conception of Realised Kind.   And there is a further objection.   The next category to Kind is the category of the Idea of the True.   Since Realised Kind removes according to Hegel the defects of the category of Kind, it would follow that, when we have reached the conception of Realised Kind, we should find ourselves already to have passed into Cognition, and, more particularly, into the Idea of the True. And this is apparently what Hegel thinks has now happened. He says (continuing the passage quoted above, *G. L.* iii. 262) "In propagation the immediacy of living individuality dies; the death of this life is the emergence of Spirit.   The Idea, which as Kind is implicit (an sich) is now for itself, since it transcends the particularity, which is produced by the living generations (Geschlechter), and has thus given itself a reality, which is simple universality.   Thus it is the Idea which relates itself to itself as Idea, the Universal, which has universality as its determination and definite being (Bestimmtheit und Dasein), the Idea of Cognition."   This, however, does not seem justifiable. But before considering this point we must determine exactly what Hegel means by the Idea of Cognition.

II.   THE IDEA OF COGNITION.

275.   (*G. L.* iii. 263.   *Enc.* 223.)   He describes it as follows. "The Notion is for itself as Notion, in so far as it exists *freely* as abstract universality, or as Kind.   So it is its pure identity with itself, which so creates such a division in itself, that what is separated is not an Objectivity, but liberates itself and takes the form of Subjectivity, or of a simple equality with self, and thus is the Object (Gegenstand) of the Notion, the Notion itself....The elevation of the Notion above Life consists in this, that its Reality is the Notion-form, freed and in the form of universality.   Through this division (Urtheil) the Idea is doubled, on the one hand the subjective Notion, of which it itself is the Reality, and on the other hand, the objective Notion, which it is as Life.—Thought, Spirit, Self-consciousness, are determinations of the Idea, in so far as it has itself as an Object, and its Determinate Being (Dasein), that is, the determination of its Being (Bestimmtheit ihres Seins), is its own difference from itself" (*G. L.* iii. 263).

This is not very clear, but, with the aid of the concrete states which Hegel takes as examples of this category, we can, I think, see what the logical conception of the category must be.   Those examples are a complete system of correct knowledge, and a complete system of gratified volition.

The conception, I believe, is as follows.   The whole Universe forms an Organic system.   The parts can only be explained or described by reference to the system, and, through the system, to the other members of it, while the unity of the system can only be explained as the unity which does connect those parts.   But the fresh element is this—each of these parts, which may now be called Individuals, has within it a system, which corresponds to the larger system—the system of the Universe.

But what sort of correspondence?   It cannot be merely that there is one part in each Individual-System for each part in the Universe-System.   For that correspondence would be equally exemplified if the Individual judged about each part of the Universe, but judged wrongly, or if the Individual willed about each part of the Universe, but willed it to be other than it is.

And it is clear, as we shall see later, that Hegel would not regard such a state as exemplifying the category.

But it is equally clear that the correspondence of the parts does not mean identity of nature. If each part of an Individual-System had the same content with the corresponding part of the Universe-System, then the two systems would have exactly the same nature. For if the parts were exactly the same in the two systems, then the relations between the parts must also be the same. And as the unity in each case is just the unity which is formed by these parts in these relations, the unities would have the same nature in each system. Thus the two systems would be of exactly the same nature, which is impossible, since one is an Individual, which the other is not, and one is the Universe, which the other is not.

The examples, moreover, show that correspondence here does not mean exact similarity in nature. My correct knowledge that A is courageous does not resemble A's courage at all closely. Nor, if my will approves the fact that A is modest, does my gratified volition closely resemble his modesty.

276. If we try to state more positively what this correspondence is, all that we can say, I think, is that each part of the Individual corresponds with a part of the Universe, and each part of the Universe with a part of the Individual; that the correspondence consists of a relation between the natures of the two correspondent terms, which is not a relation of identity; that the relation of a true belief to the fact in which it is a belief is one example of such a correspondence; that the relation of a volition to the fact which gratifies the volition is another example; and that no other example can be given.

For such a correspondence as this the expression "harmony" suggests itself, and we shall, I think, do well to use it. But it must be remembered that harmony does not here indicate the co-operation of two beings for some purpose or design outside themselves. Nor does it indicate any relation which the two harmonious beings jointly bear to a third—as when we say that the sounds of two different instruments unite to form a harmonious whole for the listener. The relation of harmony in this category is simply a relation between the two harmonious beings—the Universe and the Individual—without reference

to anything else.   (The different Individuals, indeed, are not
unconnected with each other, but it is only through their
relation with the Universe.)

Thus the advance on the last category consists in the fact
that the parts under the category of Cognition, not only, as
with Life, form a system which collectively expresses the idea
of the system, but, in addition, do this by means of the existence, in each part, of a system in harmony with the system of
the whole.

This gives a greater relative prominence, in the new
category, to the parts—*i.e.* the Individuals.   For although,
since the Universe is an organic system, they only express
the idea of that system in so far as, taken together, they form
the system, yet it is also the case that each Individual by itself
may be said in another sense to be an expression of the
Universe, since it contains a system in harmony with the
system of the Universe[1].   Whether these two characteristics
are compatible will be considered later.   At present I merely
urge that they are both to be found in the category.

It is probably the greater prominence given to the parts
in this category, which causes Hegel to speak of it as an
Urtheil (*G. L.* iii. 262, 263.   *Enc.* 223).   For, while he generally
uses this word in its ordinary sense of Judgment, he always
lays great weight on the fact that etymologically it indicates
division.

In reaching the category of Cognition Hegel says that we
have left behind the Immediacy which characterised Life.
This Immediacy, apparently, consisted in the fact that particular parts might or might not be so arranged as to manifest
the Seele of an Organism.   From the absence of any necessity
that it should be so, he apparently deduced the *possibility* of an
inadequate manifestation—though it would be impossible to
find in it the *necessity*, which he asserts, that the manifestation
should be inadequate.

If such an Immediacy did belong to the category of Life, I
do not see how it has been eliminated.   But the truth seems
to be that there is no need to eliminate it, because it should

---

[1] In this second sense it would be equally correct, as will be seen later, to
say that the Universe is an expression of each Individual.

never have been introduced.   If Hegel had proved the validity of the category of Life at all, he had proved that the parts not only *could*, but *must*, be arranged in organic unity.   That he should have thought it only a possibility is connected with his view of the possibility and necessity of inadequate manifestations, which we found reason above to reject as erroneous.

277.   This, then, is the nature of the category to which Hegel passes from the category of Life.   Is he justified in the transition ?   I cannot see that he is justified.   In the first place, the whole of Existence appears, under this category, to form a single organic system.   Now in Teleology, as we have seen, Hegel had taken all existence to form one organic system. But he gave this up in Life—gave it up, as I have tried to show above, illegitimately, and misled by biological analogies. And having once given it up, he has no right to bring it back, except by a fresh demonstration of it, which he does not profess to give us.

Even if we supposed that the Realised Kind was held by Hegel to be an organic unity (a theory which, as I explained above, I think must be rejected) the difficulty would not be removed.   For it seems clear that Hegel meant by the Kind something analogous to a biological species, of which there are more than one in the Universe, so that the organic unity of a Kind would not mean that the Universe formed one organic unity.   And, moreover, if Hegel had regarded the Realised Kind as an organic unity, his position would have been illegitimate, since the Kind when first introduced is not an organic unity, and no demonstration is given of the validity of a transition.   Thus, by basing the organic unity of the Universe in the category of Cognition on the organic unity of the Realised Kind, we should not avoid an illegitimate transition, but merely throw it a little earlier in the dialectic process.

In the second place, there is a still more fundamental objection to the transition.   So far as I can see, there is not the slightest attempt to demonstrate the characteristic which forms the essential difference of Cognition from Life—the existence, in each part, of a system corresponding to the system of the whole.   The essential characteristic of Realised Kind was the subordination of the particular Organisms to the idea of the Kind.   What the connexion is between this and the existence of the systems within Individuals is left in complete obscurity.

Hegel was no doubt justified in naming this category after a concrete state of the human mind.   For knowledge, in so far as correct, and volition, in so far as gratified, do form systems which correspond to the objects which are known or which gratify the volition in the way defined above.   Indeed, no other examples of this category can, I think, be found. Certainly Hegel does not give any other examples.   Indeed, it might be said that he has not *completely* defined the new category at all, but has left part of the definition implicit in the statement that the correspondence in question is the one of which true knowledge and gratified volition are examples.

278.   We have seen in earlier stages of the dialectic that, when categories are named after concrete states, there is considerable risk of falling into error by attributing to the categories characteristics which are true of the concrete states, but which have not been demonstrated of the categories.   Here the difficulty of avoiding this error is greater than elsewhere.   In Mechanism and Chemism Hegel is able to give other examples of the category besides those drawn from Mechanics and Chemistry.   In Life he does not himself give any examples besides those drawn from biology, but it is possible to supply the deficiency.   The unity which is expressed in the different parts of a beautiful object—a Persian rug, for example, or an Adam ceiling—is an example of what Hegel calls an organic unity.   And the distinction of the category from the biological state is rendered easier by the fact, which we have remarked, that the biological state is never a *perfect* example of the category.

Here matters are different.   No example of the category has been given, by Hegel or anyone else, except that of a system, each of whose parts is in relation, by knowledge or volition, with all the other parts.   And this would be a perfect example if the knowledge and volition had reached that perfection towards which all knowledge and volition are directed.   And, as mentioned above, it may be held that the category has not been completely defined except by reference to these concrete examples.

The danger of the error is therefore greater here than elsewhere. I do not think, as I shall explain later, that Hegel has entirely avoided it. But it has not affected his argument so seriously as it did in the category of Life.

While it is certainly appropriate to name this category after a state of the human mind, the actual name of Cognition seems unfortunate. Volition, as well as knowledge, is an example of this category, while, as we shall see, volition is the only example of one of its subdivisions. Cognition, then, would only be appropriate if it were possible to stretch its meaning to include Volition, and this does not seem possible, either with the English Cognition, or the German Erkennen. It seems to me that some more general term—perhaps Consciousness—would have been better.

279. Cognition has, according to Hegel, only two subdivisions, without any Synthesis being explicitly given. These he calls the Idea of the True and the Idea of the Good. In the *Encyclopaedia* the first of these subdivisions is called Cognition, and the second Volition, the name of Cognition being also used, as in the *Greater Logic*, for the category as a whole.

Since there is to be a harmony between the Individual-systems and the Universe-system the question naturally arises, which side is active and which side passive. The alternatives, as will be seen later, are not really exhaustive, and neither answer to the question will be finally tenable. But it is, according to Hegel, the natural way in which to begin regarding the matter. If we find two things necessarily agreeing with each other, the natural inference is that one is dependent on the other, or else both on a third. Now here there is no third. There is only the Universe-system on the one hand and the Individual-systems on the other. We seem, therefore, bound to conclude either that the harmony is produced by the nature of the Individuals being dependent on the nature of the Universe, or else by the nature of the Universe being dependent on the nature of the Individuals.

Of these two alternatives we must start with the former. If we took the latter, there would be no guarantee that the

Individual-systems, whose nature would then be taken as
ultimate, did not differ in such a way that the Universe-system
could not be in harmony with them all. In that case the
requirements of the category of Cognition, which Hegel regards
as already demonstrated, could not be complied with. But if
the single Universe-system is taken as ultimate, and the many
Individual-systems are taken as dependent on it, no such
difficulty arises.

Hegel therefore starts with the conception of the Universe-
system as determining the Individual-systems, and this gives
him

A.   The Idea of the True.

(*G. L.* iii. 274. *Enc.* 226.) The category has this name
because the only example which can be given of it is a system
of knowledge in the Individual which truly represents the
Universe-system.

280. If we compare knowledge and volition, we find that
the object of each is to produce a harmony, and that they differ
in the fact that in the one the object, and in the other the
subject, is the determining side of the harmony. This can be
tested by looking at a case where the harmony is discovered to
be imperfect. In such a case, should it occur in knowledge, we
condemn the knowledge as being incorrect; and we endeavour
to amend it by altering our beliefs till they harmonise with the
objects. With volition it is just the reverse. Here we condemn
the outside reality which does not accord with our desires, and
we endeavour to restore harmony by altering the objects so
that they may be as we desire them.

Thus in knowledge the aim of the knowing subject is that
its state should be a representation of the state of the world at
large. Of course this does not imply that the mind is purely
passive in the process, and has nothing to do but receive effects
from outside. The question is not about the way results are
produced, but about the test of them when they are produced.
However active the process of knowledge may be, the fact
remains that its correctness depends on its agreement with the
object known.

Thus knowledge is an example of this category, and it is
the only one which can be given, since volition—the only other

example of the wider category of Cognition—would not be appropriate in this subdivision.

We must of course remember, here as elsewhere, that what we are entitled to predicate of all existence is not the possession of all the characteristics of knowledge which are empirically known to us, but only those which are involved in the logical category.

It is further to be remembered that, according to the category, each Individual-system has to harmonise with the whole of the Universe-system, and that there is nothing in the Individual except this system which harmonises with the Universal. Accordingly, if we look at an actual knowing individual—such as each of us is—we find that his nature, as it empirically appears to us, fails to exemplify the category in two ways. It is too large, and not large enough. On the one hand, I do not know the whole universe perfectly. On the other hand, I am not merely a knowing being, but have also volitions and emotions.

The *Encyclopaedia*, as was mentioned above, calls this category Cognition. It is inconvenient, of course, that the same name should be used both for the wider category and for its subdivision[1], but otherwise the nomenclature of the *Encyclopaedia* seems better. For what exemplifies the category is not truths or true propositions—non-existent realities,which are just as real whether they are or are not ever known by anyone. The category is exemplified by knowledge—by existent states of existent conscious Individuals. And this is expressed more clearly if the category is called Cognition than if it is called the Idea of the True.

What have we gained by the establishment of this category? We have not proved that there is some knowledge—that some beliefs are true. The assertion that there is some knowledge could never be proved, for any proof offered would consist of assertions, which, if valid, would be knowledge. Thus the proof would assume the conclusion to be proved. On the other hand, any attempt to disprove it, or even to deny or doubt it, would equally assume its truth.

---

[1] Wallace, in his translation, avoids this inconvenience by calling the subdivision Cognition Proper.

This then, could not be proved, and, moreover, the dialectic is here concerned, not with knowledge itself, but with a category, of which knowledge furnishes indeed the only example known to us, but which must nevertheless be carefully distinguished from that example.

What is really gained by this category is that we know that the Universe is an organic system of Individuals, the nature of each of which forms another system, in harmony with the system of the Universe, and determined by it.

281.   The Idea of the True is divided by Hegel into Analytic Cognition and Synthetic Cognition.   These appear to be Thesis and Antithesis respectively, but the Synthesis is lacking.   It seems curious that he did not take Philosophical Thought as the Synthesis, since he certainly regards this as being both analytical and synthetical (cp. *Enc.* 238).

Hegel discusses Analytic and Synthetic Cognition at considerable length (*G. L.* iii. 278—319.   *Enc.* 227—232).   What he says about them is sufficiently simple and straightforward. I omit it here because it seems entirely irrelevant to the category which we are considering.   Once more Hegel has been misled by the concrete state which he has taken as an example of his category.

The distinction which he draws here is not between analytic and synthetic propositions, but that between knowledge obtained by a process of analysis and knowledge obtained by a process of synthesis.   Both of these processes can yield synthetic propositions.

Now the distinction between these two processes may be very relevant when we consider the state of knowledge as empirically known to us.   But there is no corresponding distinction to be found in the category of the dialectic, with which Hegel is dealing here.   Indeed, we may go further.   Not only are we unable to see what distinction in the category should correspond to the distinction between analytic and synthetic knowledge, but we are able to see clearly that there can be no such distinction.

For the distinction between analytic and synthetic knowledge relates wholly to the method of acquiring it.   The distinction does not exist in the nature of the knowledge, as

known. If I know that Caesar is mortal, I know the same
truth, whether I learn it by seeing him die, or by deduction
from the truth that all men are mortal. The other truths
acquired along with it by the same process may be different in
the two cases. In the first, I may learn along with the fact
that Caesar is mortal, the fact that Brutus stabbed him. In
the second, I may learn along with the fact that Caesar is
mortal, the fact that Brutus is mortal. But the knowledge
that Caesar is mortal will be the same, by whichever method it
is acquired.

This distinction can therefore have no place in the present
category, the example of which is not the acquisition of knowledge, but the possession of the knowledge when acquired.
When the dialectic passed from the lower categories of Teleology
to Realised End, it became clear that the application of the
category to any subject-matter involved, not that the Means
were becoming the manifestation of the End, but that they
were the manifestation of the End. Nothing that has happened
since that point has given us a right to change that conclusion.
The Means expressing the End have developed into the Individual-systems which harmonise with the Universal-system, but
the relation between the whole and the parts has remained
a relation of manifestation, not a relation of a process towards
manifestation.

Nor is anything in Hegel's treatment of Life inconsistent
with this view. He takes the Body, indeed, as an inadequate
and temporary manifestation of the Seele, but still, such as the
manifestation is, it is always present when the category of Life
is present. The category does not deal with the gradual
production of Life.

Thus the principle on which these subdivisions, Analytic
and Synthetic Cognition, have been introduced seems unjustified.
And the mass of detail given under them, while applicable
enough to the concrete process of acquiring knowledge, contains
nothing which has any significance with regard to the category.
I therefore believe myself justified in omitting it.

282. Hegel's error in introducing these subdivisions does
not destroy the line of his argument, for we can go directly
from the undivided category of the Idea of the True to the

next category—the Idea of the Good. Hegel himself indeed makes the transition from the subdivision of Synthetic Cognition, but, if it was not for the error which led to the introduction of the subdivisions, he could have made the transition just as well from the undivided category.

The transition, according to Hegel, rests on the necessity of Cognition (*G. L.* iii. 319. *Enc.* 232). As the account in the *Encyclopaedia* is both clearer and shorter than the account in the *Greater Logic*, I will quote the *Encyclopaedia*. The two accounts do not, I think, differ in meaning. "The necessity," says Hegel, "which finite cognition produces in the Demonstration, is, in the first place, an external necessity, intended for the subjective intelligence alone. But in necessity as such, cognition itself has left behind its pre-supposition and starting-point, which consisted in accepting its content as given or found. Necessity quâ necessity is implicitly the self-relating notion. The subjective idea has thus implicitly reached an original and objective determinateness—a something not-given, and for that reason immanent in the subject. It has passed over into the idea of Will."

It is obvious from this that Hegel regards the necessity of the harmony of the Individuals with the Universe as giving so much stability and self-centredness to the Individuals that we must add to the statement that they harmonise with the Universe, the further statement that the Universe harmonises with them. If the harmony of the Individuals with the Universe were gradually attained, then the necessity of the harmony would also be gradually attained. And since his comparison of the harmony with the concrete state of knowledge has led him to regard the harmony as gradually attained, he regards the necessity as gradually attained also. He supposes it to be attained by something analogous to the process of Demonstration, which he treats under Synthetic Cognition, and therefore does not find himself in a position to make the transition to the Idea of the Good till he has reached the end of Synthetic Cognition.

If, however, we realise that the harmony must exist in its full completeness if the category of the Idea of the True is applicable at all, we shall see that in reaching the Idea of the True we have reached the conception that the harmony is necessary. If the category is valid, then the Individual-systems are determined by the Universe-system to harmonise with it. And therefore the harmony is necessary—which is, as Hegel himself asserts, sufficient to allow us to pass to the Idea of the Good.

283. Hegel is, I think, right in maintaining that the necessity of the harmony, considered as determined from the side of the Universe, entitles us to conceive it as being equally determined from the side of the Individual. If a harmony is imperfect, if it is only accidentally perfect, or if the necessity of its perfection is due to some outside cause, there is some meaning in saying that the harmony is determined by one side rather than the other—by A and not by B. For in all these three cases a want of a perfect harmony can be conceived, and our assertion means that, in such a case, we should regard B, and not A, as defective in harmony. We say that the actions of a citizen are in harmony with the law, and not that the law is in harmony with them. For we can conceive that the citizen should cease to be law-abiding; and, if he did, we should condemn his actions, and not the law, for the discrepancy.

And, again, it might be that A could exist without being in harmony with B, while B could not exist without being in harmony with A. In this case, also, we might say that A rather than B determined the harmony, on account of the logical priority of A.

But it is not so here. The harmony between the Universal and the Individual is perfect, necessary, and not due to any outside cause, but to the intrinsic nature of the related terms. The absence of the harmony is inconceivable. We cannot therefore say that one term rather than the other is shown to be defective by any possible discrepancy, and so declare the other term to be the determinant.

Nor can we pronounce either term determinant on the other possible ground—that it is independent of the harmony while the other is not independent. For, if the category is correct, the Universe depends on the harmony quite as much as the Individual. They only exist in virtue of the harmony between their systems and the system of the Universe. But the same is true of the Universe. And therefore it is no truer to say that

the Universe determines the Individuals than it is to say that
the Individuals determine the Universe.

284.   The first use that Hegel makes of this result is to
conclude that, as one is no truer than the other, we must say
both.   To the statement that the Universe-system determines
the Individual-systems, we must add the statement that the
Individual-systems determine the Universe-system.   So we
reach

B.   The Idea of the Good

(*G. L.* iii. 320.   *Enc.* 233), which is called in the *Encyclopaedia* by the name of Volition (Wollen).   Volition must not
be taken here as meaning the desire to change, or to resist
change, which is the form in which Volition usually shows
itself.   If this were the case there would be nothing appropriate
in naming this category after it, since the category involves
a perfect harmony, and also a necessary harmony, so that there
can be no question either of promoting or of resisting change.
It is not this, however, which Hegel means by Volition here.
He means by it the judgment of the existent by the standard
of Good.   Such a judgment, of course, leads us to desire action
if it reveals a difference between the fact and the ideal, but
involves no desire of action when the harmony between the
fact and the ideal is already perfect.   Taken in this sense
Volition is an appropriate name for a category which asserts
that the Individual determines the nature of the Universe, since
in volition, as we said above, it is the object, and not the self,
which is regarded as defective if the harmony is imperfect.

The Idea of the Good is a better name for this category
than Volition in so far as it does not, like Volition, suggest the
idea of change.   In other respects, however, Volition is the
better name, since the example Hegel means to take is clearly
a psychical state and not the ethical idea of Goodness.

It is, I think, evident that Hegel took the essence of the
psychical state of volition to be as described above, since the
category of Volition, as treated by him, *includes* a state of
perfect harmony, which could certainly not have as its example
a desire for change[1].

---

[1] Lotze takes a similar view of the essence of Volition.   Cp. *Microcosmus*,
Book ix, Chapter 5 (trans. Vol. 2, p. 706).

285.   But it must be noticed that he fell into an error with regard to this category analogous to that which he committed with regard to the Idea of the True.   He conceives the category as dealing with the process of producing such a harmony, before it deals with the established perfect harmony.   This is erroneous. For, in the first place, the reasons given above (Sections 281, 282) to show that the Idea of the True deals only with a harmony inevitably and originally perfect, and not with the production of such a harmony, are also applicable here.

In the second place, even if the production of the harmony could have found a place in the Idea of the True, it could not do so in the Idea of the Good.   For at the end of the Idea of the True, the harmony, Hegel says, has been established in its necessity and perfection.   Now it is from this point that his treatment of the Idea of the Good begins.   And since his argument, as seen above, is that the necessary and perfect harmony, under the earlier category, involves necessary and perfect harmony under the later category, then the later category must have the necessary and perfect harmony throughout, even if the earlier did not.

The order of these two categories could not have been inverted.   It is impossible that the Universe-system should be determined by the Individual-systems so as to be in harmony with all of them, if the Individual-systems varied indefinitely from one another in content (cp. above, Section 279).   And the possibility of this is only disproved by showing that the Individual-systems are all determined by the Universe-system, so as to be in harmony with it.   Thus we could not have the Idea of the Good, in which the Individuals are determinant, until we have had the Idea of the True, in which the Universe is determinant.

286.   Hegel says of the Idea of the Good that it is higher than the Idea of the True, " because it has not only the value of the Universal, but also the value of the simply Actual " (*G. L.* iii. 320).   It would seem from this that the second category—the Idea of the Good—has both values, that of the Universal and that of the Actual.   As the Universality is regarded by Hegel as the characteristic of the Idea of the True, it follows that the second category contains the first, besides containing also fresh content. Its standpoint is one which finds its example, not in gratified volition by itself, but in the combination of true knowledge and gratified volition.

Hegel is entitled to take this position, for the argument which led us on to the Idea of the Good did not do so by showing that there was any contradiction in the harmony with the Universe taken as the determinant, but that the validity of that conception involved the validity of the harmony with the Individuals taken as determinant. The second conception was added to the first, and did not replace it.

This is not inconsistent with the general principle of the dialectic method, for, though the two categories in question stand, apparently[1], in the relation of Thesis and Antithesis, yet we are here so close to the end of the dialectic that its movement, according to the law laid down by Hegel[2], has become almost a direct advance from each category to the next.

It is thus the combination of the two standpoints, exemplified by knowledge and volition, which is regarded by Hegel as being higher than the standpoint exemplified by knowledge. There is nothing to suggest that he would consider the standpoint exemplified by volition as being by itself higher than that exemplified by knowledge. Indeed, his application of the dialectic to concrete facts strongly suggests that he would not consider the standpoint exemplified by volition as being higher. For nothing is clearer about Hegel than that he does not regard the concrete spiritual state of volition as higher than that of knowledge, and that he does not regard virtue as a higher excellence than wisdom.

287. Hegel clearly considers that the establishment of this category gives us the right to assert that the Universe is completely good. Can this be legitimately deduced from the result reached in the category—that the nature of the Universe conforms to a description whose only example, known or imaginable, includes gratified volition ? The question does

---

[1] This is only an inference, as no third term is explicitly given. But I cannot doubt that the term left to be supplied is the Synthesis, and that the two which are given are the Thesis and Antithesis.

[2] Cp. *e.g.* my *Studies in the Hegelian Dialectic*, Chapter IV.

not really belong to the dialectic itself, but to its cosmological applications, and does not concern us here[1].

288. The transition from this category rests on the fact that the complete harmony, with the Individual as determinant, involves (as we have previously seen) the complete harmony, with the Universe as determinant. " In this result Cognition is restored, and united with the practical Idea, the given Actuality is at the same time determined as the realised absolute End, but not, as in the process of Cognition (im suchenden Erkennen) simply as an objective world without the subjectivity of the Notion, but as the objective world of which the Notion is the inner ground and actual existence " (*G. L.* iii. 327.   Cp. *Enc.* 235).

The argument is that it is impossible to adhere to the position at which we now stand—that, in the harmony of the Universe and the Individual, the Universe determines the Individual, and the Individual also determines the Universe.

It will be remembered that the transition to the Idea of the Good was effected by the argument that, since the harmony between the Universe and the Individual was necessary, perfect, and intrinsic, any question as to which would be pronounced defective if the harmony were defective was absurd, and that, since the harmony was essential to the existence of either term, neither could be said to be logically prior to the other in the harmony.   From this the result was reached that it was no truer to say that the Universe determines the Individuals than to say that the Individuals determine the Universe.   From this Hegel starts by saying that, since one proposition is no truer than the other, both are true.   This gave us the category of the Idea of the Good (cp. above, Section 284).

---

[1] Even if the Universe were completely good, Hegel would not be justified in his corollary: "All unsatisfied endeavour ceases, when we recognise that the final purpose of the world is accomplished no less than ever accomplishing itself" (*Enc.* 234). If the Universe is seen as it truly is, then, according to Hegel, there could be no unsatisfied endeavour, or endeavour of any kind. And so endeavour could not cease because of its superfluity, since it never existed. If, on the other hand, the Universe is looked at in such a partially illusory manner that endeavour appears to exist, then the utility of the endeavour may be as real as its existence. When Hegel came to apply his philosophy to the time-world, he realised this. He did not, for example, condemn the efforts of Socrates, or of Luther, as useless.

But this, Hegel now goes on, is inadequate, and must be transcended. For the real result of what has been shown is to put the two sides of the harmony on a level, not by making them each determine the other, but by removing altogether the conception of either side being determinant. That side is determinant to which, in one way or the other, the other is subordinate. We see now that neither side is subordinate to the other, since neither is logically subsequent to the other, and neither is to be condemned as defective for an actual or possible want of harmony. The consequence of this is not that each of them is determinant, but that neither is.

Thus we see that the harmony is ultimate. It is essential to the nature of existence that it should form a Universe composed of Individuals, that the Universe and that each Individual' should form an organic system, and that the Universe-system and each of the Individual-systems should be in perfect harmony with one another.

289. Hegel takes this as the transition to the Absolute Idea. If the symmetry of the dialectic was to be preserved, he should have first passed to a third subdivision of Cognition, which should complete the triad of which the Idea of the True and the Idea of the Good are the first two members, and then, from this new category, have passed over to the Absolute Idea.

If the Absolute Idea, like Cognition, had been subdivided, the last subdivision in Cognition would have been identical in content with the first subdivision of the Absolute Idea. But the Absolute Idea is not subdivided, and the last subdivision in Cognition could not consistently with the general method of the dialectic be identical in content with the Absolute Idea as a whole. Hegel, apparently, could discover no intermediate stage between the category of the Idea of the Good, and the category of the Absolute Idea. And I can make no suggestion to fill the gap. The transition remains unsymmetrical, but not, I think, invalid.

III. THE ABSOLUTE IDEA.

290. (*G. L.* iii. 327. *Enc.* 236.) In this not only the Idea of the True and the Idea of the Good are synthesised, but also Life and Cognition. Cognition, as is natural so close to the

end of the dialectic, is so direct an advance upon Life, that we
do not find many characteristics of Life in the Absolute Idea
which were not also in Cognition.   But in the Absolute Idea,
as we have seen, the harmony is recognised as ultimate—not as
due to the dependence of one side on the other.   And in this
the Absolute Idea may be said to have returned to a characteristic which belonged to the category of Life, when the expression
of the Seele in and by the Body was conceived as an ultimate
fact, not due to the subordination of either side to the other[1].

The transition, as I said above, seems to me valid, for the
Absolute Idea, to judge by Hegel's words, does just mean what
the category of Cognition would mean after the elimination
of the erroneous conception that one side is determined by the
other.

The nearest approach to a definition given in the *Greater
Logic* is as follows: "The Notion is not only Seele, but free
subjective Notion, which is for itself and therefore has Personality; it is the practical objective Notion, determined in and
for itself, which, as a Person, is impenetrable, atomic Subjectivity, but which is just as much not exclusive Individuality,
but Universality for itself, and Cognition, and which has in its
Other its own Objectivity as Object (Gegenstand).   All else is
error, confusion, opinion, strife, caprice, and impermanence; the
Absolute Idea alone is Being, permanent Life, Truth which
knows itself.   It is all Truth" (*G. L.* iii. 327).   In the *Encyclopaedia* he says, "The Idea, as unity of the Subjective and
Objective Idea, is the Notion of the Idea—a Notion for which
the Idea as such is Object (Gegenstand) and Object (Objekt)—
an Object (Objekt) in which all determinations have come
together" (*Enc.* 236).

291.   What does Hegel mean by this?   We must first
consider a suggestion which he makes—as I think, erroneously.
We find it stated most clearly in the *Encyclopaedia*.   The
content of the Absolute Idea he says "is the system of Logic.
All that is at this stage left as form for the Idea is the Method
of this content—the specific consciousness of the value and

---

[1] Perhaps it should rather be said that this characteristic *should* have
belonged to the category of Life, since it scarcely seems consistent with Hegel's
treatment of the expression of the Seele by the Body as necessarily inadequate.

currency of the moments in its development.   To speak of the Absolute Idea may suggest the conception that we are at length reaching the right thing and the sum of the whole matter.   It is certainly possible to indulge in a vast amount of senseless declamation about the Absolute Idea.   But its true content is only the whole system of which we have been hitherto studying the development" (*Enc.* 237).   And again in the *Greater Logic*: "Thus what here still has to be observed is not a Content as such, but the Universal of its Form—that is, the Method" (*G. L.* iii. 329).

There is doubtless an element of truth in this.   The step we take in reaching the Absolute Idea is no different in character from previous stages in the dialectic process, nor is the advance we gain in it greater than in previous steps.   We have reached the absolute truth about reality now, but we had very nearly reached it in the previous category.   Hegel would be perfectly justified if he merely wished to warn us against expecting anything in the last stage of the dialectic which should be much more mystical or wonderful than the stages immediately preceding it.

But Hegel means more than this, and in doing so I think he falls into error.   The meaning of the Absolute Idea is not, and cannot be, simply that it is the idea which is reached at the end of the dialectic process.   Each category in the process asserts certain characteristics of existence, and has therefore a meaning which cannot be reduced to its place in the dialectic. In fact, it only has its place in the process by reason of the relation which the determination of existence given by it bears to the determinations given by the other categories in the process.

The Absolute Idea, therefore, has a content.   And, although much of its content is to be found also in previous categories, it is not necessary to go back through the whole series of previous categories whenever we wish to *state* the content of the Absolute Idea—though of course the validity of the Absolute Idea can only be *proved* by going through all these previous stages.   It is not necessary to go through them to state the content of the Absolute Idea because that Idea contains the truth of them all, not by containing the separate categories as a process, but by containing that part of their content which is true, synthesised into a single unity, the false and inadequate part of the content of those lower categories having been transcended.   It is not, therefore, necessary to go through the categories, nor would it be sufficient, since, after all, the Absolute Idea is an advance, even on the Idea of the Good, and so there is something in it which is not in any of the other categories.

Besides, Hegel is here inconsistent.   In the passages quoted above (*G. L.* iii. 327. *Enc.* 236.   Cp. above, Section 290) he has given accounts of the nature of the Absolute Idea which are not in the least statements of the Method of the dialectic, but, on the contrary, statements of what existence is conceived to be, when it is taken under this category.

292.   Returning to these two accounts, we find, I think, that they are what Hegel is justly entitled to assert about the Absolute Idea in consequence of the transition by which, as he has demonstrated, it is reached from the Idea of the Good. It will be, as was said above, the same in content with the Idea of the Good, except that the two sides of the harmony are no longer asserted each to determine the other.   That is, in affirming it we assert that all that exists forms a Universe composed of Individuals, that the Universe and that each Individual is an organic system, and that the relation which exists between the Universe-system and each of the Individual-systems is one of perfect harmony.

This is what Hegel is entitled to assert as the content of the Absolute Idea; and this, I think, is what he does assert.   In both the *Greater Logic* and the *Encyclopaedia*, he states that the Idea is its own Object.   The use of the word Object suggests that the relation in question is analogous to the relation between a state of consciousness and its object, while the statement that the Object of the Idea is the Idea itself suggests that the whole of the content is to be found on both sides of the relation.   So far, then, his words support my view of what he means by this category.   The fact that he says that it is the Idea which is its own Object—while, if I am right, what he means is, that, according to the Idea, the Universe is the Object—can be no objection to anyone familiar with Hegel's methods of expression.

According to the view I have put forward, indeed, there are other characteristics which must be included in the Absolute Idea. The Universe is differentiated. It consists of an organic system of Individuals. And the Subject-Object relation of which Hegel speaks is one where the Universe as a whole is Object to *each* of the Individuals as Subjects. These further characteristics are not mentioned by Hegel here. But there is nothing in what he says which is inconsistent with them. And as there is, I think, no doubt, that all of them are found in the category of Cognition, and as there is nothing in the transition from that category which could involve their removal, we are entitled to hold that they are all found in the category of the Absolute Idea.

293. We may add something which is not mentioned by Hegel, but which seems a fair deduction from his position. Each Individual, we have seen, is in harmony with the Universe, and the Universe is an organic unity consisting of all the Individuals. From this it follows that each Individual is in harmony with all the other Individuals. This statement would not be an adequate substitute for the previous statement—that the Universe and each Individual are in harmony. For, in saying that the harmony is between the Universe and each Individual, we bring out the fact that the harmony is between the whole and its part—a fact which is essential to the category. And this is not brought out when we say that each Individual is in harmony with all other Individuals. But if one statement is true the other will be. And, when the results of the dialectic are to be applied to concrete problems, it may be a matter of some importance to remember that each Individual's harmony with the Universe implies his harmony with all other Individuals.

It may be objected that the new statement ignores the organic unity of the Universe. It is not the case that the Universe is equivalent to the Individuals in isolation, or as a mere aggregate, or as a mechanically determined system. It is only equivalent to the Individuals when they are joined in just this organic system. And, it might be said, this is ignored if we treat the harmony of each Individual with the Universe as involving its harmony with all other Individuals.

I should reply to this that it is the objection itself which fails to do justice to the organic unity of the Universe, and so falls into a kind of spiritual atomism. For it assumes that it is at any rate conceivable that Individuals could exist as isolated, or as merely aggregated, or as mechanically determined. Now this is just what the dialectic has disproved if it has done anything at all. It has shown, not only that the Individuals are in fact connected in an organic unity, but that it is essential to their nature that they should be, and that if they were not connected in this particular way they would not be Individuals at all. Thus to speak of an Individual is to speak of an Individual in organic unity with the others, just as to speak of a triangle is to speak of a figure whose angles are equal to two right angles. To object that, when the Individuals are mentioned without mentioning the organic unity, that unity is neglected, is to ignore this essentiality of the organic unity to the Individuals, and it is thus the objection which is unduly atomistic.

294. In this category the dialectic ends, and we reach, according to Hegel, the absolute truth, so far as it can be reached by pure thought. "All else," as he has told us, "is error, confusion, opinion, strife, caprice, and impermanence." There are, he asserts, no defects to be found in this conception, which compel us to proceed to a higher category to remove them. There is, indeed, one defect which reveals itself here, as in every other case where pure thought is taken in abstraction from the other elements of existence, and by means of which Hegel's philosophy is driven on, beyond the Logic, to the conception of Nature, and from that to the conception of Spirit—the final and supreme truth about all existence. But with the Absolute Idea we reach the highest and final form of pure thought.

The proof that this is the final form of pure thought must always remain negative. The reason why each previous category was pronounced not to be final was that in each some inadequacy was discovered, which rendered it necessary, on pain of contradiction, to go beyond it. Our belief in the finality of the Absolute Idea rests on our inability to find such an inadequacy. Hegel's position will hold good, unless some future philosopher shall discover some inadequacy in the Absolute Idea which requires removal by means of another category.

Most of the space devoted by Hegel to the Absolute Idea, both in the *Greater Logic* and in the *Encyclopaedia*, is concerned with questions relating to the dialectic method. That such questions should be discussed here follows, of course, from the position, discussed above, that the content of the Absolute Idea is the dialectic method itself. But, in any case, the end of the dialectic would be a natural place for a review of the method which had been followed. To discuss the dialectic method would, however, be beyond the object I have proposed to myself in this book.

295. Is the Absolute Idea exemplified in any concrete state known to us, in the same way that the category of Cognition was ? It seems clear to me that Hegel regarded it as exemplified by consciousness of some sort. In the first place there are the references to personality in the passage quoted above from the *Greater Logic* (iii. 327). The Notion is here, "as a Person, impenetrable atomic Subjectivity." This does not, I think, indicate that the nature of the Universe as a whole is exemplified by personality, since the Universe would never be described by Hegel as impenetrable or atomic. It is, I think, the parts of the Universe which are to be regarded as having these characteristics, and as therefore having a nature exemplified in personality. In the second place, we have the statement that the Idea is its own Object, and again that the Absolute Idea is the truth which knows itself. Moreover, the harmony in the Absolute Idea is the same as the harmony in Cognition, except that neither side is taken as determinant. Now Cognition was regarded by Hegel as exemplified in states of consciousness.

But what sort of consciousness gives us an example of the category of the Absolute Idea? It cannot be knowledge, or volition. For knowledge, as we have seen, exemplifies the Idea of the True—the category in which the Universe is the determinant of the harmony. And volition exemplifies the Idea of the Good—the category in which the Individual is also the determinant of the harmony. In the Absolute Idea neither side of the harmony is determinant.

Hegel does not, so far as I can see, consider this point at all. I believe that the state of consciousness which would exemplify the Absolute Idea is love, since in love we have a state of harmony in which neither the subject nor the object can be considered as determinant. To discuss this here, however, would take us beyond the sphere of the Logic, since love, though it may exemplify the Absolute Idea, is not itself a category, but a concrete state of spirit[1].

Would Hegel have agreed with this ? As I have just said, he does not consider the question in the Logic. On the other hand, we are not left without means of judging what his opinion would be. For, according to Hegel, the Absolute Idea must be true of all that really exists, and Spirit really exists— in fact, nothing but Spirit exists. If, therefore, among the various forms under which Spirit appears to us, we can find one which adequately expresses the nature of Spirit, while none of the others do so, then that form will be an example of the Absolute Idea (and, also, though this does not concern us in the Logic, the only instance of it).

There is no doubt, I think, that Hegel believes himself to have, in the *Philosophy of Spirit*, a dialectic process such that the last term, and the last term alone, gives us the truth about Spirit. This then would seem to be the example of the Absolute Idea. But this term is not love, but philosophy. Whether Hegel was justified in holding this may be doubted[2], but the fact that he did hold it seems to indicate that he would not have accepted love as the state of consciousness which is an example of the Absolute Idea.

On the other hand, in the *Philosophy of Religion*, "the kingdom of the Holy Ghost" is apparently taken as the absolutely true description of Spirit. And that is represented as a Community bound together by love. The question must, I think, remain undecided.

296. A Commentary such as this necessarily throws more emphasis on points of difference than on points of agreement.

---

[1] For a discussion of this question cp. *e.g.* my *Studies in Hegelian Cosmology*, Chapter IX. especially Section 284.

[2] Cp. *e.g.* my *Studies in the Hegelian Dialectic*, Sections 204—206.

I should wish, therefore, in concluding the exposition of Hegel's philosophy which has been the chief object of my life for twenty-one years, to express my conviction that Hegel has penetrated further into the true nature of reality than any philosopher before or after him.   It seems to me that the next task of philosophy should be to make a fresh investigation of that nature by a dialectic method substantially, though not entirely, the same as Hegel's.   What results such an investigation may produce cannot be known till it has been tried, but much of Hegel's reasoning seems to me to vary so little from the truth, where it varies at all, that I believe the results, like the method, would have much resemblance to Hegel's own.